Patrick Lindsay was born in Sydney ⟨...⟩
The Australian newspaper before ⟨...⟩
a reporter and presenter for the Ni⟨...⟩
He began writing books full-time in late 2001. His bestselling
The Spirit of Kokoda: Then & Now was published in August
2002. *The Spirit of the Digger* is the culmination of many years
of research, which included trips to Britain, Papua New
Guinea, East Timor, the World War I Western Front battlefields and Gallipoli.

THE **SPIRIT** OF THE
DIGGER

Then & Now

PATRICK LINDSAY

MACMILLAN
Pan Macmillan Australia

First published 2003 in Macmillan by Pan Macmillan Australia Pty Ltd
St Martins Tower, 31 Market Street, Sydney

Extracts: George Aspinall quotes from *Changi Photographer* reproduced by permission of ABC
Books and the copyright owner; *A Military History of Australia* by Jeffrey Grey reproduced by
permission of Cambridge University Press; *Crisis of Command* by David Horner reproduced by
permission of the Australian National University and David Horner; *Those Ragged Bloody Heroes*
and *We Band of Brothers* by Peter Brune reproduced by permission of Allen & Unwin.

Every effort has been made to contact the copyright holders of material reproduced
in this text. In cases where these efforts were unsuccessful, the copyright holders are
asked to contact the publisher directly.

National Library of Australia
Cataloguing-in-Publication data:

Lindsay, Patrick.
The spirit of the digger: then and now.

ISBN 0 7329 1181 8.

1. Mateship (Australia). 2. Social interaction – Australia.
3. Australia – History, Military. I. Title.

302.30994

Set in 13/15pt Granjon by Midland Typesetters
Maps by Laurie Whiddon
Printed in Australia by McPherson's Printing Group

Dedicated to the memory
of Phil Rhoden,
wise warrior, true friend
and to
Diggers, then & now

For Lisa
and
Nathan, Kate & Sarah

Contents

The Bali experience

11.08 pm Paddy's Irish Pub, Kuta Beach, Bali, 12 October 2002

The young woman was catapulted across the room and cannoned into Peter Hughes, crashing him to the floor as he waited at the bar for his first shout at Paddy's Pub.

'At first I thought, why did she do that? Next, I was wondering why I couldn't stand up,' Peter recalls.

As he was regaining his senses, Peter remembers realising there had been an explosion and thinking it must have been a gas cylinder going off. By that stage, his instincts for self-preservation were kicking in. He noticed his T-shirt was on fire and snuffed it out.

'I had this sensation of floating in slow motion and all of a sudden looking around and seeing everything black and realising something's gone off. I saw red embers. No fire. Just red embers.'

Peter Hughes, owner of a roof tiling business in Perth, had only arrived in Bali late that afternoon for his annual holiday. It was familiar territory to him and his mates, North Melbourne AFL players Mick Martyn and Jason McCartney and an old friend from Perth, Gary Nash. In fact, this was Peter's eleventh trip here. His 21-year-old son, Leigh, had accompanied him on the previous six but this time Leigh had gone to Phuket in Thailand with his football team.

Peter and his mates met at the pool bar in the Hard Rock Hotel where they were staying. Peter hadn't seen Mick and Jason for eight months and they spent the rest of the afternoon catching up around the hotel pool.

'I remember thinking how great it was to be back in paradise with my friends and the gentle Balinese people I'd come to really appreciate.'

Around 9 pm the group headed off to the Macaroni Bar in Jalan Legian, across the road from Paddy's Pub.

'We ordered some pasta and sat around eating and chatting, having a laugh and planning where we were going to go out partying on what is traditionally a big night out, our first night in Bali.'

By the end of dinner they'd agreed on the Sari Club as the place to 'kick on'.

'But, on the way to the Sari Club, Jason, for some reason, headed into Paddy's Bar. The bar was about half full. On the way in we met two girls Jason knew, and I went to the bar to order drinks for everyone. I gave the drinks to the others and returned to the bar to get mine.'

Peter had reached the bar when a massive explosion erupted and he collided with the young woman who seemed to be floating through the air.

'People were screaming and the sound of shattering glass was terrifying. Everything went black and then seemed to glow red. I got up and helped the girl to her feet. I was standing, bloodied and on fire, looking for Jason, Mick and Gary. But it was too black to see and the people were frantic. People were jumping over everybody and the sight of detached legs, arms and people on fire was indescribable. Everybody was trying to get out and the screams were piercing.'

Peter cannot remember how he made it out of the inferno in Paddy's and staggered into the street. He had just enough time to look towards his hotel when another, even bigger, explosion from the other end of the street virtually blew him back inside Paddy's. The second blast was from the nearby Sari Club, Peter's group's first choice for the evening.

'When I walked out of Paddy's I automatically looked left because that's where I had come from, that's where our hotel was, that's where I came out of the restaurant. As you walk out, the Sari Club is on the right. If I had looked right, I would have died.'

The lethal shower of shrapnel generated by the second blast was designed to maximise injuries to anyone within range. When Peter came to after the second blast,

'Two girls were screaming at me to help them so I went and helped them out. Their clothes and skin were on fire. But somehow this seemed normal to me.'

Peter helped the girls out into the street. As he did, his senses were assaulted by the sight of the headless, limbless, charred bodies that littered the scene. For the first time, Peter saw his own injuries. He knew he was burnt badly but he felt no pain. The second blast had wounded him in the chest and stomach with shrapnel and, as someone pointed out, his right calf had been blown out.

'I had no pain. There was no pain. What they say now is that it was just adrenaline going. I was probably fighting for my life from that point without realising it.'

Peter knew his hands were burnt. That had happened when he pulled the girls free.

'Sometimes I don't know whether I did or I didn't. It's like a dream. But I know we were grabbing people and it wasn't just me, it was a whole heap of Australian people – that was the most amazing thing of all.'

Almost immediately, the Australians at the scene began bonding and helping each other. Peter Hughes remembers noticing how many people of other nationalities seemed paralysed into inaction while the Australians seemed to react instinctively.

'I remember watching for a minute or two and it was like the world had been put into slow motion. In this time, all I remember seeing was Australians.'

::

I had already begun my research for *The Spirit of the Digger* when, like all Australians, I was stunned to hear the news of the Bali bombing in October 2002. As I watched the chilling television images and listened to the stories of individual lives snuffed out and shattered, I was struck by the spirit of the victims and those who rushed to their aid.

I realised that the spirit of the Digger was being played out right before my eyes. The Aussies in Bali had no slouch hats, no uniforms, but there was no mistaking the spirit. General Peter Cosgrove, the hero of our intervention in East Timor, saw it:

'They are our real people. Australians automatically form teams. They bond. We can't see another Australian without feeling an immediate and strong sense of identity. You've immediately got a team. I mean in a situation like that, people who wouldn't even have noticed each other in the club saw each other in the shattered aftermath, turned to each other and took care of each other, forming these immediate, lifesaving little teams, and that's because we instinctively trust each other until something happens to say the trust was misplaced.

'And that's why Australians are, almost as a fundamental premise, so good when they put a military uniform on. You don't have to put a uniform on to have the qualities of a Digger. When you do put the uniform on, we expect the qualities of a Digger, and you don't have to dig very deep to find them.'

That is the essence of this book. All Australians have the spirit of the Digger within them. In times of crisis – terrorism, bushfires, floods, accidents, disasters, conflicts – the spirit shines through. It's a spirit we must cherish.

ONE

The essence of the spirit: Diggers talk

'The Digger' is a key piece of the complex jigsaw puzzle that makes up 'The Australian'. However, defining the Digger is like defining 'class': it's hard to describe, but you know it when you see it. The Digger is an Australian Everyman. Soldiers are only as good as, and reflect, the community from which they are drawn. Australians have the essence of the Digger within them. The spirit emerges when the individual calls on it in times of need.

The image of the Digger is derived from an intricate amalgam of qualities: each has been proven in the heat of battle and has been personified at various times by remarkable members of the tribe. Chief among these qualities are mateship, courage, compassion, endurance, selflessness, loyalty, resourcefulness, devotion, independence, ingenuity, audacity, coolness, larrikinism and humour.

Mateship is the essential binding force of the Digger, and examples of it are legion: from the two Light Horsemen at The Nek at Gallipoli, who swapped places with other Diggers in the line so they could charge to their deaths shoulder to shoulder, through to 'Dasher' Wheatley's refusal to leave his wounded mate's side in Vietnam in the face of certain death. The Diggers' mateship extends beyond comradeship. It develops into a mutual respect and acquires an almost spiritual quality, which binds men for life. It enables them either to embrace or to overlook their mates' foibles and to draw on a seemingly limitless depth of commitment to each other. It helps to form teams with a combined strength far exceeding the sum of those of the members.

Courage, both physical and moral, is a core element. It comes in many forms: from the sustained inspirational bravery of men like Albert Jacka in World War I, who by all accounts won his VC many times over, to the timeless valour of Bruce Kingsbury, who charged into immortality on the Kokoda Track. But most Diggers recognise the crucial value of moral courage and accord it a respect, albeit often underplayed, that surprises many observers.

When you think of **compassion**, you think of Diggers like 'Weary' Dunlop and his fellow doctors on the Burma–Thailand Railway, Bruce Hunt, Albert Coates, Roy Mills and others as they tended to their frail mates in unspeakable conditions. You think of the way Diggers across the years have been able to switch without difficulty from the role of the warrior to that of the peacekeeper or the rescuer or the rebuilder of shattered lives in times of disaster.

Diggers from all wars have drawn on reserves of **endurance**, which have enabled them to overcome odds that would have defeated lesser soldiers: from the original Anzacs during their eight-month nightmare at Gallipoli to the prisoners of war who endured years of despair and cruelty. From the hellholes of the Somme to the Rats of Tobruk, Diggers have endured unimaginable privations to ultimately triumph against all the odds. Men like John Metson, who, shot through both ankles, crawled for two weeks through the New Guinea jungle rather than burden his mates, symbolise the levels of endurance to which the spirit of the Digger can rise.

The **selflessness** of men like Simpson with his life-saving donkey on the slopes of Gallipoli through to Charlie McCallum at Isurava, wounded three times, with Bren gun in one hand and Tommy gun in the other, holding off scores of Japanese while his mates escaped, has inspired countless other

Diggers to follow their noble leads. From the start, once the Digger left his home shores he committed himself to his quest, as Charles Bean noted of the First AIF:

> *'The fond dream of the return home was silently surrendered by many without a word, or a sign in their letters. The ambitions of civil life had been given up; men's keenness now was for the AIF – for their regiment, battalion, company – and for the credit of Australia.'*

The Digger comes in all shapes and sizes and from all backgrounds and walks of life. He (and now she) has something of the Australian ethos of the volunteer for, historically, most Diggers have not been regular Army soldiers but volunteers for a specific cause. And they have returned without regret to their former civilian lives after their conflicts ended. Even our National Servicemen volunteered for service in Vietnam.

Originally, many Diggers came off the land: practical, self-reliant men accustomed to hardship; skilled horsemen; good shots; men good with their hands. But even when, in later years, the vast majority of the Diggers came from the cities, there seemed to be little loss in effectiveness as a force. Wally Thompson, a former Regimental Sergeant Major of the Australian Army (a post established to give Diggers a direct conduit to the Chief of the Army), has studied the makeup of the Digger and the way it's changed:

> *'In the First World War when Bluey rode up from the bush, he could shoot, ride, swear, a great all-rounder. But Bluey was maybe not the bloke I wanted in my section or company or the battalion because he would tend to be an individual. Individuals can be very dangerous. They can shine when it's necessary but they've got to learn to be part of the team. The crucial thing is the team effort. It's not me, me, me or I, I, I. Everything is in the way you train them. The spirit is there but it's all in the way you train them.*
>
> *'It goes back to the First World War. You can see the difference in the beginning at Gallipoli: it was chaos. And it was the same in the beginning in France and Belgium, particularly in*

France at Fromelles. It was up the guts and it was sheer bravery but ridiculous bravery. A great example was at The Nek in Gallipoli. They knew they were going to die for nothing but they went ahead because they wouldn't let their mates down.

'But it was bad leadership from the top. Later on in the battles in France, they thought there's got to be a better way and they started "fire and movement". The Germans used it, and the French, and we did. So we didn't just go straight in, we'd put a gun down and fire and move. In other words we were learning to work as a team. And things like The Nek, where there was no teamwork, could have been Gettysburg or Waterloo.

'But I also contradict myself here too because you still need those Blueys in the platoon — just not in that style of up-the-guts. You need him when the chips are down, things are crook, morale's low, you've taken a few casualties, a few killed, it's not a good day. That's when the Digger humour comes into it. Not so much a bloke doing something himself but an act, like jumping up into a shell hole and saying "Bugger it, I'm gonna have a wash". It's the joke, the laughter, it gets people going. I think it's the ethos of Australia, our character.'

This larrikin approach and the humour that travels with Australians wherever they go have become ingrained in the Digger. Whatever the occasion, no matter how desperate, no matter how solemn, the Digger will find the humour in it, as Peter Cosgrove recalls:

'I can remember when I was the Director of Infantry and I was watching a whole group of infantry soldiers in the Duke of Gloucester Cup Section Competition go through some very arduous military tests.

'They'd been hard at it for days, all trying in their Section groups to outdo each other, just punishing themselves to be the best. It was late on the last day of the competition and I'd brought a whole lot of venerable old retired officers by Land Rover up this extraordinarily steep bush track. You'd get sunburn on the roof of your mouth walking up it.

'The Land Rover was groaning its way up in low gear past

these sweating soldiers who were climbing this hill on the way. We popped out from the vehicle up the top, fresh as daisies, and we're watching these kids struggle the last few metres across the finish line.

'And there's some kid with a machine gun and a very heavy load plodding up this hill. He looked up, he saw me and he suddenly assumed this very worried expression. He looked at me and said: "Oh, hello Sir. How are you?" I said: "I'm alright soldier." And he said: "You're not tired or anything are you Sir, because this hill's very steep?" That, to me, was typical – and wonderful – the irreverence and the fact that, at the end of the test, this bloke still had a spark of humour left in him.'

The irreverence is interwoven into the traditional Digger's disdain for traditional military 'spit and polish'. From their earliest days, this attitude has been mistaken for a lack of discipline. But, clearly, when it mattered, the Digger matched any army for discipline under fire. Wally Thompson:

'People say Australian soldiers are not well disciplined and that's a myth, especially in the present day. They may be a little bit raucous and play up a little bit on leave but that's spirit and you want that spirit. But in the field, on operations, they are moulded together as one.

'It really is quite incredible. I had three tours in Vietnam and I saw it. Larrikinism is a bit of spirit. In many ways our country is drifting away from that. We're getting a bit more selfish in our ways and I think the military pulls people back into reality and says mate you're not as good as you think you are – it's a great leveller.

'It doesn't matter how good you think you are, it's how good the group thinks you are that counts. It's like somebody who thinks he's a bit of a goer; there's always someone who can do him. It's that spirit and the caring for each other.'

Peter Cosgrove believes one of the cornerstones of the good Digger is his reliability. His word must be his bond:

'If the fellow says I won't let you down, I'll be there or I'll guard this or I'll take care of you, then that's written in stone. And it's

this bond of trust that is the core of mateship. Mateship can't exist without trust and reliability and we elevate mateship but it must be built on the fundamental obligation felt by the individual to keep his or her word.'

Like all successful teams, the Australian Army fosters a healthy level of competition within its ranks. As former Vietnam vet, retired Major, Dennis Ayoub observes, competition often puts things into perspective:

'An engineer commander once told me: "In every group of men, each one of those men can do one thing, at least, better than you can." I always bore that in mind. There was always one who could run further and faster than anyone else, one who could do more chin-ups, another who was the best plant operator, the best grader operator. There was always recognition for the best. The bloke who was best at it would always get that job.

'It's very important that soldiers are felt to be important. Diggers know they are part of a team and each one knows he's a pivotal person in that group because of his excellence at something or the team's representative at one specific area. A natural hierarchy will develop and they'll work within the best skill divisions.

'As an officer you must know and understand that and you must foster it and work within that teamwork. But soldiers who are very good at things can become hard to manage, like very bright kids at school. So you must work to stop them being bored and keep them occupied. Often a good way to do that was to pass on their skills and information to new members of the team or other units; cross pollination.'

Peter Cosgrove sees the value of the competitive spirit in the Digger:

'Our infantry soldiers are an extraordinary bunch of people and they rate themselves really highly. They don't often leave you wondering about how good they are and how they compare with any other soldiers in the army.

'That can be galling to equally feisty blokes who drive tractors or huge trucks or who service artillery pieces or who have changed

the tracks on an armoured fighting vehicle. These are all blokes who do a tough job well so there's a little bit of that sort of internal professional rivalry, which is fine. It's a bit like the Australian use of the term "Bastard". With just a couple of nuances of difference in the way you use it you can be greeting your oldest friend, or putting an eternally damning curse on somebody.

'But you know, I think Australian soldiers have got a healthy respect for each other, helped along a bit by the fact that whenever you see an infantry organisation you don't have to look very far to see the other parts of the army that support oper-ations in there close by.'

When the Anzacs fought alongside the British, at Gallipoli and later in France, they first had to prove themselves as worthy soldiers. Having done that, they found the British officers still regarded them with disdain because of what they perceived as the 'unmilitary' relationships between the Australian officers and their Diggers. In his book *Digger*, John Laffin wrote of the British officers:

'They were appalled to find that, in action, private soldiers often called officers by their Christian names.

'A Queensland captain was sharply rebuked by an English colonel for telling his men details of a projected attack. The colonel said testily that it was not done for officers to discuss battle details with private soldiers. The captain, whose name is unknown, said: "I don't regard them as private soldiers, sir, they are my mates. Naturally I want them to know why I'm asking them to risk their lives".'

Much of this difference in approach can be attributed to the old British military class structure, where the upper class dominated the top ranks and the lower levels came from the middle and lower classes. From the start, by necessity, the Australian Army had a strong egalitarian attitude. The lack of an established class structure meant that most commissions were earned on merit. The heavy casualties suffered by our AIF in World War I, with the consequent rapid promotions across the board, saw tested leaders rise through the ranks.

Their experiences as private soldiers gave them an appreciation of the Diggers' problems, and the fact that the officers earned their promotions by performance meant they generally earned the respect of their troops. This system has persisted to the present day. As Wally Thompson points out, the Digger is still a key element in the Australian Army:

'Wars may be fought with weapons but they're won by men with courage and fighting spirit to close with the enemy. Good leadership, good planning, good equipment and weapons and good training are all ingredients. But, in the end, it's the soldiers and how they execute the plans and orders, using their field skills and weapons with confidence, who will win the firefight or the battle – soldiers with pride in themselves and the steadfast knowledge that their mates are trained to the task and will not fail them in the test of battle.

'When you go and look at a war memorial, you'll see private, private, private, corporal, private, sergeant, private, corporal, private, lieutenant, private, private. The soldiers do the fighting. They do the bleeding and they do the dying. And we must never forget that.'

History has shown that the Digger will perform super-human feats if he has faith in his mates. He's generally convinced he won't be the one to be killed, as an old Digger told Dennis Ayoub:

'He said: "I wasn't concerned about the one that had my name on it. I was worried about the one that had 'To Whom it May Concern' on the fucking thing!" Most of us believed that if someone was aiming at you, you'd probably be killed outright, shot in the head or the heart. The one to worry about is the one which you were going to cop out of the blue, a ricochet, or over-spray or something like that!'

And the Digger can cope as long as he knows his mates will look after him if something does happen. Wally Thompson:

'We have a thing in our army: we don't leave our wounded. And that's terribly important. It all comes down to the lowest denominator – mates. It's as an extended family: don't pick on

my brother – I can have a fight with my brother but I'll fight with him against anyone else.'

The core strength of the Australian Army lies in the quality of its sub-units – the section, the squadron, the platoon, the battery and the company – and the quality of the men who command these units. As we've seen on many occasions, in many conflicts, it doesn't matter how good a soldier's equipment is if he doesn't have the necessary fighting spirit. Conversely, as Vietnam showed, a poorly armed force with an unquenchable desire to win can upset even the most powerful army. To Wally Thompson it makes sense to view the army as a human body:

'The officers are the head, the brain, the orders and the policies; the backbone is the sergeant, as it's always been; the arms and legs are the junior NCOs which make the thing move; the actual body is made up of the soldiers. Of course, the Company Sergeant Major is the heart because he is the link between the brain and the body.'

Of course, the NCOs have always held the view that the officers command the army . . . but the NCOs run it! The interplay between, on the one hand, the NCOs and their officers and, on the other, the NCOs and their troops is crucial. Some relationships have proven themselves over time, as Vietnam vet, retired Colonel, Mike McDermott points out:

'There is a master-apprentice relationship between the sergeant and the officer in the Australian Army. The sergeants take on the job of keeping you alive and making sure that you don't do anything stupid.

'Early in my time in Vietnam, I ran along the beach chasing some VC with a machine gun and starting firing at them and my sergeant grabbed me and said: "Sir, for Christ's sake, don't do that again! I've lost a few platoon commanders and I don't want to lose any more!" His name was Brian London and he got a DCM, the next one down to the VC.

'The master–apprentice relationship is part of the system. Generally the sergeant is an older bloke than the officer. I was 21 and Brian was about 33 and he'd been to Vietnam before and he'd done a lot before I got there. They don't countermand you. Rather, it's: "Sir, that's an interesting plan. Not the silliest I've seen from you. Some of us might survive that plan" – non-confrontational language which just guides you.'

The Army converts most soldiers into short-term goal seekers. It's the nature of much of the work and it's the best way to minimise breakdowns in communication and to avoid confusion in the field. Dennis Ayoub knows how it works. He rose from the ranks to retire a major:

'The Digger is normally a very, very manageable person. But he's also an intelligent and wily dude. He's a rat-cunning sort of a bloke who doesn't thrive on bullshit for a start.

'He's fairly pragmatic. He'll accept his lot but if he can see another way of doing things he's not averse to saying: "Yeah that's very, very good but why don't we just walk over here and, like the young bull, old bull thing, just take the whole lot." They are also not averse to saying that something's wrong. In fact I think almost all Australian soldiers are potential union delegates. One thing you often hear is "Ayorta", as in: "Ayorta do it this way, it's much quicker".

'If you give a Digger a logical and substantial reason for doing something, he'll do it for you. If you bullshit to him, you'll never get him to do anything for you.'

Over a lifetime's experience, Wally Thompson has developed some basic rules:

'Keep orders to a minimum. Pass the information through the chain of command. Let the soldiers see the importance of their closest commander, their leader, the section commander.

'Mutual respect must be upheld to all soldiers at all times by all ranks, including officers and NCOs. The company must have cohesion to be an effective fighting unit. The respect must be seen between the officers and the NCOs and between the soldiers themselves.

'Treat NCOs and soldiers as you would like to be treated yourself, firmly but fairly. There's no room for standover merchants or bullyboys in the NCO ranks.

'You must show strength of character and toughness when and if required. Never let a fault or a sloppy activity become norm. Set high standards and enforce them. The Diggers must see you have both physical and moral courage.'

There is a sense of instinctive leadership in the Digger: a strange dichotomy in which many Diggers are content to allow someone they respect to lead them while, at the same time, maintaining a sort of 'watching brief' on them. Peter Cosgrove believes this attitude contributes to a higher standard of leadership by keeping those in command on their toes:

'Our Diggers have got this sort of restless ingenuity. And a sense of irreverence, too, because they're not sitting back there thinking Senior Lance Corporal is going to give me an order and that will be good. It's more along the lines of when's the dopey so-and-so Lance Corporal going to get here and figure out what we figured out ten minutes ago: that it's raining or it's going to rain, or that if we don't move soon we won't get a feed.

'So it's this sort of cheerful pressure on those who are appointed as leaders, which actually makes them much better [leaders]. You don't prance around with a sort of conferred and acquiescently-agreed mantle of authority as a leader in the army. You work all the time to establish and reaffirm your credibility and it can last just a few seconds: if you come out with something dumb; if you miss the obvious point; if you're cranky for no reason; or if you're dismissive of this sense of initiative. And you've also got to play within the boundaries because with that comes a tinge of irreverence which is the Diggers, to some extent, always mildly pushing the envelope.'

To Wally Thompson, an important distinction must be made between 'leaders' and 'commanders':

'They are two different things. A commander commands resources. A leader actually leads men. I believe a leader can go down to about company level, sub-unit level, where the strength

of our armies has always been – the companies, the platoons and the sections.

'*The battalion* [has an objective] *but it's the companies, the platoons and the sections which actually achieve it.*'

To the Digger, the section commander has a key role. Most commanders recognise that the section commander – the corporal or the lance corporal – is the backbone of the Army. Wally Thompson:

'*Diggers idolise their section commander. On operations, you can get by with a mediocre officer and a good sergeant, or vice versa, but you cannot survive with bad section commanders. They almost never get proper recognition either.*'

Dennis Ayoub recalls how his perspective about his commanding officer, Major Sandy McGregor, and his style of leadership changed once he himself became an officer:

'*When I first met him I thought he was an arrogant sort of bastard. Diggers are fairly irreverent blokes. They don't like officers. They don't like officers because they're not supposed to like officers. It's not that the officer wasn't a good fellow or wasn't a capable or able bloke.*

'*Sandy McGregor was a capable and able bloke, a very good commander and a very passionate bloke but a tough bastard as well. Because he was the officer, we didn't like him. Anything that he said was all bullshit and had to be treated with a certain amount of caution. He was to be treated like a politician because they're unbelievable buggers.*

'*Later when I became commissioned I saw him in an entirely different light. He was trying to extract the best by his leadership and by the use of some very good qualities that he has: one was leading by example, one was being a little over-exuberant, so much so that he would allow the blokes to say "Oh for Christ's sake Sir, that's bloody ridiculous! This is the way we should be running things."*

'*So he'd learn by allowing them to have sufficient confidence to speak up and thus spreading the knowledge base so he was able to barnstorm an idea.*'

Sandy McGregor's methods clearly worked. He was able to mould a disparate group of Diggers into a cohesive force of 'tunnel rats' in Vietnam. More than that, his leadership opened the way for many of his troops to develop their own individual leadership skills:

'We had three majors, 14 warrant officers, we had several sergeants – all out of that troop. When they came back to Australia, they really blossomed.'

They also bonded extremely closely, many remaining lifelong mates, with two of them so close that when Billy Coolburra was stricken with kidney failure a few years ago, his mate 'Snow' Wilson gave him one of his kidneys.

One of the constants in the Australian Army has been a strong emphasis on training and leadership. It has never skimped on resources in its officer training and has been rewarded with a stream of world-class military leaders. In essence, leadership in our Army, from the level of section commander to the chief, can be reduced to four elements: planning, directing, monitoring and controlling. Former Colonel, Ted Love, explains:

'Planning is done with the help of other people, like staff officers. You need advice and how much depends on how much time you've got to make the decision.

'Directing is not some pompous bastard standing up and saying "Here are the orders". It's making sure the staff put out orders that are sensible, clearly phrased without misunderstanding. I think it was Ulysses S. Grant who said something like: "A good order now is better than a perfect order too late".

'Monitoring means that because every plan will change when the thing starts you've got to be able to adjust down the track. And controlling is part of adjusting. Read the battle, the intelligence, the people, the circumstances.

'That's where the Australian army is very good at preparing, say, majors, for higher command at staff college and testing whether they can do all those four things. If you look at history

you'll see that when things go bad it's almost always one of those four things which has failed.

'Even at its most basic level of operation, if a corporal commanding a ten-man section – the lowest combat or working unit in the army – can't do those four things, then he, his men and his platoon commander have a problem. His leader must take control of him.'

Some will argue that the Digger is largely a myth. They claim that, as a fledgling nation, we needed heroes and we created them at Anzac, and we've built on that myth ever since.

It's true that mankind has always had its myths. Almost every movie can be broken down into some form of mythical journey. But myths are to some degree based on fact. And any examination of the essence of the Digger stands up to detailed scrutiny. In fact, if anything, many of the remarkable feats claimed of the Digger are actually underplayed. Countless heroic acts by Diggers have gone unnoticed and unrewarded in all wars in which they have participated. The system of decorations and awards for bravery adopted by the Australian Army has always militated against the fair recognition of the valour of the men involved. The nature of the Digger has usually meant he has been reticent about talking about his combat experiences. Yet every Digger with combat experience can give scores of examples of heroic acts that he has personally witnessed, which have gone without recognition. There is a humility and self-effacement that seems to be part of the returned Digger's makeup.

As a general rule, Diggers don't 'big-note' their own achievements. Part of the tradition has always been to shrug off achievements with a silent grin. The only time this attitude softens is when Diggers feel they must speak up so their mates receive their due, especially if the mates have died. It's also common for the survivors of major battles to tell their tales once they feel they have reached an age when they can no longer take every day's dawning for granted. They are almost always motivated by the desire to make sure their departed mates receive due recognition – no more, but certainly no less.

While the Americans and, to a lesser extent, the British have filled the silver screen with epics based on the heroics of their soldiers, Australian films about Diggers are disproportionately thin on the ground. Many of our most decorated Diggers are little known to the Australian public – unlike their American counterparts who, through movies, are often household names.

Perhaps this will change with the groundswell of interest in the achievements of our Diggers. This is part of a nationwide movement of exploration of what it means to be an Australian. The exciting thing about this is that our youth is in the vanguard. The fact that Anzac Day at Gallipoli has recently been expanded to a two-day commemoration to accommodate the crowds travelling to the peninsula from Australia and the growth in the numbers of Australians trekking the Kokoda Track are testament to the movement and the roles played in it by our young. Substantial increases in Anzac Day march crowds; growing numbers of boys and girls marching, wearing their grandfathers' medals; a maintenance, and perhaps even an increase, in the level of respect which the community retains for the Dawn Service and Anzac Day ceremonies; and the remarkable popularity of the Australian War Memorial in Canberra, are all pointers to the extent of the movement.

We are justifiably proud of the heritage our Diggers have bequeathed us. They have had an impact in world conflicts far in excess of their numbers. They have won respect from much larger armies and governments wherever they have fought, and from countries around the globe in which they have maintained the peace with justice and dignity.

Old soldiers are often criticised for being preoccupied with the past. Some have no choice, and are condemned to flashbacks and nightmares. Others only visit sporadically, on Anzac Day or at unit reunions. A few choose to spend time in the past as an escape from the present. But most don't live in the past, they simply honour it. They will never forget the sacrifices of their mates, who gave their tomorrows for our todays. The serving Digger cannot afford the luxury of living in the past, as Wally Thompson says:

'Soldiers know about the past but they can't concentrate on the past. They must work for the future to work to make them the best and you've got to make them believe they're the best. You've got to instil pride, first as an individual in the recruit training stage, and that's quite a challenge for many. Then, when we get them into the company, we try to develop collective pride, pride in the group they're in — an esprit de corps, pride in yourself and your unit. You will not fail. You won't leave your mates behind. We're a team. We're brothers in arms.

'I'm sure the blokes in the Second World War tried to be as brave as the blokes in the First War. We used to talk about the battles in Korea, at Kapyong and Maryang San, and in Vietnam at Long Tan and Coral.

'But you don't dwell on it because that's the past and because a unit did something in the past doesn't mean they're going to do it in the future. It all depends on them: their pride in themselves; then in their sub unit; and then in their unit.'

In many ways the Digger is a study in contradictions: he doesn't crave war yet he will fight with unequalled ferocity; he hates spit and polish but will hold his discipline under the most trying conditions; he is tough yet compassionate; he hates his enemy until he surrenders, then he is generous in victory; he despises histrionics but will cry unashamedly at the loss of a mate; he believes he's invincible but he's not afraid of death; he will refuse promotion but unhesitatingly take command in a crisis; he will poke fun at his leaders but defend them with his life; he represents an arm of the nation's authority, yet he hates authority.

TWO

Today's Diggers

Junction Point Bravo, Bobonaro Province, East Timor
(near the Tactical Coordination Line)

The moon is just a sliver of a crescent, barely enough to etch an outline around the clouds that ring it. The bush is shrouded in inky darkness. If you look up you can just make out the blurred edge of the treetops where the earth ends and the sky begins. At ground level you can scarcely see the outline of your hand in front of your face. Crickets chant their mantra as a warm breeze rattles through the treeline. But the wind cannot combat the overpowering humidity, which draws beads of sweat from the slightest exertion.

Corporal Brett Woodward is just metres away but blends into the darkness like a spectre. He guides his men with hand signals as he steers them through the thick scrub towards their objective.

Section Two Three Bravo, of the 5/7th Battalion Royal Australian Regiment (known here in East Timor as Ausbatt VII), is out on a covert night patrol. Its mission: to set up an observation post overlooking the border with Indonesian-controlled West Timor and to observe there, unseen, overnight for smuggling or militia incursions. The border is known as the Tactical Coordination Line – effectively a Demilitarised Zone – established in 1999 by the United Nations to protect

Roma

Leti

Kisar

Wetar

Arwala

Luna

Airpanas

Selat Wetar

Tutuala

Lospalos

Loré

Baucau

Viqueque

Manatuto

Ataúro

DILI

Aileu

Ainaro

Ermera

Suai

Liquica

Maliana

Atambua

Batuolong

Kefamenanu

Kalabahi

Alor

Pante Macassar
(Oecusse)
EAST TIMOR

Soe

Pantar

EAST TIMOR

INDONESIA

Kupang

Andonara

Lomblen

Larantuka

Solor

Kewapante

Flores

Roti

Baa

Rote

N

kilometres

0   100

the sovereignty of the world's newest country, East Timor, in its transition to independence.

The men of Two Three Bravo were dropped quietly in the bush, well off the main roads, around sunset. They've been on the move now for about an hour and, despite the darkness, the humidity is still oppressive and evident in the glow on their faces and the dark sweat stains spreading on their brown-green jungle uniforms. Corporal 'Woody' Woodward, his face fractured by camouflage paint, has an air of quiet confidence as he directs his men through the bush. Despite the state-of-the-art camouflage uniform, the massive pack and modern weapons, you can imagine him as a section leader at Gallipoli, Tobruk, Kokoda or Long Tan. And the Diggers he's leading today would not have been out of place alongside him at any of those iconic battle sites. The first thing that strikes you is how young they are: five of them are 19 or 20. But in every war most of our Diggers have been around this age.

Despite their youth, the Diggers of Two Three Bravo know their stuff. They've trained long hours in the bush around their Darwin base in preparation for this deployment. They're keen and they're keyed up – well aware that contact is distinctly possible, either with the militia forces still operating across the border or with smugglers trying to sneak fuel and other contraband into East Timor. The men of Two Three Bravo are also aware they're following in illustrious footsteps. Sixty years ago, during World War II, the Diggers of 'Sparrow Force' fought in these hills in a remarkable guerrilla campaign against a massive Japanese force which had invaded Timor and which planned to use it as a base to attack Australia. The Sparrow Force Diggers won the hearts of the Timorese. Some Timorese fought alongside the Australians. Many helped supply them and warn them of Japanese approach. Some of the Portuguese also actively supported the Australians in their fight behind enemy lines. Sadly, thousands of these patriots paid with their lives for their loyalty. Some historians claim that as many as 60,000 Timorese were killed by the Japanese during their occupation.

Now the Diggers have returned, and they have once again connected with the people of this beautiful but troubled land. They know they have heavy responsibilities as representatives, of both Australia and the United Nations. They are in East Timor in a different role from their forebears of Sparrow Force. The modern Diggers are here as peacekeepers under the mandate of the UN. One of the great ironies surrounding their return is that this time they're working alongside Japanese soldiers: a battalion of engineers from our former enemy is helping rebuild roads and infrastructure just a few kilometres away from the main Australian Forward Operations Base. The locals are aware of the irony too and have noted that it coincides with the late arrival of the wet season – for the first time since the Japanese paid their unwelcome visit six decades earlier!

Australia has had a chequered relationship with Timor. Except for Papua New Guinea, it's our nearest neighbour; after Indonesia, Australia is Timor's nearest neighbour. The island has had a turbulent history, which has retarded its development. Initially it was a pawn in the colonial struggles between the Portuguese and the Dutch. Then it endured invasions by the Japanese in World War II and the Indonesians in the 1950s and again in the 1970s.

Timor is the biggest of the Lesser Sunda Islands, situated towards the end of the long Indonesian Archipelago, about 800 kilometres northwest of Darwin, between the South China Sea and the Indian Ocean. Today the island is divided politically roughly in half, with the western portion controlled by Indonesia and the eastern half now struggling to develop as the world's newest independent country. East Timor has about 750,000 people, West Timor perhaps another three million. Its inhabitants are of Malay and Papuan origin, with about one-third of the East Timorese population from the Tetum people. They speak Portuguese, Tetum and Bahasa Indonesian. The East Timorese are more than 90 per cent Catholic and less than 2 per cent Muslim. The island is long and narrow – about

110 km wide and 480 km wide – and heavily mountainous. It's reminiscent of parts of Papua New Guinea, although its mountains are smaller and the jungles less dense. Despite its beauty, East Timor's climate is harsh. Much of the island is semi-arid, yet the annual wet turns the mountainsides into torrents and washes away much of the soil, restricting cultivation largely to subsistence levels. Paradoxically, the wet season provides the farmers with their once-a-year chance to sow the crops of their staple diet, rice.

The East Timorese population was first drastically reduced by the Japanese invasion in World War II and then again in the years following the Indonesian invasion in 1975, where estimates of those killed range from 100,000 to 200,000 people.

To understand the island's convoluted pedigree we must look back 500 years to when the first European contact began, around the beginning of the 16th century, when Portuguese traders arrived, chasing sandalwood and beeswax. The Dutch, also in search of colonial expansion, followed early the next century, and the two colonial powers started a drawn-out dispute over control of the territory. The Treaty of Lisbon in 1859 split Timor between them – the Dutch taking the western half, the Portuguese the eastern, plus the enclave of Oecussi on the western side (which was the original Portuguese settlement).

That's pretty much how things stayed until the advent of the Republic of Indonesia in 1950, which saw West (Dutch) Timor subsumed into Indonesia. It's currently known as the Nusatenggara Timor province.

Australia's direct involvement began during World War II, when Timor suddenly acquired major strategic importance as a stepping stone for a Japanese advance on Australia. It loomed as a perfect air base for bombing and fighter attacks on the Australian mainland. To combat this threat, in December 1941 the Australian Army sent Sparrow Force, about 1400 soldiers, to help reinforce the tiny Dutch and Portuguese garrisons then on the island. The main force of the Aussies was centred on Koepang in the far southwest corner of Timor, where they defended nearby Penfui Airfield, base to a flight of RAAF Hudson bombers. Another Independent Company of Diggers based themselves at Dili (the modern-day capital of East Timor) on the north coast.

In mid-February 1942, just as Australian and American reinforcements were aboard transport ships bound for Timor, their convoy was attacked by Japanese fighters and forced to return to Darwin on 18 February. The very next day the anticipated invasion hit Dili as part of the Japanese sweep through the Pacific following Pearl Harbor. There the Diggers inflicted considerable casualties on the Japanese before successfully withdrawing to the centre of the island. At the same time a massive Japanese assault force, including tanks and paratroopers, landed at Keopang and tried to overwhelm the Australians there. The Diggers fought with great deter-mination, virtually destroying the paratrooper force (killing around two-thirds of them), but inevitably the numbers – about 1000 against a Japanese force which grew to 20,000 – began to take their toll. Split in half, surrounded and burdened with the growing weight of sick and wounded, the Australians fought for three days and nights. Then, almost out of food, water and ammunition, they were faced with an ultimatum: surrender or annihilation. At 9 am on 23 February, the bulk of Sparrow Force surrendered. But a group of about 250 of them escaped and headed east to join the Independent Company in East Timor.

These gallant Diggers then began a year-long guerrilla cam-paign of harassing the Japanese. Many East Timorese risked their lives and many forfeited them, helping the Australians in their covert conflict. The guerrilla warfare waged by those elements of Sparrow Force is an excellent example of the initiative, endurance, courage and independence which we have come to expect of the Digger. Out of contact from the end of February until 20 April when Darwin picked up their first message, the Diggers ignored repeated Japanese calls for them to surrender and many subsequent attempts to flush them out and hunt them down. By this stage the guerrillas had grown to around 700. They were supplied by air and sea and by the local Timorese and Portuguese people, and they were able to tie down the vastly superior Japanese force of more than 20,000. One of the Diggers, a former Western Australian kangaroo shooter named 'Doc' Wheatley, was said to have accounted for 47 Japanese.

The Sparrow Force survivors were ultimately recovered and returned to Australia. The Japanese wrought their customary vengeance on those left behind.

Six decades later, Australian Diggers have returned to play their role in helping rebuild East Timor. Section Two Three Bravo has a small but crucial job in ensuring that the brand new nation's borders are secure. Like so much of the Army, the patrol is a cross-section of middle Australia.

The oldest in the party is the section second-in-command, Lance Corporal Billy Boulton, from Queensland, at 34. The youngest is the First Scout, Private Joshua Nicholas, from Tasmania, at 19. Despite his youth, 'Nicko' is a qualified sniper, and he cradles his F88 Steyr semiautomatic assault rifle with practised hands as he scans the darkness with a slow, deliberate sweep. Only when he has looked and then listened does he move ahead. Behind Nicko, the second scout, 'Griggsy', 20-year-old Private Wayne Griggs from Perth, signals all clear to his section leader, Corporal 'Woody' Woodward, and moves off. Woody turns and signals the rest of the patrol to move off. Billy Boulton nods and steps lightly through the undergrowth – no mean feat considering that he, like the others in the patrol, is carrying gear weighing around 50 kilograms. Most carry three or four days' rations, at least 15 litres of water, and an amazing assortment of ancillary gear, including first aid packs, satellite navigation apparatus, night vision goggles, bivouac bags, mozzie nets, camouflage make-up, ammunition and F1 grenades. Two of the patrol, 20-year-old Private Brent 'Thommo' Thomson from Wagga Wagga and 19-year-old Private Clinton Holdsworth from Brisbane, are 'assault gunners' and carry the modern equivalent of the WWII Bren gun, the F89 Minimi automatic light support weapon. Like the Steyr rifle it fires 5.56 mm calibre rounds, but it has a magazine holding 100 rounds, to the Steyr's 30, and can be used to telling effect in a firefight. (Looking around you can see an obvious change in the weaponry: the Steyr's butt and its magazine are made from high-strength plastic, making it lighter and easier to maintain than its predecessors with their wooden butts and metal magazines. The magazine is transparent so a soldier can see how many rounds he has left without removing it.)

The veteran in the group is Private Scott Dudley, from Sydney, who's been in the army for seven and a half years. He provides much of the humour – as the resident 'angry ant' – and a lot of the common sense, as he insists the youngsters do the 'hard yards' and keep their minds focused on their tasks. 'Duds' is also the mechanical expert. He takes that role for the company as well and should be promoted to corporal by year's end. Private Matthew McMahon, the inevitable 'Macca', is a rangy 20-year-old from the western New South Wales town of Narromine. Macca carries himself with the laconic spareness of the typical Australian 'cocky' (or boy from the bush). In the absence of Private Nathan Charles, 24, from Brisbane, who is away on a communications course, Macca is the radio operator and must carry the communications equipment in addition to his normal gear. Macca is also qualified in combat first aid and is the team's medic.

The patrol's enthusiasm is impressive. They are enjoying the challenge of trying to move and work as a tightly knit team, each constantly glancing back to Woody or Billy to make sure everything is on track and to watch for their individual commands. Woody is very clear about his role:

'The section commander's job is to train his men, leading them into combat or operations and, at the same time, take an active involvement in their personal life. We have to rely on each other so much that if they have any personal problems which will affect their work, I want to know about them – relationship issues, financial problems, health, whatever.

'In the first instance I'll offer a helping hand – suggestions, counselling. If it's serious then the army has systems in place which can help them. My concern is that the problem can't affect our team.'

Woody and Billy are still building their working relationship. Billy joined the section from another company only about a month ago. A former factory worker, he's been in the Army almost five years. He joined relatively late, seeking goals and some structure in his life. Now 34, he's six years older than his leader Woody and has 15 years on some of the men. But he brings life experience and a worldliness which balances the unbridled enthusiasm of the youngsters. Woody recognises Billy's strengths and is consciously cultivating their partnership:

'The strongest link in the section has to be between the section commander and his 2IC. If that link isn't there, it's going to cause breakdown throughout the whole section. In a perfect world, everyone would get on really well as best mates and work together at the same time. That doesn't always happen. We're fortunate at the moment because we're all mates as well as colleagues at work.'

For months before Section Two Three Bravo was posted from its base in Darwin to East Timor, Woody has worked on building teamwork and maintaining their enthusiasm:

'If I wasn't trying to enhance their knowledge and to constantly push them, then I wouldn't be doing my job because they wouldn't be developing. They'd be sitting there idle, and idle soldiers are definitely not a good thing. The main emphasis is on a team rather than on individuals, but within the team you

must focus on the individuals and highlight and correct any problems, weaknesses and downfalls so the team can reach its full potential.'

The Digger has always had a low tolerance of soldiers who are not team players, as Woody explains:

'One of the first things we do with new members of the section is to encourage them to become a team member as much as possible. We try to make the transition from someone being an outsider to becoming a team member as smooth as possible so we can work more effectively. Otherwise, someone who isn't a team player will create a lot of stress within the group and the army will usually try to find him another role.'

In Digger-speak, a non-team player is 'Jack' – as in 'I'm alright, Jack'. He's a soldier who lacks respect, from the humble foot-soldier right up to the man at the top. Chief of the Australian Defence Forces, General Peter Cosgrove:

'You know, "Jackman" is probably one of the more printable things a non-team man is called. If a guy is "Jack", he doesn't pull his weight. If he doesn't pull his weight, if he suits himself, if he's unreliable because he'll just look after number one, if he doesn't do his job, then the Diggers will often say: "Oh. He's a Jackman." One of the worst insults or reputations you can have is to be a Jackman and that's a testament to the fact that our men and women are so interrelated, so mutually dependent on each other.'

There are no Jackmen in Two Three Bravo. All through the night they silently take turns in staggered pairs at watch over-looking the Tactical Coordination Line – the no-man's land between East and West Timor. Using night vision goggles, they constantly scan the river and its banks, which is the effec-tive border. At random intervals Woody sends out a two-man patrol to edge closer and make sure nothing is missed. But despite a few false alarms – mainly locals using the river as a toilet – dawn arrives with no contacts.

Once back from their patrol and even when relaxing in their hut at their Forward Operating Base at Maliana, the men of

Two Three Bravo remain on alert. They take their rifles (or, in Digger terms, their 'gatts') with them everywhere – even to the showers or latrines, even when they go on training jogs. When on operations, their entire world must fit into their identical 75 cm by 125 cm trunks at the foot of their stretcher beds. In our digital world, these trunks can contain far greater recreational equipment than in years gone by. Today's Digger has come a long way from the days of two-up. Walkmans, laptop computers, DVDs, video games, sound systems, digital cameras – all ease the long hours when the Diggers must, like all soldiers since Rome's Legions, 'hurry up and wait'. Eminem's latest CD provides the soundtrack as the boys head off to shower, grab breakfast and clean their gear ready for the next patrol. When they get back someone has swapped Eminem for, of all things, Paul Simon.

'What's that shit, mate?' asks Nicko.

'Paul Simon,' replies Billy, without a hint of shame.

'How eighties, mate!' comes from the back of the room.

Then, as if directed by some unseen conductor, they all start singing along to Paul Simon's 'Call Me Al' and break up laughing.

From the start, the Australian Digger has built his team-work around a curious amalgam: of mateship interlaced with 'piss-taking' humour; ingenious attempts to find better ways to carry out his tasks, interwoven with constant 'grizzling' about his predicament; pride in his work, leavened with a cavalier depreciation of his real value; love–hate relationships with officers whom he sees as coming from the 'dark side', balanced with a deep and lasting respect for those leaders who earn it; all wrapped in a cocoon of mutual protection centred on the core values that all Diggers share as a 'family'.

Peter Cosgrove has watched the Digger evolve first-hand for more than 30 years. He sees many things as constants:

Some of the vernacular has changed, the sort of taste in music has changed, the externals have changed but fundamentally they're exactly the same.

Cosgrove views the Digger as an ordinary Australian who has taken on an extra 'mantle' of responsibilities:

'The mantle is partly professional training, partly a mountainous aura of tradition and responsibility that goes with the notion of being a Digger.

'I see him as an ordinary Aussie, superimposed with the extra notion of being a soldier who values trust, mateship, loyalty and initiative. One of the great things that differentiates Australian soldiers from those of many other countries is that our soldiers are craving an opportunity to be heard, to express, to participate, to contribute, to innovate.'

Today, as Chief of the Australian Defence Force, General Peter Cosgrove relishes the rare opportunities he gets to talk to his Diggers:

'When I get an opportunity to talk to them at any length – a length more than two or three minutes – after the guy's got over the culture shock of talking to a General, after just a very short time, they think "Well, this guy's not going to bite my head off" and you start having a bit of a gossip. The years fall away from me and I could be a young and quite confident officer again. So I'll never lapse back to being perhaps the brand new boy, but I feel in conversation with the soldiers that the years have gone away and I'm talking the same sorts of Diggers I knew so well when I was a young officer.

'And the same sort of things get up their noses: people mucking them about; giving them four or five different versions of what's going to happen next; being treated like mushrooms – where's my mail, would be nice if we could get a hot meal hot and a cold drink cold, who's the idiot who designed the "no gear" policy. Among others it was probably me! The thing I find about soldiers too is if you can talk to them about what you want to do and why you're doing it, why you're asking them to do it, even if you're any number of ranks removed from them, which I tend to be these days, they appreciate it. So they don't want you to run round sort of babying them to make them happy. They hate to be taken for granted and not told why something which is obviously

hard needs to be done that way.

'So to me it's a two-way street, where you prise these charac-teristics out of Diggers then you've got to acknowledge them in the way you actually relate to them. Very few martinets, author-itarian sorts of popinjays, flourish in the army. Not just the soldiers but also the other leaders in the army don't like that style and somebody will either adjust their style or find a different employment.'

In some strange way, that feeling is consistent with Australia's return to East Timor. At the end of World War II Indonesia proclaimed its independence, and its driving force, President Sukarno, set about bringing his dream – an Indone-sia made up of the old Dutch East Indies – to reality. In so doing, many would argue that he replaced an ancient colonial regime with a modern one. In 1949, Indonesia came into being when the Netherlands gave up its colonies in the Dutch West Indies, including West Timor.

East Timor languished as a neglected Portuguese colonial outpost until a military coup in Portugal in 1974 weakened its hold over its colony. This provided the East Timorese with a tantalising chance of independence the following year when the Portuguese abruptly pulled out after 400 years of colonial rule. The result was a power vacuum. But just nine days after the Democratic Republic of East Timor was declared an inde-pendent nation in December 1975, Indonesia invaded and annexed it on 16 July 1976.

Only three nations, Australia, India and Papua New Guinea, officially recognised the annexation. It had the tacit compliance of the United States. The United Nations passed a resolution condemning the invasion but took no action. Resolution 3485 (XXX) read: *'Recognising the inalienable right of all peoples to self-determination . . . Calls upon all States to respect the inalienable right of the people of Portuguese Timor to self-determination.'*

Talk but no action. It was the Cold War. The USA and her allies wanted Indonesia, the world's biggest Muslim country, as a trading partner and ally. Compounding that, the main political force in East Timor championing independence was Fretilin, then dominated by Marxist doctrine.

In fact, Indonesia's invasion and its brutal occupation of East Timor largely escaped international condemnation. The tiny island's resistance movement was violently suppressed by Indonesian military forces, and as many as 200,000 Timorese are thought to have died from famine, disease and fighting since the annexation. It wasn't until the early 1990s that Indonesia's human rights abuses finally attracted international attention – largely due to the work of two East Timorese activists, Bishop Carlos Filipe Ximenes Belo and José Ramos-Horta, who won the Nobel Peace Prize in 1996 for their efforts.

Indonesia did an about-turn on its stance on East Timor in 1998, following the departure of the intractable President Suharto. The new president, B.J. Habibie, surprised the international community by agreeing to a referendum on East Timorese independence. But in the lead-up to the vote pro-Indonesian militia and the separatist guerillas clashed repeatedly, forcing two postponements. Eventually, on 30 August 1999, 78.5 per cent of the population voted for independence from Indonesia. Violence exploded immediately as pro-Indonesian militia and Indonesian soldiers turned on the East Timorese and their possessions. Buildings were torched, services such as electricity, phone and water were destroyed, and many civilians were killed. Around one-third of the population fled into West Timor or overseas.

It was in this chaos that the Australian Digger again proved his worth to the people of East Timor. The UN Security Council passed Resolution 1264 (1999), calling for the creation of an International Force in East Timor (INTERFET) to intervene in East Timor. The force, to be led by Australia, would address the deteriorating humanitarian and security situation. The Australian Commander of Interfet, the then Major-General Peter Cosgrove, had orders to: restore peace and security in East Timor; protect and support the UN Assistance Mission East Timor (UNAMET) in carrying out its tasks; and, within the capability of the force, facilitate humanitarian assistance operations.

The Diggers of Interfet left Australia on 19 September 1999 with the warm wishes of most Australians, as Peter Cosgrove remembers with pride:

'I've never seen such an outpouring of concern, sympathy, empathy, identification as we experienced when we headed off into Timor. We were heading off into the unknown and in those first few weeks I believe you could have cut the emotional outpouring with a knife. It was coming in through letters, radio broadcasts, television, the whole nine yards. The force was overwhelmed with these messages of concern, which uplifted them greatly.

'And that was from people who were perhaps playing their vicarious role as a Digger. A lot of mums and dads and brothers and sisters but, also, a lot of people who simply wanted to identify with the team – "Team Australia", but also "Team Australia in East Timor".'

Peter Cosgrove was the man for the job. He was imbued with the spirit of the Digger from birth as a third-generation Digger. His maternal grandfather served in both World Wars and his father was a WWII veteran and professional soldier:

'My Dad was, I knew – from what I knew as a young fella and then confirmed when I was in my very early years in the army – that he was rock solid. His word was his bond. John Cosgrove was reliable. If he said he would do something then everybody knew that he would move heaven and earth to do it. So his mates, his superiors, his subordinates could rely on him. So it was this notion that at the core of a soldier is somebody who must and can be trusted.'

The Army seemed the logical career path when Peter Cosgrove left school:

'I grew up in a family where the men wore khaki. But, notwithstanding the fact that I loved what I knew of the army through

my dad's service, it didn't make me necessarily an organised, self disciplined, highly self-confident individual. These are things you have to inculcate and grow. I don't think I shone through on the interview board as being "Oh, we must have this guy".'

In fact, the young Cosgrove only just made it into Duntroon:

'I know I squeaked into Duntroon because in this day and age you can ask to see your files. I'm well aware that the board wasn't wholly persuaded of my field marshal-type qualities at that time so the casting vote of the chairman was necessary to get me onto the successful candidates list.'

That chairman knew his stuff. Because, once he knuckled down, Peter Cosgrove emerged as one of our finest soldiers. From his first combat posting in Vietnam, within a year after receiving his commission, 22-year-old Lieutenant Cosgrove stood out. He won a Military Cross for bravery within a month of arriving in Vietnam as a platoon commander and revealed himself to be an outstanding leader of men. It was the start of a glittering career, which would culminate in his appointment in 2002 as the Chief of our Defence Forces.

Ironically, the Interfet deployment was our biggest since Vietnam, but from the start Peter Cosgrove was aware his men faced a very different task this time. Vietnam was high-intensity, all-encompassing modern warfare. East Timor loomed as a jigsaw of multinational cooperation in border and personnel protection, peacekeeping, diplomacy, humanitarian aid and nation building.

Just as he did in Vietnam, Peter Cosgrove rose to the occasion. He showed the leadership and determination necessary to establish the credibility of his force. And this, at the start, was not easy. Interfet arrived with about 5000 troops. Indonesia then still had 15,000 troops in East Timor – troops which, either with or without orders from their superiors, had participated in or stood by as pro-Indonesian militia destroyed much of the country's infrastructure and killed many of its inhabitants. Cosgrove's force, with his Diggers at the front, had stepped in between two deadly foes in full fight, with all the hazards such an exercise involves. But Interfet had arrived with such speed and had deployed with such precision that many observers believe they gave the impression of being a far larger force. Peter Cosgrove immediately sought and quickly achieved a balance between the threat of force his troops represented and the desire to end the violence peacefully. In all his work, he was aware of his responsibility to the Diggers:

'I think that people want to be reassured that when their sons and daughters have to apply violence it's a matter of regret, not because they did the wrong thing, but that violence was necessary.'

At this stage Peter Cosgrove also revealed his great capacity for diplomacy and his ability to explain the role and the actions of the soldier in simple, positive terms:

'At one stage in Timor there was border incident where an Indonesian policeman shot, a number of Indonesian policemen were shooting with automatic weapons, at our soldiers. Another Australian soldier in a slightly different position to the ones who were being shot at could see these men shooting at his mates and did the right thing — shot one of the policemen, killed him. There was no rejoicing over that. It was a matter of regret, of necessity, but of regret.

'Part of the public explanation of what had occurred was this: "How sad. If that man had not been shooting at our soldiers, he'd be alive today". But you know, the message here was: "Don't shoot at Australians or that might happen to you". But it could have been put the other way: "You shoot at Australian soldiers, you learn your lesson". That wouldn't have gone down well. I mean, the expression of it that way. I guess "he's learnt his lesson" would have sounded like rejoicing. So it just seems to me that in certain sorts of conflicts your people are hoping for the fact that the force can operate in a humane way.'

Peter Cosgrove's experience as a soldier tells him that in many other conflicts it's just not possible to exhibit the same level of overt humanity:

'When we were in Vietnam, we were sneaking around the jungle never knowing when we would come across a superior force who would beat the living daylights out of us. I mean, at Long Tan a reputed 2000 enemy force conducted human wave attacks, hour after hour, against a company's worth, perhaps 120, of our soldiers. There was not a lot of compassion in evidence there, you didn't have time for it. You either had temporary, momentary compassion for your own, [within your own] shrinking circle of Australians – how many of us are left? But there's a time and place, and I think we would have maximised the times and the places.'

Peter Cosgrove has often reflected on the contradictory nature of military leadership, in which the need for uncompromising decisiveness must be balanced against the need to maintain one's personal principles:

'I've got to be capable of being extraordinarily tough because in the end you need to employ a high level of ruthless and dispassionate logic when you are seeking to make hard decisions that put people in harm's way. As soon as you know what it is that must be done, cannot be avoided, you then need to engage immediately the other side, or hopefully the other part of the character which says, now how can we do this at minimal cost? And I hope that that's the compassionate side. In different jobs it ebbs and flows.

'When I was a young platoon commander in the midst of battle I had to be tough as nails, prepared if necessary to walk past a wounded colleague, a comrade, in order to prosecute the attack. You know, the most I might do is say "you fix him", but I had to be able to walk past that person. I mean, when my three soldiers were wounded my job when I got there was to first and foremost find out if the enemy was still there, what we were doing about it. If we didn't have that evidence, was the place secure? Thirdly, is somebody attending to the casualties? Next and most important I had to call for the helicopters to come in and take them away. And that's before I could even say "Oh it's Bill and Tom and Joe who've been hurt. Oh, how badly are they hurt? Well ..." I found out about how badly they were hurt as part of the calling for the helicopter, because part of the thing is you say how serious are these wounds, so you do have to have ... you have to be able to grip your own sense of compassion under certain circumstances, but that doesn't mean you should be absolute because if you are you're in big trouble. So I think it's more appropriate to display, exhibit, compassion as you get more senior in rank because your decisions will be quite far reaching, less instantaneous, so I should think that stifled compassion is more appropriate in the urgent and instantaneous needs of combat. But in any more measured activity you should-n't be afraid of saying "well, I'm going to do this but now I'll also start to measure how it can be done with a minimal human cost".'

In many ways Peter Cosgrove himself reflects the traits we admire in the Digger – courage, leadership, initiative and compassion:

'I think we carry our national characteristics with us, we don't subordinate any important element of the Australian character in the making and the life of a Digger. For example, we still very much have a sense of social justice which applies not just inter-nally to the army but in our dealings with other people. So I would be amazed if Australian soldiers seeing people of other nations suffering hardship, which they do if they go to an area of operations, they will see people who are down and out, if this doesn't strike a tremendous chord in the Digger's heart.

'I can recall in the Oecussi enclave a young Corporal from Support Company 3RAR. These troops were our security force down there and I was down visiting them. I used to visit them on frequent occasions. I was way down in one end of the Oecussi enclave about as remote as you can get and in amongst a group of about 10 or 15 3RAR soldiers when this corporal said: "Sir, can we get a doctor down here?" And I said: "Why, are you crook?" He said: "No, we're alright and we see our doctor or the medico from time to time when we need them but where I am I'm down right on this little village and there's just us infantry *soldiers here and we need a doctor and it's for the locals". I said: "Yeah, well I suppose I could look into that but you know we're still struggling to get the medical system laid out here in all of East Timor." I said: "What's the story?" He answered: "Well, about a week ago a bloke brought his wife to me and she was having a baby and he was tearing his hair out because she was in very strong labour and he didn't know what to do and we just got on with it." I said: "What do you mean?" He said: "Well, we delivered the baby." I said: "Was that a first for you?" He said: "Absolutely." He said in the end it was reasonably uncomplicated, everything worked out OK and baby's alright, the mother's made a good recovery and that's fine. I said: "Oh good. All's well that ends well." And he said: "Yeah but yesterday a lady presented with a breech birth . . . I'm not real good on those!"'*

Interfet's mission to restore 'peace and security' to East Timor has been judged a resounding success by most observers. The commander received accolades both from the UN chief administrator, Mr Sergio Viera de Mello, and from the leaders of the struggling nation, Mr Xanana Gusmao and Mr José Ramos Horta.

At a farewell ceremony in Dili, when General Cosgrove relinquished command of Interfet, Xanana Gusmao read a passage written by a soldier from Sparrow Force: 'Money cannot repay the East Timorese for their loyalty in saving the lives of Australian soldiers.'

Mr Gusmao then spoke directly to General Cosgrove: 'General, you have now paid the debt and the East Timorese people honour you for that. We thank you personally and we thank all Interfet from our hearts. When the children of our nation learn of the sacrifices made by all of our martyrs, they will learn also of the role of Interfet.'

General Cosgrove was visibly touched by the emotional response of the local population: 'We're absolutely delighted with the signs of affection and regard that have been given to us by the East Timorese leadership and the people.'

Later he added: 'It was an emotional moment for me and probably quite a few of my military colleagues to see that a military force can come into a country for five months and walk away with the people cheering it.'

Peter Cosgrove and his men have added to the reputation of the Australian Digger with their performance in East Timor. Their successors in the Australian battalions there have maintained the standard. They captured the hearts of most Australians with their approach to what was, particularly in the early stages of their deployment, a very difficult task. Above all, Peter Cosgrove's clear speaking and honest, compassionate leadership stand out like a beacon in a grey world of self-serving jargon-spouting heads of government and business who masquerade as presidents and premiers but are rarely more than 'presenters'.

THREE

The origins

Australia's military history began with the First Fleet in 1788. Four companies of the Marine Corps, totalling 212 men, were among the 1030 souls crammed into the 11 vessels that sailed into Port Jackson on the afternoon of 26 January 1788. The 548 male and 188 female convicts guarded by the Marines were the first of about 160,000 shipped from Mother England from that day until the last convict ship disembarked its sad cargo in Western Australia in 1868.

The birth of modern Australia was unique. No other nation has had to endure such a beginning: a bizarre social experiment in which a country simply exiled its problem citizens to what was then the equivalent of another planet. Britain may have had good trade and strategic reasons for establishing an outpost in this strange new land – trade with China and the East Indies and a naval base to neutralise French, Spanish and Dutch interests in the region – but the most pressing problem was finding a destination to which they could send the convicts previously dumped in America.

So the First Fleeters were dispatched to an unknown land, inhabited by a remarkable people who had been thriving there, hidden from the rest of the world, for at least 500 centuries before the Romans conquered barbarian Britain. In the introduction to *A Military History of Australia*, Jeffrey Grey makes a powerful point:

'. . . at the heart of white settlement of Australia, as elsewhere, lies the violent dispossession of the previous tenants, an aspect of our history with which many Australians have still to come to terms. The conflict between whites and blacks on the frontier of settlement was neither unique, nor uniquely horrible, but the failure to acknowledge its existence and the baleful consequences for Aboriginal people which flow from it is not only a profound discredit to us as a community, but suggest something of the in-security which has run through sections of the white population since the mid-nineteenth century: as we took this country, might it not yet be taken from us?'

What was unique was that these English outcasts not only survived the dislocation, the loss of their families, the strange land with its inhospitable climate, but prospered and created what has become one of the most advanced nations in the world. And they did it without the kind of civil war which many countries had to endure before finally achieving nation-hood. Surely their achievement is extraordinary. Perhaps it is not so surprising that these early Australians passed on some powerful character traits to their progeny.

Clearly, the convicts, and the free settlers who later joined them, sowed some of the original seeds of the Australian national character. Among them must have been independ-ence, energy, endurance, courage, ingenuity, resourcefulness and adaptability, along with a disdain for – even a hatred of – authority.

The calibre of the convicts varied widely. While the vast majority came from the oppressed lower classes, the harsh penalty system that prevailed in England swept up a substan-tial number of better-educated unfortunates. In England at the time, more than 160 offences carried the death penalty: from treason and murder down to deer-stealing and even cutting down trees. The next worst penalty was transportation, and that was imposed for crimes that included stealing goods valued at more than a shilling. Soldiers could find themselves on the boat for failing to salute an officer (a tradition the

Diggers of later centuries were to carry on with pride). Convicts from England, Ireland, Scotland and Wales blended their various national character traits into what soon became a vibrant, sometimes violent melting pot. Only the toughest survived and the most self-reliant and adaptable prospered.

But, as Tim Flannery points out in the introduction to his anthology, *The Birth of Sydney*, the influences on the Australian character were not limited to Old England:

'One might imagine that Sydney was a purely British creation, but that would be quite wrong. Quite apart from the Aborigines who had been there for 50,000 years, the Maoris and the Pacific Islanders, West Indians and Americans, Malays and Greeks put in early appearances, just to name a few.

'Within a few years, Muslim sailors would be constructing extravagant temples and filling the streets of the town with exotic Eastern festivals.

'It's important to note that this great social experiment was taking place in a strange natural environment whose impact was to be profound, for the timeless interplay between earth, water, air and fire that helps shape all cities was felt in Sydney from the very first day.'

Nevertheless, the dominant heritage brought to Australia had its roots in the rich tapestry of British history, which drew on influences from the Roman invasion, through the Middle Ages and down to the colonial era. It bred what the English historian Lawrence James described in his book *Warrior Race* as a 'warrior elite'. In Britain this warrior elite evolved into a ruling class, which won and maintained political power by their skills at arms:

'Its carefully cultivated concepts of personal courage, honour and self-respect based on indifference to danger lay at the heart of chivalry. It survived, blended Christian ideals of social responsibility and Renaissance notions of virtue, and was bequeathed to subsequent generations.

'The result was a persistent faith in the peculiar moral qualities of gentlemen which qualified them to command in war.

Their outlook and values made them the natural leader, which was why victory at Waterloo was allegedly won on the playing fields of Eton and why the RAF was desperate to recruit former public schoolboys with an aptitude for sport and experience as prefects to fly Spitfires in 1940.'

Another of the legacies of the Middle Ages was the crucial importance of a warrior's reputation, as James points out:

'It was a sentiment shared by warrior elites irrespective of nationality. Just before battle was joined at Bourgtheroulde in 1124, a Norman knight steadied his brothers-in-arms by telling them that their resolution and valour were soon to be assayed publicly. Reputation mattered, the more so if those who aspired to it were of noble ancestry. Courage transmitted, as it were, through the blood brought with it a special responsibility . . .'

The land Down Under worked on its settlers to mould different characters. The isolation, the Spartan conditions and the cruel land forced the early settlers to band together, and fostered the notion that the servant was as good as his master.

Life in Britain developed with the ruling classes passing on their positions of power, wherever possible, to their children. They created protective mechanisms in virtually all walks of life to protect the system and therefore their power and wealth. Schools, the Church, the armed services, professions, the civil service, political parties, sporting bodies and clubs, even Parliament itself, all served to maintain the system and the class structures that supported it.

For example, amateurism in sport originated in England: not as some noble Olympic ideal but as the result of the landed gentry trying to protect their control of many sports. They did that by insisting that anyone who couldn't afford to play 'for the love of the game' (because he had to earn a living) was to be either excluded or categorised as a 'professional', and therefore treated using different rules. In fact, until after World War II, English county cricketers were divided into two classes: 'players', or those who were paid to play; and 'gentlemen', who played for the love of the game. Although members of the same team, they often changed in different dressing rooms and took the field through different gates. Amateurs were introduced as 'Mr Jardine', while the professionals were called 'Larwood'.

Britain was an 'upstairs–downstairs' society, where the aristocracy and the landed gentry lived high on the hog and those languishing at the bottom of the scale 'knew their place'. This approach had particular resonance in the military, where wealthy families purchased army commissions for their sons. Virtually all officers were 'born to rule', as Lawrence James writes:

> 'It was not just that the Renaissance gentleman had learned how to ride and had mastered the difficult skills of swordsmanship. Or that he was accustomed to giving orders and expected respect and obedience. Or, and this concept had its roots in feudal society, that he had been taught to feel a moral duty towards his inferiors.
>
> 'Honour gave him the ultimate right to command. Bravery and courage were contagious. Men who did not comprehend the niceties of honour were more prepared to risk their lives when they saw those who did hazarding theirs. Moreover, a gentleman was obliged to defend his honour with force, hence the duel was a public test of courage in the face of death. All the virtues prized by the medieval knight were cherished by his successor, the gentleman officer.'

Imagine how offensive this system was to those early Australian settlers. And imagine the reaction of British officers when exposed to the colonial reality. Even when the colony was opened to free settlers from around 1820, it retained a strong military flavour. Some early problems with the New South Wales Corps, which centred on illegal trading in rum (a common occurrence at the time among colonial troops) and led to clashes between the military and the early governors, resulted in 1808 in the overthrow of Governor William Bligh (who seemed to make a habit of it). The following year Governor Lachlan Macquarie replaced the NSW Corps with his own regiment, the 73rd. This began a succession of 26 British infantry regiments, which would garrison the Australian colonies until 1870. As Jeffrey Grey notes, there was not a great difference between many of the early troops and those they were guarding:

'Many officers were frequently absent from their regiments, often insubordinate, and just as frequently drunk. Their attitude to their military duties was casual, and day-to-day administration and training was very largely the province of NCOs.

'Officers had little to do with the rank and file who were in any case separated from their superiors by a yawning social gulf. "Whoever 'listed for a soldier'," wrote one such in 1805, "was at once set down among the catalogue of persons who had turned out ill". Another ex-soldier, writing in the 1840s, noted that the British Army "as is well known, is the dernier resort [the last resort] of the idle, the depraved and the destitute".'

Essentially, the British Army had degenerated to the stage where it consisted of the bottom-dwellers of the society, led by officers who, in the main, where aristocratic amateurs. Indeed, even the great Duke of Wellington once remarked of his force:

'I do not know what the enemy will make of them but, by God, they frighten me.'

But while generally maintaining the colonials' pre-existing negative attitudes against the rule of law and the military, the various regiments did make some positive contributions. They established the Mounted Police in New South Wales, helped to build fortifications, guarded goldfields, treasuries and government buildings, and attempted to keep the peace. As the years passed, the military control over the colonies lessened and their involvement with the communities became more cooperative. For example, military engineers surveyed much of early Sydney and helped build roads and bridges and ports, and soldiers were often used as firefighters.

There must have been a considerable dampening in the antipathy towards the military and, indeed, the Mother Country as the years progressed and the numbers of free settlers grew. The pro-Empire sentiment expressed by those who willingly fought to defend British interests in the second half of the 19th century is testament to that change in attitude, and was a precursor to the enthusiastic response in the rush to Britain's defence at the outbreak of World War I.

Our first soldiers sent to fight overseas were the four regiments, including 1475 volunteers, sent by the colonies to assist in the New Zealand Maori Wars. They had little chance to develop any definable national character as a force and, in fact, were even called the Waikato Militia (because that's where they were fighting). But the first Australians to be killed in a foreign war ironically fell fighting in the land of our greatest ally, New Zealand. Four Victorians from the 1st Waikato Regiment (largely recruited from Australians) died during a skirmish with Maori insurgents at Mauku, near the Waikato River, on 23 October 1863. Another 1200 Australian volunteers joined the following year and some took part in the first pitched battle in which the Australians fought, at Te Ranga in the Tauranga District. The battle forced the surrender of the Ngaiterangi Tribe and was the last substantial engagement of the Waikato campaign. Many Australian volunteers accepted the offer of land in New Zealand as a reward for their service, but most had drifted back to Australia by the 1870s.

The first genuinely Australian military force – one drawn from volunteers – to fight overseas was raised in 1885. It came about as a result of the Australian colonies' response to the actions of the Dervishes of the Sudan. Under their leader, Muhammed Ahmed, known as the Madhi (or 'expected one'), the Dervishes, an Islamic sect, overran the British garrison at Khartoum and killed them all, including the famous British General Charles 'Chinese' Gordon. Gordon was widely loved and, in a surge of colonial patriotism, the government of New South Wales offered to send 750 troops to help recapture the Sudan. Drawn from volunteers it acquitted itself well, fighting alongside units as famous as the Grenadier Guards, the Cold-stream Guards, the Scots Guards and the Royal House Artillery. The Australians served from 29 March through to 13 May, but saw only sporadic action.

The Sudan episode was a dress rehearsal for the next time the Empire called for assistance from its loyal colonies, and it came soon enough.

On 11 October 1899 the South African republics of the Transvaal and Orange Free State declared war on Britain. Australians leapt to the defence of the 'Mother Country'. Thousands volunteered to fight against the Boers, the descendants of the original Dutch settlers in South Africa, who were trying to free themselves from what they saw as British interference in South Africa. New Zealand, Canada, Ceylon and India also rallied to Britain's side. The conflict had been simmering since the First Boer War of 1881. It was to be our first major conflict.

Within three weeks of the declaration of war, 200,000 Sydneysiders lined the city's streets to farewell the first troops to leave for the war. At the end of November around 1200 left in a convoy from King George's Sound, Western Australia. By the time they reached Cape Town, they found that a contingent of the NSW Lancers, which by coincidence had been undergoing training at Aldershot in England, had been diverted to Cape Town on the way home and was already in action.

The Australians quickly impressed. Many were included in the specially selected Imperial Light Horse which defeated a force of Transvaalers at Elandslaagte on 21 October 1899. They set the tone for the impression created by the Australian troops during the war, as recorded later by one of their commanders, British Major General E.T.H. 'Curly' Hutton:

'No man, be he Cromwell or Napoleon, could drive Australian troops. But a strong and capable leader no matter how strict,

*could lead an Australian army to emulate – aye and surpass, if
need be, the finest and most heroic deeds recorded in the annals
of the British Army.'*

Clearly, some of the key ingredients in the makeup of the
future Digger were already evident: his independence and his
fighting spirit.

During the course of the Boer War, Australia sent 859
officers and 15,064 men (12,000 before Federation and 4000
after), including 16,357 horses and around 220 guns and
wagons. A total of 57 Australian contingents took part: 15
from New South Wales, eight from Victoria, nine each from
Queensland, South Australia and Western Australia, and
seven from Tasmania. Our casualties totalled about 1400, of
which 251 were killed in action and 267 died of illness.

Our troops generally fell into three groups: those funded by
local government or private subscription; the Imperial
Bushmen, who were backed by the Imperial War Office; and
the Commonwealth Contingents, raised after Federation but
paid for by the British.

The first Australians to die in the war were two troopers
from the Queensland Mounted Infantry, who were killed at
Sunnyside on New Year's Day 1900 – the first day of a new
century, which would see at least 100 million more die in
wars – 100,000 of these were Australians.

From the start, the Australians established a reputation as
resolute fighters. The Boers also quickly won grudging
respect for their courage and their unconventional guerilla
tactics. On 9 February 1900, 20 West Australian troopers, led
by Captain Hatherly Moor, were on patrol with a squadron of
Enniskillen Dragoons east of Slingersfontein. They clashed
with a Boer commando unit of about 400 men. The West
Australians were assigned to cover one of the flanks, and
withstood a series of withering attacks by the Boers who
attempted to encircle the force. In *100 Years of Australians
at War*, George Odgers records the appreciation of one of
the Boers at the West Australian troops' fighting qualities in

the face of overwhelming numbers:

'We tried to crawl from rock to rock to hem them in but they, holding their fire until our burghers moved, plugged us with lead. To move upright to cross a dozen yards meant certain death. They did not play wild music. They only clung close as climbing weeds to rocks and shot as we never saw men shoot before and never hope to see men shoot again.

'Then we got ready to sweep the hill with artillery but our Commandant, admiring those brave few who would not budge before us, in spite of our numbers, sent an officer to them to ask them to surrender, promising them all the honours of war.

'But they sent us word to come and take them if we could. "Go back and tell your Commandant, Australia's here to stay," they said.

'We tried to rush them under the cover of the artillery fire but they only held their posts with stouter hearts and shot the straighter when the fire was hottest. We could do nothing but lie there and swear at them though we admired their stubborn pluck. They held the hill till all their men were safe and then dashed down the other side. They made off carrying their wounded with them. They were but twenty men and we were 400.'

The NSW Lancers and the Queensland Mounted Infantry were prominent in the conflict. They helped establish the Australian tradition of always leading the way in an attack. One of the company commanders of the Queenslanders was the remarkable Captain Harry Chauvel, who would later rise to Lieutenant General and lead the famous Desert Mounted Corps in World War I – at five divisions, the biggest cavalry force of modern times under the command of one man. Chauvel and his men were prominent in the relief of Kimberley and Mafeking, but perhaps the most outstanding achievement of the Australian forces in South Africa occurred after the war had degenerated into a guerilla-style conflict, at Elands River.

Attracted by a large storage dump at an outpost at Elands

River in western Transvaal, a large force of Boers attacked the small Australian garrison. Under the command of General Koos de la Ray about 3000 Boers, with accompanying artillery, laid siege to a garrison of about 300 Australian troops and 200 Rhodesian volunteers. The siege began on 4 August and continued with constant shelling from five Boer artillery pieces for ten days. After six days, the Boer commander demanded that the defenders surrender. He was met with this response from the British commander, Colonel Hore:

'I cannot surrender. I am in command of Australians who would cut my throat if I did.'

The garrison outlasted the siege. Their furious defence had dissuaded the Boers from attempting a frontal assault on the position. The Boers finally admitted the position was beyond them and retired. Two days later the garrison was relieved by a force under General Kitchener.

The famous British detective novelist Sir Arthur Conan Doyle wrote in his memoirs of the Boer War:

'This stand at Brakfontein on the Elands River appears to have been one of the finest deeds of arms of the war. Australians have been so split up during the campaign that although their valour and efficiency were universally recognised, they had no single large exploit which they could call their own. But now they can point to Elands River as proudly as the Canadians at Paardeberg . . . they were sworn to die before the white flag would wave above them.

'And so fortune yielded, as fortune will when brave men set their teeth . . . when the ballad makers of Australia seek for a subject, let them turn to the Elands River, for there was no finer fighting in the war.'

The Australians fighting in the Boer War made significant contributions in virtually all the areas in which they fought. Their overall impact was watered down because the force was split up and incorporated into so many other units, but six Australians won Victoria Crosses.

The first VC awarded to an Australian serviceman was won

by Captain Neville Howse, from the NSW Medical Corps, at Vredefort in the Orange Free State on 24 July 1900. Howse risked heavy cross-fire to cross open ground to pick up a wounded man and drag him to safety. He would serve with distinction in World War I and become the Federal Minister for Defence after the war.

Lieutenant Guy Wyllie and Trooper John Bisdee, of the Tasmanian Imperial Bushmen, both won VCs for rescuing wounded on the same day during the battle at Warm Bad in Transvaal on 1 September 1900. Lieutenant Fred Bell of the WA Mounted Infantry won his for gallantry on 16 May 1901 at Brakpan, Transvaal, and Trooper James Rogers of the South African Constabulary was awarded his VC for repeated acts of bravery in Thaba Nchu in the Orange Free State on 15 June 1901. On 23 November 1901 our last Boer War VC went to Lieutenant Leslie Maygar of the 5th Victorian Mounted Rifles, for gallantry at Geelhoutboom in Natal. He would later die gloriously in the great charge of the Australian Light Horse at Beersheba in World War I.

By late 1900 the Australians in South Africa were becoming disillusioned at the conduct of the war. The fighting was now predominantly sporadic guerilla warfare and the Boer civilian population was caught up in the process. The British 'scorched earth' approach, which involved burning Boer farms and imprisoning their families in the newly created 'concentration camps', alienated many of the Australians. After they began to show open disaffection, the initial contingents were progressively returned home from December 1900. There they received an enthusiastic welcome.

But the war continued and fresh volunteer contingents, the Bushmen and draft contingents, were raised in Australia and sent to Cape Town. Some incidents involving these men revealed a darker side to the conflict.

First, at Wilmansrust on 12 June 1901, the 5th Victorian Mounted Rifles was ambushed by Boers at night. Caught completely unawares, the unit lost 18 killed and 42 wounded in the initial onslaught and the rest either fled or were temporarily captured. The Boers destroyed or stole the Victorians' horses; then, unable to travel with prisoners, they freed them. Their British commander, Major General Stuart Beatson, labelled his troops a 'fat-arsed, pot-bellied, lazy lot of wasters' and another British officer called them 'a lot of white-livered curs'. Not surprisingly the troops reacted, and three of them were subsequently charged after being overheard telling their mates they should not take the field again under Beatson's command. The three Australians were court-martialled, found guilty of inciting mutiny, and sentenced to death. The sentences were later commuted to prison terms. Nevertheless, the incident was raised in the new Australian Parliament, with the issue centring on the British control of Australian soldiers. This led the then Prime Minister Edmund Barton to question the British government, which intervened, found flaws in the courts martial, and released the men before they had completed their sentences.

A far more serious incident occurred towards the end of the war when three officers from the Australian Bushveldt Carbineers, a special force which had been conducting a guerilla campaign in northern Transvaal against the Boers, were charged with the murder of Boer prisoners. One of the officers, Lieutenant Harry 'Breaker' Morant, had a strong public profile as a bush poet and balladeer for *The Bulletin*. He and Lts P.J. Handcock and G.R. Witton were found guilty by a British court martial. Morant and Handcock were sentenced to death but Witton's death penalty was commuted to life imprisonment. Morant had admitted shooting the prisoners but claimed he was acting under orders that no prisoners were to be taken. He won lasting fame for refusing a blindfold and for calling to the firing squad: 'Shoot straight you bastards! Don't make a mess of it!' The actions of the three Australians won little sympathy or support at home, although it contributed to the view that Australian authorities should control any disciplinary action against our soldiers.

In the aftermath of the Boer War, the British Elgin Commission commented favourably on the dash, the courage and the initiative of the colonials, including the Australians. Several witnesses before the Commission expressed the view that the Australians were 'soldiers of great potential'. But the Commission also pointed to some interesting shortcomings in the Australians: they were good horsemen but poor horse masters; their marksmanship needed work; and their officers were poorly trained.

Many of the British officer class believed that the Australian Army, with its citizen soldier base, would not be able to stand up against a fully professional army. They maintained this view right up until the Anzacs proved it wrong at Gallipoli. General Sir Ian Hamilton, who would lead the Anzacs at Gallipoli, held that view too, but he did see the potential of the individual Australian soldier:

> 'The best assets of the Australian land forces . . . are to be found in the natural soldierlike spirit, in the intelligence, and in the wiry and athletic frames of the bulk of the rank and file . . . Patriotism, keenness, study and careful instruction, strain and struggle at the heels of practical experience and habits of discipline, but rarely quite catch them up.'

Hamilton's eyes would be opened at Gallipoli.

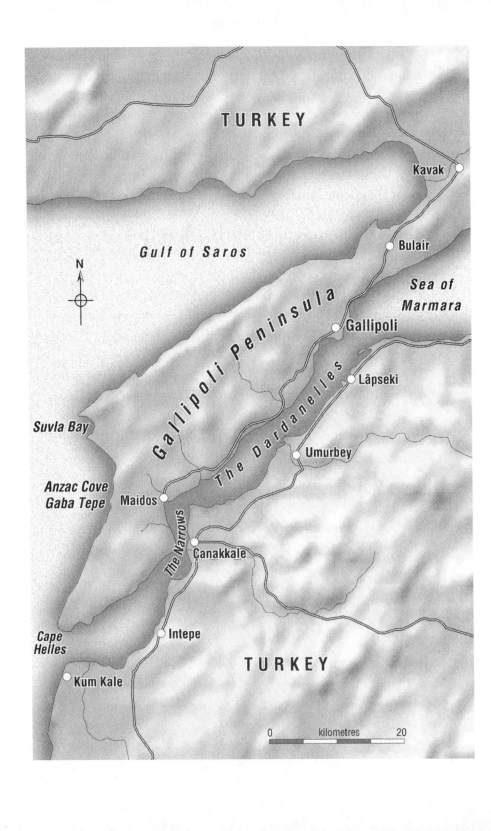

FOUR

Gallipoli: The spirit of Anzac

It has been raining for three days as winter creeps across the peninsula. The land seems to bear the drenching with quiet resignation. So does the lone shepherd, who turns his face from the stinging squalls that whip across the waters of the Dardanelles and lash his flock as they trudge along the shore-line. The sheep need little encouragement when the shepherd urges them into a stone-lined opening in one of many manmade grassy hillocks. As they file into the shelter, the shepherd relaxes and lights up a smoke. His face is weathered like the rocks around the cavernous entrance, lined with hard experience.

It is a scene typical of this land and of its people – one of adaptation, endurance and survival. The shelter has been here for centuries. Originally it was part of the network of massive gun emplacements protecting the waterway that divides Europe and Asia. Today local shepherds use it to shield their flocks from the worst of the Turkish winter.

Our guide here is Captain Ali Efe, a compact, courtly man with beautiful manners and a ready wit. He's the ideal size for his former profession, a submarine commander in the Turkish Navy patrolling the Black Sea during the Cold War. After retiring he studied history at the University of Istanbul, majoring in World War I. Now he acts as a special guide to the battlefields of Gallipoli. 'My name is Ali Efe . . . a small

Turkish name for a small Turkish man,' he says, offering a welcoming hand.

Aged 66, Captain Ali knows the land here intimately. As a child he spent long days roaming the Gallipoli battlefields with his father, Ahmet. Ali's dad was well versed in the history and folklore of the place – as well he might be. His father, Hussein (Ali's grandfather), died fighting the Anzacs.

Hussein Efe was a fisherman who came from an ancient village, now known as Guzelyali (or 'beautiful beach') but originally called Dardenos (after which the Dardanelles were named) on the Asian side of the Dardanelles, about 15 kilometres from Çanakkale, the closest large city on the Asian shores of the Dardanelles. Hussein died during the terrible fighting at a tiny ridge the Turks called Kanlisirt (or 'Bloody Ridge'). The Australians know it as Lone Pine. Ali's dad, Ahmet, was just six months old when his grandfather was killed.

Captain Ali is deeply connected to the land he loves. Like the trees here, the poplars, pines, apple, peach, almond and olives, he draws sustenance from the land. Ali also understands the Australian fascination with Gallipoli. He shares our reverence for the place and the actions that occurred here:

'The Anzac soldiers on the battlegrounds, with their blood, gained the Anzac spirit and they gave that Anzac spirit to the people of Australia and New Zealand. It is the best gift. It was won by their blood. If you gain something with your blood it should be a sacred thing.'

Captain Ali feels a powerful personal connection with the campaign:

'My grandfather was 22 years of age when he lost his life on Lone Pine. He had a baby son. That six-month-old baby son became my father. We are part of the land here.'

This land has always lived under threat of invasion. For thousands of years it's been sought after and fought over. You can see that in the structure in which the flock shelters. Massive stone walls, sunk deep into the earth and built to withstand the heaviest bombardment, open out to reveal a honeycomb of passageways and rooms which protected men and munitions. The air is cool and dank and the walls and ceilings are black with mould. It's part of a labyrinth of similar fortifications woven into the surrounding countryside on both shores of the Dardanelles.

These fortifications played a special, if indirect part in Australian history. From these chambers Turkish gunners fed ammunition to great guns which bombarded the British fleet in March 1915 as it tried to force its way up the Dardanelles to Constantinople (modern-day Istanbul). The success of the Turkish soldiers who manned these chambers in repelling the world's greatest naval power led the Allies to change to Plan B: land attacks on the peninsula. These in turn gave birth to the Anzac legend.

Today, the only sounds here are the occasional low bleating from the flock and the whistling of the wind as it plays across the entrance to the bunker. But it's easy to imagine the deafening blasts of 18 March 1915 and to see those gun-layers straining every muscle to maintain the supply of explosives to the gunners outside. The British fleet was trying to bludgeon its way through to Constantinople. It had the finest ships afloat, 18 battleships in all, each bristling with massive guns and all spewing their deadly missiles at the shore batteries. The Royal Navy, along with ships from its French allies, planned to stand off the coast, out of range of the shore batteries, and use the greater range of its guns to blow the Turkish defenders aside. Even now, deep in the chambers, you get a fleeting impression of the claustrophobic fear that must have pervaded the place as the artillerymen heard the cacophony of destruction above them and waited for what must have seemed their inevitable turn to be blown into atoms.

But the Turkish defenders fought with superb tenacity and the Allied fleet was soon caught in a deadly quandary. The Turks had mined the straits. The British knew that. They had tried on many occasions to sweep the waters prior to the massed fleet attack. But the Turkish guns had rained fire down on the minesweepers and forced them to back off before they could complete the work. This placed the British East Mediterranean Fleet's naval commander, Vice-Admiral Sackville Carden, in a dilemma. He couldn't defeat the shore batteries until he brought his fleet into the Dardanelles so they could wreak their havoc from close range, but he couldn't risk bringing the fleet in closer until he'd swept clear the mines.

Carden was a cautious, even ponderous leader, believed by many to be dominated by the bombastic First Lord of the Admiralty, the young Winston Churchill. Churchill saw the Gallipoli campaign as a great career move: a bold gamble, which could open up the route to Russia, bring critical supplies to the beleaguered Tsar's armies and force the Germans to continue fighting on two fronts. Churchill, along with the British Secretary of State for War, Lord Kitchener, was convinced the Turks lacked the heart for a prolonged conflict. The British High Command also believed that, once the Turks had seen the might of the Allied Fleet in action, they would throw in the towel. Another theory adopted by the Allies was that, because Constantinople was largely made up of wooden buildings, it was susceptible to the threat of massive fires that might result from naval bombardment once the fleet reached the city. The feeling was that the Turkish administration would surrender rather than risk such a terrible conflagration.

Churchill harried Carden until he tossed the dice and ordered his fleet into the Dardanelles. Carden was taken sick on the evening of the attack and Vice-Admiral De Robeck took over command.

The inevitable happened. After some early successes against the shore guns, first the ageing French cruiser *Bouvet* and then the British warships *Irresistible* and *Ocean* struck mines. The *Bouvet* went down almost immediately, losing almost all her crew. The *Irresistible* and *Ocean* were both disabled and eventually sank, and many other ships were hit. Fully one-third of the fleet was sunk or disabled in one day.

De Robeck pulled back his badly mauled force and licked his wounds.

The desperate Turkish defenders forced the British to change their attitude and their plan of attack. They would now try to take the peninsula with land forces supported by the Navy. For the men in the shore batteries along the Dardanelles it was a mighty victory. Ever since, 18 March 1915 has been revered in Turkey as the day their brave gunners overcame all the odds to send the invaders packing. It was yet another battle honour in the long history of the defenders of the Dardanelles.

We are at one of history's great gateways. Since the middle of the 15th century, huge batteries of guns on either side of the straits have barred passage to ships intent on sailing up through the Sea of Marmara to attack Constantinople, which stands astride the Bosphorus, one foot in Europe, the other in Asia. This thin, 60 kilometre-long channel, which opens the way from the Mediterranean via the Aegean Sea, through the Sea of Marmara to the Black Sea, has witnessed some of history's most critical turning points. It has seen many great armies on the march. Almost all of them have passed through, heading to other conquests.

Agamemnon tried it more than 3000 years ago when he arrived with 1000 'black ships' transporting 100,000 Greek warriors attacking the Trojans, the inhabitants of the city of Troy on the Asian side of the channel. Then Xerxes, the Persian, swept through here on his way to Athens in 480 BC. In 334 BC Alexander the Great travelled in the opposite direction, bound for India.

The place where the shepherd shelters with his flock is called The Narrows. Europe and Asia almost touch here. Just 1.5 km separates them: 1500 metres – the distance Murray Rose, Keiren Perkins and Grant Hackett swam to win gold at the Olympics – between forts, which dominate the high ground on either side of the water as it flows to the Aegean. On the Asian side, the Cimenlik Fortress (meaning 'grassy', because part of it is hidden under the earth) guards Çanakkale, a city which grew up around the fort between the port and the Saricay ('yellow') River. On the European side, the heart-shaped Kilitbahir ('lock of the sea') Fortress stands sentry to the town of Eceabat. Mehmet II, conqueror of Constantinople, built both fortresses halfway through the 15th century. Legend has it that his great guns could fire cannonballs only about 800 metres, just over halfway across The Narrows – hence the need for the twin fortresses to cover the full span of the channel.

There is still no bridge across The Narrows, and travellers must make the crossing by car ferry. During the crossing you get an inkling of how invaders must have felt running the deadly gauntlet between the fortresses.

In so many ways this is where the legend of the Anzac began. It happened by accident. It arose from adversity. It ended in defeat. But somehow, from the dregs of an ill-planned, poorly executed and ultimately pointless campaign, three nations drew positives. The armies and the peoples of Turkey, Australia and New Zealand all emerged with enhanced reputations. Though suffering grievous losses (more than a quarter of a million killed and wounded), Turkey emerged with renewed national self-respect. And both Australia and New Zealand emerged with a brand new repu-tation. As captain Ali points out:

> *'You can imagine the Turkish defenders' surprise when they discovered the invaders who landed at Ari Burnu* [from then on to be known as Anzac Cove] *had travelled halfway around the world to try to steal their country.'*

For most of the young Australians who answered the bugle call when Britain declared war on Germany on 4 August 1914, it was a chance for a great adventure. The respected WWI war correspondent and historian Charles Bean likened it to a crusade. Perhaps it's the same with all wars, but this was Australia's first chance to play a role in a world conflict.

The Prime Minister, Joseph Cook, said simply that when the British Empire was at war, so was Australia. And the Labor leader, Andrew Fisher, fully agreed, famously promising 'our last man and our last shilling' to the cause. Australians and Kiwis volunteered in their thousands for this great adventure. Men came from the bush, from country towns and from the Big Smoke. Bean believed the Aussie soldier had a head start because of his upbringing:

'The Australian was half a soldier before the war; indeed throughout the war, in the hottest fights in Gallipoli and in the bitterest trials of France or Palestine, the Australian soldier differed very little from the Australian who at home rides the station boundaries every week-day and sits of a Sunday round the stockyard fence.'

In these heady early days, only the finest specimens were accepted into the Australian Imperial Force, the First AIF, and then only after having passed rigorous physical examinations. The successful recruits had to be at least 5 feet 6 inches tall, with a chest measurement of 34 inches. They had to be at least 19 years old and not older than 38. Those with flat feet or physical defects were rejected out of hand. Those with poor teeth – a far more common occurrence in those days – were also turned away. These restrictions naturally eased as the war dragged on, but the first waves of men who would earn the title 'Anzacs' were the cream of the crop. More than half of the 416,000 Aussies who enlisted during the course of World War I had worked with their hands as labourers or tradesmen, and one in every seven came from the land. Interestingly, about one-third of the volunteers had been born in Britain.

The New Zealand volunteers joined the Australians at Albany in Western Australia and then the force embarked for an unknown destination. This turned out to be Alexandria in Egypt, where they were put into strict military training. Not surprisingly, the young Anzacs didn't take the military life too seriously, and spent much of their time looking for a good time in Egypt.

Charles Bean believes the word 'Anzac' was actually coined in the weeks before the Australian troops left Egypt on their way to Gallipoli, and gives the credit to an Aussie lieutenant, A.T. White. Author John Laffin, in his book *Digger*, mentions that others have variously credited the Gallipoli campaign commander, Sir Ian Hamilton, the Australian detachment commander, Lieutenant General Sir William Birdwood, and Major C.M. Wagstaff, among others. But Laffin believes the most likely explanation is that some unknown clerk saw 'Australian and New Zealand Army Corps' on cases of supplies and shortened it to Anzac on telegrams. The top brass saw the sense of this, and the rest is history.

The actual planning for the Gallipoli landings fell to the Scottish-born British General Sir Ian Hamilton. On 12 March, Kitchener appointed Hamilton commander of the forces supporting the British Navy's attempt to force the Dard- anelles. By then 'Johnny' Hamilton was 62 and had been a serving soldier for 42 years, with active service in South Africa, Burma, India, Afghanistan and the Sudan. Clearly he was a brave soldier, with two unsuccessful recommendations for the Victoria Cross. He'd been recently responsible for England's land defence and was keen for a final combat command. Kitchener gave Hamilton the British Regular Army's 29th Division, two divisions of Anzacs, the Royal Naval Division and a French contingent, a total of about 70,000 troops. (We now know the High Command's secret plan was that once Hamilton's force had taken Constantinople and defeated the Ottoman Empire, it would be given to the Russian Tsar Nicholas II.)

Hamilton's state of mind and the level of his preparation can be seen in excerpts from his *Gallipoli Diary* published in 1920, some of it from notes he dictated in 1915:

'But my knowledge of the Dardanelles was nil; of the Turk; of the strength of our own forces next to nil. Although I have met K [Kitchener] almost every day during the past six months, and although he has twice hinted that I might be sent to Salonika,

never once, to the best of my recollection had he mentioned the word Dardanelles.'

In essence, Hamilton's plan relied on two diversionary actions and two main attacks. The first diversion was assigned to the French army, which was to land on the Asian side, near Troy, and to carry out feint attacks to keep the main Turkish units occupied on that side of the Dardanelles and out of the major operations on the peninsula. The second feint was to be made by the Royal Naval Division on the isthmus, near Bulair, where the Turks expected the real thrust.

The genuine attacks were to be made, first, on Cape Helles, which was assigned to the 29th British Division, which would land at five beaches, code-named S, V, W, X, Y, on the toe of the peninsula and, second, by the Anzacs at Brighton Beach, halfway along the peninsula's Aegean coastline.

The 29th British Division and the First French Division joined the Anzacs in Alexandria, and then General Hamilton took his force across the Mediterranean and through the Aegean Sea to the Greek Islands of Lemnos, Skyros and Imbros. When Hamilton inspected the troopships there, he found they'd been very poorly loaded and withdrew to Alexandria for reorganisation. It was a major error. Vital weeks were lost while the Turks worked relentlessly on their defences. The Aussies of the 3rd Brigade spent the time training on Lemnos, climbing high cliffs and getting used to their massive packs, which weighed more than 40 kilograms; with additional ammunition they reached up to 68 kilograms!

By this stage, the Turks were well aware of the imminent invasion. The British intelligence and security had been laughable, and reports of the intended campaign had been published in Egyptian newspapers. Although they were still recovering from their losses in the Balkan Wars, the Turks knew they were fighting for their families and their land. Under the overall command of the German General Otto Liman von Sanders, who had been seconded to beef up their military, they rushed to shore up their defences. General von Sanders placed

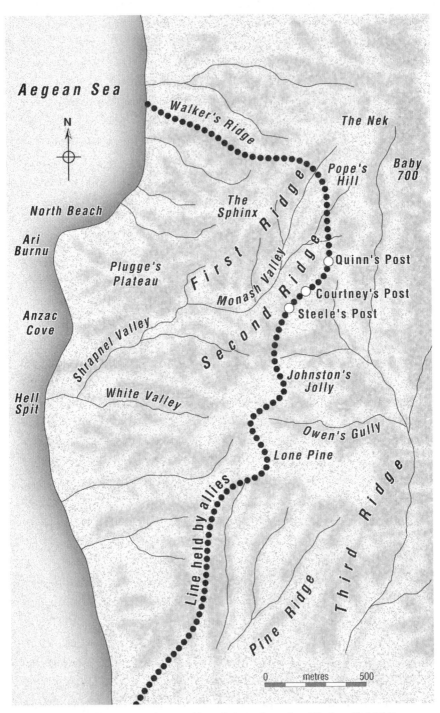

Allied positions on the Gallipoli Peninsula, 25 April 1915

two strong divisions on the isthmus, where he was sure the Allies would make their major landing. (In fact, many military experts now believe that had the Anzacs or the British 29th Division, or both of them together, with the support of the British Fleet, landed there as von Sanders feared, they could have cut the peninsula so that the Turkish Army there had no supplies from the mainland and would have had two choices: surrender or fight to the death.) General von Sanders also positioned two divisions near Troy on the Asian side and another about 8 kilometres inland from Brighton Beach at Bigali.

Before dawn on Sunday, 25 April 1915, around 4.30 am local time, the Anzacs began their terrible journey into immortality. Even as they started landing on the peninsula, as so often happens under combat conditions, the plan began to unravel.

Brighton Beach was a good choice. It was long and flat, with more flat ground just behind it leading into the Wolf Valley. The Anzacs could land, move up the Wolf Valley and then turn left and capture the main objective of the whole exped- ition, the high ground near Sari Bair and Chunuk Bair. This high ground held the key to the whole campaign. If the Anzacs took it they could position long-range guns there and dominate the peninsula, destroying the Turkish installations and cutting the peninsula off from the mainland. Then they could silence the big Turkish guns from close range, put in their own artillery, allow minesweeping, and open the way for the British Fleet to steam straight up to Istanbul.

But the Anzacs were not landed at Brighton Beach. Instead, in the confusion, they were set down almost 2 kilometres north of their intended destination in totally different terrain. The Australian 3rd Brigade was dropped off around a small headland which the Turks called Ari Burnu (or Bee Point). The South Australians and Tasmanians landed to the north of Ari Burnu and the Queenslanders and South Australians landed to the south, along the beach that would become known as Anzac Cove.

The Anzacs' major objective was to capture the high ground. Ironically, when they began their landing there were virtually no Turkish defenders on the high ground. Just behind Ari Burnu, on the first ridge, about 160 Turkish troops waited. Turkish High Command had neither expected nor even imagined any landing around Ari Burnu, because the terrain behind it was like a natural castle, with steep slopes up to sharp ridge lines and a maze of dead-end gullies. The closest substantial Turkish force was near the high ground, in a small village called Bigali, where there was a mobile Turkish division, the Turks' only reserve division.

Captain Ali explains how the Turkish defenders felt as they prepared to meet the invaders:

'We have two old sayings: One, it is the responsibility of any man, if he is a man, to sacrifice his own life to defend his own family members. And two, if a man is trying to defend his own wife, his own family, he'll be two times stronger than normal.'

In addition, the Turkish soldiers' religious beliefs sustained them:

'We are generally a secular country but we have some strong religious beliefs. One is that when a Turkish soldier is killed on the battleground, his spirit goes directly to paradise. So, Turkish soldiers were not scared to die in battle. In fact, they hated dying in a hospital.'

The Turks facing the Anzacs had the strongest possible motivation for fighting to the death:

'The Turkish soldiers' wives stayed at home on the farms, continuing production, harvesting and supplying yoghurt, milk, fruit, vegetables and repairing their men's uniforms and shoes. They stayed very close to the battlegrounds and indirectly encouraged their men to fight to the death to protect them. The soldiers were defending their own homes, their own families, not just their country in general.

'Finally, the bitter and determined resistance by Turkish soldiers fighting on the peninsula was due to the quality of the men involved. The defenders had been selected one by one from

thousands off the farms and out of the local villages, mainly from country areas, often from the mountains. They were not pampered city people. They knew the land intimately, were hardened and accustomed to living rough.'

One of the Turkish officers silently waiting for the invasion was Major Mahmut Bey, quoted in *Bloody Ridge Diary* by Hasan Basri Danisman:

'On 25th April, 1915, at 0430hrs, when intensive enemy fire raked out shore, we blew our whistles, reserve companies were called to arms and took positions at the double.

'With naval gunfire concentrating mostly on our advanced skirmishing line, the shoreline was covered with heavy black smoke, tinged with blue and green. Visibility was zero. In comparison to the volume of fire poured on it, the targeted area was disproportionately small. Many shells fell in close proximity of each other and shrapnel exploded in rapid succession . . .

'Two of our 37.5 guns were knocked out and many of our advanced positions and communication trenches were levelled. Foxholes, meant to protect lives, became tombs.

'. . . the enemy approached the shore in lifeboats. When they came into range, our men opened fire. Here, for years, the colour of the sea had always been the same, but now it turned red with the blood of our enemies.'

These were the implacable foes the Australians faced as they struggled up the rocky gullies above Anzac Cove. Albert Facey, a 20-year-old private, was in the second wave of the landings. He recalled his feelings in his autobiography, *A Fortunate Life*:

'This was it. We were scared stiff – I know I was – but keyed up and eager to be on our way. We thought we would tear through the Turks and keep going to Constantinople. Troops were taken off both sides of the ship on to destroyers . . . all went well until we were making the change to rowing boats . . .

'Suddenly all hell broke loose; heavy shelling and shrapnel fire commenced. The ships that were protecting our troops returned the fire. Bullets were thumping into the rowing boats. Men were

being hit and killed all around me. When we were cut loose to make our way to the shore was the worst period. I was terribly frightened. The boat touched bottom some thirty yards from shore so we had to jump out and wade to the beach. The Turks had machine guns sweeping the strip of beach where we landed . . . there were many dead already when we got there. Bodies of men who had reached the beach ahead of us were lying all along the beach and wounded men were screaming for help . . . we used our trenching tools to dig mounds of earth and sheltered from the firing until daylight . . . the Turks never let up . . . the slaughter was terrible.'

The small initial Turkish defensive force fought to the last but took a heavy toll on the attackers, as one of the original Anzacs, Private Gordon Craig, later explained in a letter to his brother Ken as he lay recuperating from wounds in Egypt (published in *Simply Hell Let Loose* published by the Department of Veterans' Affairs in 2002):

'A tug took us within 100 yards of the beach and we had to row the rest of the way. The shrapnel was bursting all round us, also machine guns, rifle shot.

'We lost a lot of men before we landed but our boat got safely ashore.

'Well we landed. We marched about 100 yards and then took a rest and then word came up to go up into the firing line at once. We threw our packs away and then got on with the game. The country was so rough and scrubby that you couldn't see where you were going and the shrapnel was bursting all round us and the bullets were so thick that we thought they were bees buzzing about us.'

Private Craig typified the Anzacs as they experienced their baptism of fire. His letter also reveals traits common to many of his mates – individual initiative, and a healthy cynicism for officers who refuse to take command:

'By this time we were all mixed up with different companies and I heard one of our officers call out "Are there any men about here?" So I called out that I was there. So we advanced together.

We came to a gully and we laid there for a rest. The shrapnel was worse than hell, was getting nearer to us every minute, so I said to the officer that we ought to get into the firing line and try and pot a few Turks before we throw a seven. The rotten beggar wasn't having any so I left him.'

Private Craig finally made it to the front line and made his presence felt before he became another casualty in the firestorm:

'Then I got up to the firing line. I was lying next to a major who was shot in both legs. He asked me what sort of shot I was so I told him not bad, so he told me to try the range at 500 yards, but my shot went over their heads so tried 450 and got right on to them. It was awful hearing the wounded crying out and seeing the dead lying round you.

'Well, after a while a bullet hit me, and just grazed my wrist enough to burn the skin. I didn't take any notice of that, but about five minutes after one got me clean through the arm. I tried to go on but was settled. Just as I got hit the chap next to me got one also.

'I then made my way back to the beach. I reckon I have more luck than Jessie the elephant not getting hit on the way back. When I got back the doctor dressed my wounds. I went into the hospital boat. We lost 15 men on the boat. There were about 5000 to 6000 wounded and killed the first day.'

The courage under fire shown by the Anzacs during the first day of the landings impressed all observers, including the Turks. There were countless stories of individual acts of bravery in the most extreme circumstances. Most went unrecorded. Charles Bean reports on the actions of Lance Corporal Noel Ross, who, on the afternoon of the second day, noticed some movement among what had been presumed to be dead bodies, which lay where they'd fallen during the dawn landing in the deserted landing boats along the shoreline at Anzac Cove. While he watched, a figure scrambled out of a boat and hobbled along the beach. He immediately drew Turkish sniper fire and collapsed:

'Ross went out with four men along the beach to bring him in.

When they had gone a few hundred yards, the sand and the stones about them began to be whipped by Turkish bullets. They dropped behind the bank of the beach, and, dodging from shelter to shelter, reached a point within hail of the wounded man. He was lying out in the open, but, little by little, crawled to cover. He had been shot through both knees and nearly collapsed, but his spirit was high, and they brought him back. There were four others in the heap, he said, still alive. There had been eight but four died before the dawn.'

Sergeant Baker later wrote to his friend Vera Johns back home of his feelings at the landing (the letter was published by the Australian War Memorial in its magazine *Wartime*):

'Their fire was getting absolutely murderous, but our chaps advanced again and again and were dropping in all directions, but would not be stopped.

'That Sunday [April 25] *should live in history, for the Australians proved what stuff they were made of and many a one made a hero of himself. And many a poor fellow died urging his mates onward with his last breath.*

'... Many of our officers were shot down and most of the time we had no orders at all, but had to rely on ourselves to do the best we could. Whenever we did happen to see an officer the order was always the same: "get ahead lads and stick it into them".'

Sergeant Baker spoke of the growing pride with which the Anzacs were beginning to view themselves:

'Our lads all the time were behaving splendidly. We had often been told that a soldier dies of fright the first few minutes when he first goes under fire, but dear Vera that is rot. It makes you feel a bit uncomfortable but it also makes you want to get at the enemy and give him a bit of his own back – with interest. One bad point about our fellows was that they were too eager and rushed ahead in any sort of order, often exposing themselves unnecessarily.'

The raw horror of war was exposed in every form:

'Here is a tragic happening, Vera – a chap that had half his face blown off was seen to coolly finish himself off with his own rifle.

One of his mates was with him at the time.'

This selfless approach was typical of the response of the Anzacs, who seemed to instinctively band together right from the start of the campaign. The mateship that developed amid this tragic loss of the flower of Australian and New Zealand manhood somehow ennobled their terrible ordeal. It grew to represent something more than friendship, or camaraderie, or comradeship. It was greater than the shared experiences of brothers-in-arms, although all these things are elements of mateship at its purest level. Mateship has a spiritual element, which sets it apart from the esprit de corps experienced by many other soldiers. Many nations' soldiers have a powerful esprit de corps which sustains them in crisis. But most centre on their regiment or colours or corps and extend to include the soldiers serving in or under them. For the Anzacs – and for the Diggers who followed them – mateship centres on the soldiers themselves and it extends outwards from there. At Gallipoli, mateship formed a cocoon that enveloped the Anzacs and made their existence there bearable. It gave them greater confidence because of the unconditional communal support that surrounded them, and it created a teamwork that produced a force far in excess of its individual components. At its centre was selflessness. This was wrapped in mutual respect and sealed with an unbreakable determination not to let each other down. As it has in subsequent conflicts, mateship often meant the difference between life and death at Gallipoli as the Anzacs alternately fought and began to dig themselves into whatever defensive positions the terrain allowed.

During the chaos of that first day one small piece of Australian history almost went unnoticed. Captain Joseph Peter Lalor of the 12th Battalion was ordered to bring re-inforcements across Malone's Gully to the beleaguered 2nd Battalion under the command of Captain (later Sir Leslie) Morshead. Lalor was the grandson of the Eureka Stockade's Peter Lalor, who led the 'Diggers' of the Victorian goldfields in their rebellion at Ballarat in 1854. At Malone's Gully Lalor was supposedly carrying the same sword his grandfather had wielded at the Eureka Stockade as he prepared to order his men to charge the Turkish positions. According to Bean's report:

'Lalor stood up to see and resolved to charge forward. "Now then 12th Battalion", he cried; and as he said those words a Turkish bullet killed him.'

A grudging respect for the enemy began to emerge among the Anzacs as the days wore on, as Lieutenant Richard Thomas Tarrant of the 2nd Battalion, 1st Infantry Brigade, later wrote to his mother, as quoted in Neville Kidd's *An Impression Which Will Never Fade*:

'On Tuesday morning the 27th (Harry's birthday) at 6am, I was sent out on a patrol to look for "snipers". Those are men who must be looked upon as having grit, even though they are Turks. They creep up by themselves, as close as they can, and "pot" anybody off that comes within sight. They nearly always lose their lives as they are sure to get caught.'

Lieutenant Tarrant and his men continued advancing through the rugged country, finding shelter from the constant Turkish fire in every dip in the ground:

'I got under cover as well as I could and tried to push forward. But it was slow work. We had to wait for a few minutes here as we were under heavy machine-gun fire. My next move was about five yards, as every time one exposed himself he was a "goner". The Turks at this time were only about three or four hundred yards away, to our front and well entrenched, whereas we were only lying on the ground. We could not get a good view as we had scrub all round us, and we were at a disadvantage. Altogether, we were only in the firing line, at this point a while when my little turn came.

'The two men on my left were "outed" and the man on my right also went under. Someone on my right was also crying out – "For God's sake finish me off. Shoot me someone." Reinforcements were being mown down in trying to come to me. I seized a man's rifle on my left and fired about twenty rounds, when

I felt a sharp pain on my left leg between the knee and the instep. It was just like being hit with a brick, edge on, thrown with some force. I found it was no good lying there, and waited until another officer came up, and then tried to stand up, but over I went and my heel turned around and looked at me. I was pulled back by the right foot for about thirty yards into a trench onto a dead man.

'I could not have been there long when another man fell across me wounded. I was dragged back a little further and had my leg roughly dressed. One man from old G Company stayed with me until I was carried away on a stretcher. He was shot through the right shoulder. He was able to walk back to the Dressing Station, but I could not get rid of him.'

It was an often-repeated scene as officers and men stuck by each other. Lieutenant Tarrant's comrade could have moved out of the danger zone to safety, but he stayed with him until they could both reach safety together. It was an unsaid connection, wordlessly appreciated by both parties. And many of the Anzacs showed that, despite the horrors they were enduring, they still retained their essential humanity, like Lieutenant Roy Harrison, writing to his cousin Emily from Gallipoli (also quoted in *An Impression Which Will Never Fade*):

'The first day we landed the smell of crushed wild thyme was beautiful and, strange to say, it made more impression on my mind than a lot of things that happened that day. We use the thyme for seasoning our stews, etc now. We had a little soup today.'

Roy Harrison was one of the lucky ones who survived the landing unscathed. More than half of the first wave of troops landing were either killed or wounded. The Anzacs soon established their beachhead around Anzac Cove. It extended along the shore for a little more than a kilometre and then, in a wedge pointing inland for a little more than a kilometre, a total area of about 160 hectares within a perimeter of about 2 kilometres. To see why they were held up in their advance, we have to look at what happened on the other side of the front line.

::

The commander of the Turkish reserve division that happened to be positioned at Bigali, inland from Anzac Cove, was to change the whole outcome of the campaign with his actions early in the invasion. That man, Lieutenant Colonel Mustapha Kemal, would go on to become the first President and founder of modern Turkey and be known as Ataturk, which literally means 'Father of the Turks'. Kemal wasn't even a full colonel, let alone a general, when the invasion occurred. But he was a man destined for greatness.

About five minutes after the Australians landed at Anzac Cove, a salvo of massive British naval shells exploded on top of the first ridge above the beachhead. It was the first salvo of the campaign. When Kemal heard it he immediately woke and called his commander for instructions. But the commander, General von Sanders, was out of his HQ and at the isthmus, responding to the British feint there.

Kemal the instinctive leader now emerged. He used his own initiative and gambled. First, he gambled with his own life, because he had no authority to deploy his troops. They were a critical reserve unit and had he failed he would almost certainly have been executed (this was the way in the Turkish Army). Then he gambled again. And it was to be a decision that changed the outcome of the entire campaign. Kemal sent his troops not to the actual landing area at Anzac Cove but straight to the high ground, about 3 kilometres inland from it. When siting defensive positions, soldiers always identify what they call 'the ground of tactical importance'. They define that as: 'the ground which, if held by the enemy, makes your position untenable'. Kemal knew the high ground near Chunuk Bair was that ground: whoever held it held the key to the peninsula. Kemal ordered his famous 57th Regiment there.

Ironically, when he did so, the Turks and the Anzacs were about the same distance from this key ground. But because the Anzacs had been landed at Anzac Cove and not at the intended Brighton Beach, they were forced to slog their way through a hailstorm of shrapnel up the steep gullies above Plugge's Plateau as they headed for the high ground.

The Turks had a much easier route. Kemal rushed a considerable distance ahead of his men to observe the landings. To get a better view, he had moved in front of the defensive lines at the high ground when a group of the first Turkish defenders rushed past him in full retreat. They told him they were out of ammunition. Suddenly the first Anzacs appeared behind them. Kemal was as close to the Aussies as he was to his own lines. He again acted instinctively. He ordered the wavering Turks to fix their bayonets, form a line and take cover. When the Anzacs saw the Turks taking cover, they followed suit. Kemal grabbed his chance. He rushed back and immediately ordered his men into their defensive positions on the high ground. They reached the ground of tactical importance just ten minutes ahead of the Anzacs.

It was ten minutes that changed the campaign. You can even argue it was ten minutes that changed history. If the Aussies had beaten Kemal's men to the dominating heights at Chunuk Bair, it's unlikely the Turks could have sustained their remarkable defence of the peninsula. Had the Allies overrun them, there's little doubt Constantinople would have fallen. Supplies would have been rushed to the faltering Russian Army and, once bolstered in material and morale, it might not have collapsed as it did in 1916, opening the way for the communist revolution the following year. Russia might have gained Turkey (as was the secret Allied plan), the Tsar might have had sufficient clout to stave off the communist risings, and Ataturk would never have risen to power.

But Kemal's leadership ensured that the campaign would drag on. His historic orders to his men as they waited for the Anzacs' assault set the tone for the campaign:

'I do not expect you to attack, I order you to die. In the time which passes until we die, other troops and commanders can come forward and take our places.'

One of the first major tests faced by the Anzacs came on 19 May. The previous day, the gallant Australian General Sir William Throsby Bridges, commander of the 1st Australian Division and the father of Duntroon, had been killed by a sniper. On 19 May two events occurred that have gone into Australian folklore: first, the remarkable Private John Simpson 'the man with the donkey' was killed by shrapnel in Monash Gully as he brought in yet another two wounded men on his donkey; second, the Turks launched a massive counter-attack, aimed at sweeping the Anzacs back into the sea.

The Turkish commander, General Liman von Sanders, gathered four divisions, 42,000 troops, in the valleys behind the front lines facing the Anzac beachhead. It was more than twice the number of the Anzacs. Von Sanders gambled on an all-or-nothing surprise massed assault. But, warned by British naval reconnaissance aircraft, the Anzacs were ready. When the Turkish attack came, the Australian rifle and machine-gun fire was withering. The Turks fell in their hundreds. Entire companies were wiped out. When von Sanders called off the slaughter after eight hours 10,000 Turks had fallen, 3000 of whom were killed. The Anzacs lost 160 killed and 468 wounded.

The day after the 19 May counterattack, unofficial truces broke out along the front line as each side recovered the dead and wounded from no-man's land. On 24 May the grizzly task was completed under a formal armistice. These ceasefires gave the two sides their first opportunity to eyeball the men they were fighting. Tokens were exchanged – photos and smokes. This first tentative peaceful contact sowed the seeds of the respect with which each side would view the other after the campaign. The Anzacs began calling their enemy 'Johnny Turk', or 'Jacko' or 'Abdul', with the typical ambivalent Australian respect for an honourable foe. There would be no lessening of intent to defeat the Turk, but the Anzacs now knew they were fighting men who were, like them, doing their best for their country.

By June and July the campaign had degenerated into static trench warfare – a constant round of sniping, grenade throwing, tunnelling and patrolling, along with the ever-present artillery bombardment. While the fighting may have ebbed somewhat and casualties eased, the toll taken on the Anzacs by their cramped, unsanitary environment was rising sharply. Incessant flies and the constant lice in their clothes added to the dysentery, enteric fever and diarrhoea that raged through the position. Even morale weakened under the strain of constant combat and the enervating heat. As one Anzac said: *'Of all the bastards of places this is the greatest bastard in the world.'*

He wasn't far wrong. Charles Bean reported that life at Anzac *'differed from experience on the main fronts in that the troops were nowhere away from shellfire and had practically no chance of rest in peaceful conditions.'*

Until late in the campaign, Anzac was deprived of any canteen or even Red Cross stores, and mail came fortnightly. The Anzacs had no delousing apparatus for the fleas and the lice infesting their trenches and no proper dental treatment. By the end of July, Bean noted that the 25,000 Anzacs on Gallipoli were being depleted by around 200 men a day, who were being sent to hospital in Egypt because of sickness. The Regimental Medical Officer of the 15th Battalion AIF wrote:

'The condition of the men of the battalion was awful. Thin, haggard, as weak as kittens and covered in suppurating sores. The total strength of the battalion was two officers and 170 men. If we had been in France the men would have been sent to hospital.'

Charles Bean described the sight of Anzac Cove, which was piled high with the detritus of war:

'Anzac Beach was a sight perhaps never before seen in modern war – a crowded, busy base within half a mile of the centre of the front line; and that strongly marked and definite entity, the

Anzac tradition, had, from the first morning, been partly created there.

'From the moment of launching the campaign it was the resolve of those Australian soldiers who would usually be regarded as non-combatants to show themselves not a hairs-breadth behind the combatants in hardihood.'

Roy Harrison wrote to his Emily on 24 July:

'The heat is great, consequently few of us feel inclined for meals when they are ready. Then again, the strain of 90 odd days on end in the trenches with shellings and blowings ups etc, long hours and interrupted rest, pulls one down. Personally, there is no feeling of illness, but I can't bear half the fatigue I could three months ago, and most of the others feel the same way.

'It's over three months since I slept with my boots off, and how I look forward to even one night in a bed with clean sheets and a real pillow, and by the way, something SOFT to sit on. The ammunition box for a seat is very uncompromising and though better than no seat at all, suffers when compared with the lounges of the old "Derfflinger", which brought us from Alexandria.'

To break the deadlock, General Hamilton called for more troops. Kitchener sent five more British divisions to be used on the peninsula (English, Irish, Scottish and Welsh troops). They were to be landed behind the salt lake at Suvla Bay, perhaps 8 kilometres north of Anzac Cove. When they arrived their commander, Lieutenant General Sir Frederick Stopford, was overcautious and wasted three days with his troops waiting on the beach for heavier artillery pieces to be sent from Egypt. In addition, the beachhead was chaotic, with the final two divisions landing on top of the three earlier divisions.

Had he moved immediately, Stopford might have turned the tide. He could have advanced to join the Anzacs and over-whelmed the Turks facing them. At the time Stopford's force landed, on nearby Chocolate Hill, just 1500 Turkish defenders prepared to confront the 70,000 fresh British soldiers. But General Stopford waited offshore aboard the yacht *Jonquil* for his guns to arrive.

The Turkish commander, General von Sanders, did not hesitate. He rushed his two divisions from the isthmus to confront the British. Some of the bloodiest fighting of the entire campaign was about to erupt. Ironically, the attacks on both Lone Pine and The Nek, two of the most famous battles of the whole campaign, were designed as feints to try to divert Turkish defenders away from the planned British landings at Suvla.

Today, after three days of squalling rain, Lone Pine is drying under a gentle winter sun. A wind ruffles the leaves of the solitary Aleppo pine tree which stands sentinel to the neat rows of gravestones. Like most battle sites, Lone Pine retains an aura. You may visit it alone but you will feel the presence of other souls there. And that's not surprising, for, in an area about the size of two tennis courts, more than 4000 Turkish soldiers and 2200 Anzacs fought and died for their countries.

Today they rest here – the vast majority together in a mass grave under an impressive stone memorial that commemorates those with no known graves and, spread in front of the memorial, rows of individual headstones honouring those who died here and were identifiable.

Even today one is struck by the shocking cost of life for such a tiny area of territory. The site is a flat, open space on the top of an exposed ridge with views back to the Aegean Sea and the Greek islands beyond. The battles here were war reduced to its most primitive and most visceral: hand-to-hand combat to the death. Here brave men fought like gladiators, with bayonets, rifle butts, fists and boots, as the trenches filled with the lifeless bodies of the vanquished. Still they battled on, literally standing on the corpses as the conflict raged for four days and four nights.

On the very first day of the Anzac landings, around noon, some Victorians from the 6th Battalion made it up here to Lone Pine. The Anzacs originally named the spot Lonesome

Pine after an American song, 'On the Trail of the Lonesome Pine', which was very popular around the start of the war. Over time it became known as Lone Pine. (The Lone Pine that thrives here today is a descendant of the original, which was destroyed during the fighting. After the Aussies captured the position, one of the Anzacs who lost a brother here picked up a cone from one of the dead tree's branches and sent it home to his mother as a keepsake. She raised a tree from seed shed by the cone. She later presented that tree to the Australian War Memorial in Canberra where it still thrives, southwest of the main building. Seedlings from this tree have subsequently spread around Australia and one was returned to its original site, here where it all started.)

The Turks had a perhaps more appropriate name for Lone Pine. They called it Kanlisirt, or 'Bloody Ridge'. This hallowed ground came into prominence because the Anzacs were called on to assault the Turkish trenches here as a diversion to cover the landing of the British reinforcements at Suvla Bay under the tardy General Stopford. A simultaneous, virtually suicidal attack against the entrenched Turkish machine guns by other Anzacs along another exposed ridge line at The Nek was the central assault in Peter Weir's evocative movie *Gallipoli*.

During the battle at Lone Pine, the Turkish trenches were in several rows right under where the main Australian memorial stands today. The Australian trenches were in six rows under where the gravestones now lie. Just a couple of cricket pitches separated the two front lines.

The mateship we have come to expect from Australians banding together, especially in times of crisis, was present while the Anzacs counted down the final minutes before the assault, as Charles Bean reports:

'By 5 o'clock the 1st Brigade was in position, crowding below the openings in the underground line and on the firestep of the old, deep, open trenches fifty yards behind. "Can you find room for me beside Jim here?" said an Australian who had been

searching along the bays. "Him and me are mates an' we're going over together".'

Under a full moon, on 6 August at 5.30 pm, Australians from the 1st, 2nd, 3rd and 4th NSW Battalions, 7th Victorian Battalion and 12th Battalion, South Aussies and Tasmanians, all original Anzacs, rose from their trenches and surged towards the Turkish trenches. They wore white armbands and white patches on their backs so they could recognise their mates in the silver moonlight.

At the end of the four-day battle, for the first and only time since the landings, the Turks withdrew. But they set up a new trench line just 39 metres behind their previous positions. So, for the sake of two tennis courts' worth of land, 6000 souls perished.

Lieutenant Malcolm Cotton took part in the Lone Pine assault and later wrote to his family about it while recovering from wounds he received there:

'We charged over to the Turks' trench about 5.30pm on the 6th [of August] *under deadly machine gun fire and rifle fire but I managed to get there alright although I don't know how I did it . . .*

'The shelling they gave us and the bombs were pretty hot the whole time. About midday or a little after, they made a bomb counter attack. They threw over about 50 bombs [grenades] *in as many seconds and I tell you things were pretty lively for a while . . .*

'About 10 bombs were picked up and thrown out of the trench before they exploded, grand work. I eventually got it and I am glad I can write the fact and more so pleased that I can say my wounds are only slight. Poor Rube Cradick was shot dead on the charge.'

Lieutenant Roy Harrison was also there, as he wrote to his cousin Emily:

'The signal for the assault was 3 short whistle blasts. The whole line moved as one man, but instantly the Turks opened a terrific fire, and almost at once, the dust thrown up by bullets and shells striking the ground, hid everything a few yards away, from view.

The fight was terrific for a time, and one corporal from B Co is credited by several of the men with having killed 17 Turks with his rifle and bayonet before being killed himself.

'*The Colonel and I crossed with the 4th wave, and as their machine guns and artillery were waiting for us, we got some hurry up. Those of us who were lucky enough to miss the bullets, tumbled into the enemy trenches without loss of time. The place was choked with dead and wounded, and in many places, it was impossible to avoid walking over the dead.*

'*When light came, the second morning after the assault, the trenches were 3 deep with dead and wounded and in one partic-ular trench, were three and four deep. To pass along, it was necessary to crawl over the dead and the living . . .*

'*The sights and sounds come up to anything I have yet read, and surpassing my wildest dreams as to what war really meant.*

'*My old platoon was with the first wave, and not one man answered the roll call, when we were relieved by fresh troops on the 8th.*'

Of the 27 officers and 576 men who were with Roy Harrison at the start of the attack, 21 officers and 420 men perished. The Anzacs won nine Victoria Crosses in eight months at Gallipoli, seven of them in three days at Lone Pine: Lance Corporal Leonard Keysor; Lieutenant William Symons; Corporal Alex-ander Burton; Corporal William Dunstan; Private John Hamilton; Lieutenant Frederick Tubb; and Captain Alfred Shout. Not surprisingly, the valour of the Anzacs impressed the Turks, as Roy Harrison attested:

'*One Turkish sergeant who was captured, said: "We will go out to meet the French, we will wait for the British to come up to our trenches, but the Australians we will not face and no amount of driving will make us do so." That is a reputation to win, and the Turk himself has the name of being a very stubborn man when fighting on the defensive.*'

Roy Harrison, a hardened veteran now after three months of constant fighting, revealed the changes to the Anzacs since their baptism of fire at the Anzac landings. He compared the sense of anticipation before the landing to that before the Lone Pine attacks:

'The night before the landings was similar in a sense, but there was unrestrained skylarking and fun generally, for we were all strangers to war. On the night preceding Lone Pine, however, everyone knew exactly what to expect, and there was no foolery.'

The Lone Pine Memorial, the main Australian memorial here, marks the maximum Australian advance into the peninsula during the entire eight-month campaign and is a paltry 1.2 kilometres from the beachhead at Anzac Cove. At the end of the Lone Pine battle, the dead were piled like bags of grain in the Turkish trenches. It was in the full heat of the Turkish summer and the bodies began decaying quickly. The Turks stopped firing from their new trench line and the Anzacs realised it was a message: bury the dead. The Australians buried all the dead in the first, second and third Turkish trenches, the deepest of the trenches, and turned it into the largest mass grave on the peninsula.

One of the Turks buried in that mass grave is Captain Ali's grandfather, Hussein:

'The Turks and the Australians lie in the same graves here – not just side by side but embracing each other. That is why the Lone Pine memorial is sacred to both sides.'

As he speaks, Ali's keen eye has spotted something in the earthen mound below where we have been sitting, contemplating the enormity of the losses. Every time it rains heavily here, more relics are exposed. In the midst of the weatherworn pebbles leached from the ancient ground, a mottled pink-white shape stands out. Ali picks it up and brushes it. Now it is clear. It is a spent .303 Anzac bullet, one of thousands that sought out Turkish targets. It calls to mind a graphic demonstration of the intensity of the fire here. In the museum at Gabatepe a couple of kilometres south of Lone Pine, a glass cabinet displays a dozen or so fused bullets – bullets that have not only struck each other in flight but have become embedded in each other. Can you imagine the odds of that happening, even once? How much of a hailstorm of lead must have flown here for so many to have been found?

A few metres away, at the edge of the road, Ali stops again. This time the rains have unearthed an even more poignant reminder of the cost of these battles. These are clearly shards of human bone – leached and pitted and brittle but, without doubt, human and sacred. Ali carefully retrieves them and moves them out of harm's way for later interment. Turkish or Australian, it matters little: these bones were once vital and full of promise.

The High Command ordered the Anzacs to mount another heroic and ultimately pointless assault at around the same time as Lone Pine. The charge at The Nek was aimed at holding the Turks' attention away from the British landings at Suvla Bay. Once again the High Command wanted to tie up potential Turkish reinforcements against the landings. It chose the famous Australian Light Horse troops (without their mounts, which were languishing back in Egypt).

The Nek is a narrow saddle which runs east–west along the ridge line between two hills, Russell's Top and Baby 700. It drops away sharply on both sides into a valley 150 metres below. The Turkish positions were perfectly sited, eight lines of trenches rising with the hill line to the top of Baby 700. Implanted in these fortifications were five nests of machine guns, positioned so they could bring deadly fire from the high ground on any movement below.

By the time the dismounted 3rd Australian Light Horse Brigade was in position for the attack, the supporting actions which should have given them some glimmer of success – a Kiwi attack on the Turkish rear and seizures of key Turkish posts next to The Nek – had either failed or were running late. The only real hope for the Light Horsemen was the planned artillery barrage, which should have battered the Turkish defenders. The bombardment was planned to run for half an hour from 4 am, with a final three minutes of intense shelling. The Australians were set to charge in four lines, each of 150 men (there was no room for more on the ridge), at exactly 4.30 am. Bean reports what happened:

'The first line stood with its feet on the pegs in the trench walls, ready to leap out. But for some reason that may now never be discovered – probably an error in timing watches – this shelling suddenly ceased when the watches of the Light Horse Officers showed on 4.23 – that is, seven minutes before the time of the attack; and when, at 4.30, Lt-Colonel A.H. White of the 8th Light Horse gave the word "Go", and, followed eagerly by the 150 men of the first line, scrambled from the deep trenches, there burst out within three or four seconds from the Turkish trenches, packed with men, such a torrent of rifle fire, growing quickly to a continuous roar, as soldiers can have seldom have faced.

'The Australian line, now charging, was seen suddenly to go limp, and then sink to the earth, as though [said an eye-witness] *"the men's limbs had become string". Except those wounded whom bullets had knocked back into the trench, or who managed to crawl a few yards and drop into it. Almost the whole line fell dead or dying within the first ten yards. White and every other officer was killed. Three or four men reached the Turkish parapet and the burst of their bombs was heard above the uproar.'*

Now, put yourself in the minds of the men of the second line, waiting in the trench for the signal to charge. They have heard the hellish firestorm and the cries of the wounded and dying. As they tend the wounded thrown back at them, they know what lies ahead for them. (There were reports of men farewelling each other, knowing full well their fate was sealed.) Nevertheless, when the whistle is blown, they leap up without hesitation. Charles Bean:

'The fusillade, which had slightly abated, instantly rose again to a roar as if some player had opened the swellbox of an organ. The second line, running hard, got a little beyond the first before being mown down.'

The commander of the men who formed the third line questioned the wisdom of continuing the slaughter. But there were reports that some men from the earlier charges had made it to the Turkish positions – red and yellow flags carried by the Anzacs were believed to have been seen on the enemy parapet. The brigade major decided these men must be supported. So the third line answered the whistle and was cut down. The fourth line was held back for what must have been an agonising half hour while their leaders sought further confirmation that the attack should press ahead despite the evident slaughter. Finally, a tragic misunderstanding saw an officer, who was unaware of the reasons for the delay, calling for the final charge. The right side of the last line, believing the order had been confirmed, leapt into action:

'The tempest broke out again. With a call "By God! The right has gone!" other leaders leapt out with their men, and the fourth line went, and most of it was swept away like the others.'

Dawn revealed a chilling sight. Strewn in a reddening heap, like cast-off rag dolls, the pride of the Light Horse lay in an area no bigger than a tennis court in front of the Australian trenches. According to the official history:

'At first here and there a man raised his arm to the sky, or tried to drink from his waterbottle. But as the sun of that burning day climbed higher, such movement ceased. Over the whole summit the figures lay still in the quivering heat.'

Of the 600 Light Horsemen who charged at The Nek, more than half became casualties and 234 of them were killed. The Turks had another name for The Nek. They called it Cesarit Tepe (or 'Hill of Valour').

The mistakes of the early stages of the campaign were still being repeated in late August. In an attempt to link the Anzac and Suvla lines, the commanders sent in a raw AIF battalion, without the benefit of reconnaissance, to assault the Turkish stronghold on Hill 60. As Charles Bean repeatedly points out bravery alone could not overcome lack of battle experience or proper preparation. The 18th Battalion AIF, newly arrived on the peninsula, was thrown at the Turkish defences to try to consolidate the tenuous foothold that British and other Anzac forces had secured. The Anzacs of the 18th fixed their bayonets and charged in two lines. They were immediately caught in a murderous hail of machine guns and grenades. Somehow they managed to grab a section of the Turkish trenches but in doing so they lost 11 officers and 372 men out of their original strength of 750; half of these casualties were killed.

One of the wounded officers was a 25-year-old chemist from Armidale in northern New South Wales. Lieutenant Arthur Rafferty had been at Gallipoli for less than a month when he led his platoon at Hill 60. After mounting a machine-gun position during the firestorm, his left arm was shattered by a burst of Turkish fire. He was evacuated to London, where doctors reset his arm and tried to save it. But his health was gravely impaired by the injury and the long journey to London. His arm turned gangrenous, and in early November it was amputated above the elbow.

Arthur Rafferty was just one of many Anzacs who endured suffering even after they'd survived battle injuries and been safely delivered to hospital. Imagine the pain and anguish he endured as he fought to regain his health and retain his arm. A photo taken in a London park while he was recuperating before the amputation shows a disconsolate man in full uniform propped with his back to a tree as he examines his bandaged arm. Yet after the amputation he showed the remarkable resilience of so many of the Anzacs. He was playing tennis and riding within weeks. He returned to administrative duties in England and France and, on his return home, took up a soldiers' settlement property where he raised cattle. He broke in stockhorses, shod them and rode them over the roughest terrain, and dealt with the bushfires and floods. His daughter, Joan Murray, fondly recalls seeing her friends imitating her father by tying their left arms behind their backs and trying to draft cattle. The only thing Arthur needed help with was trimming his nails.

::

Eighty-six years later, an Australian army officer walked through the poppy fields on the flat ground in front of Hill 60. Colonel Don Murray came to Gallipoli with the Australian cricket team in his role as Australia's Military Attaché to the Australian High Commission in London. He devised and organised the plan for Steve Waugh's team to re-create a legendary sporting moment by emulating the famous Anzac cricket match at Shell Green at Gallipoli on 17 December 1915. That match formed part of the deception of normality designed to cover preparations for the evacuation, and was played despite the constant menace of artillery shells passing overhead. The recreation was a moving experience for the Aussie Test cricketers, and provided inspiration in their preparations for the forthcoming Ashes series.

While the cricketers enjoyed some quiet time walking among the hallowed land near Lone Pine, Don Murray went alone to Hill 60. Here, his grandfather, Lieutenant Arthur Rafferty, fought and was wounded. Don Murray:

'I was quite taken. It's a beautiful place. The cemetery is down on the flat, surrounded by poppies. It was a beautiful day when I went there and I was quite affected by it. To me it was just marvellous and it closed off many of the things which I knew of my grandfather when I was a boy.

'My recollections of him were that he was basically fairly irreverent about most things. He used to make me laugh although he was a straightforward man.

'I had known him as a young boy when we always used to take holidays up there. I was always amazed at the things he could do with one arm, whether it was to play tennis, ride a horse or shoot, or even open a bottle of rum. And I was always drawn to him.

'I think I was about 13 when he died and it was the first time there had been any tragedy in our family. And I also admired his

sense of humour. I always admired my grandfather as a man from the bush, a man who could do anything – an indestructible Anzac was my impression of him.'

After Lone Pine and The Nek, things changed on the peninsula. The trench stalemate gradually brought a mutual respect. As Captain Ali points out:

'There is the same tradition in any army that says if you cannot defeat your enemy you should respect him: he is at least as strong as you are.'

The casualties lessened on both sides and by mid-November the killing had slowed almost to a stop. What was the point of killing without any gain? Both armies remained remarkably close to each other with a warren of trenches and communication tunnels carved into the landscape. It was in this deadly proximity that Turks and Anzacs revealed the characteristics which would eventually lead to the mutual respect that persists today. Ali explains:

'The Turkish elderly local people recalled the Anzac battles as the "gentlemen's war" and they became gentlemen. In the early days of the conflict both Turks and Australians threw many grenades. But the detonation system of grenades was adjusted to not less than ten seconds – enough time for each side to become very proficient catchers who could lob back the bombs to the thrower. But who could be sure just when the grenade would go off. Too many brave men on each side were being blown apart or horribly mutilated.'

One day the Australians decreased their bombardment of grenades. The Turks got the message and reciprocated. Soon the Turks stopped throwing them at all. The Australians followed. A gentlemen's agreement had broken out. It was a tacit agreement that appeared in other areas.

The Anzacs were rationed to 2 litres of fresh water a day for all their uses. Because of the paucity of fresh water, the Anzacs went down to the sea whenever possible to bathe and to wash their clothes, usually the only set they had, and for what they called 'chatting', or patiently crushing the mites that gathered in the seams of their uniforms and caused terrible itching and rashes. Ali says:

'The Turks could see them bathing from Baby 700, Hill 60 and Olive Grove [all hills] *but they didn't shoot at them because they were not carrying any weapons. Gentlemen's agreement number one. The first time most of the Turks had tasted chocolate was when the Anzacs, near Quinn's Post, tossed some of their rations instead of grenades. Turks retaliated with plenty of tomatoes and apples. One day a white handkerchief tied on a bayonet was shown in Turkish lines. A Turkish boy jumped out and ran to the Australian lines with some bags. He dropped them into the Anzac trenches and ran back. The Aussies opened the bags and found them full of tobacco – the Turks had plenty of fine cut tobacco in their rations. But they had no papers to roll the tobacco. The message with the bags said: "I tobacco . . . you papier. Everyday. Everyday."'*

The Anzacs understood perfectly. They gathered all the paper they could find – rollies, newspapers, old letters – and over the following days the exchange continued. Virtually no firing, but huge puffs of smoke rising from both sides as they enjoyed their unofficial ceasefire.

Captain Ali believes Lone Pine has a special symbolism for both sides in the conflict:

'In 1990, the 75th Anniversary of the Anzac landings, I had the privilege and honour of guiding two original Australian Anzacs for the commemorations. Near the Lone Pine tree, one of the Anzacs said to me: "Ali?"

"Yes Sir."

"We believe we gained the true Australian spirit on Lone Pine."

'I said: "Sir, you know we gained Ataturk on the same area."

'And the second Anzac said: "So that is why the Lone Pine area is so important in the history of both Australia and Turkey."'

The bald statistics eloquently spell out the futility of the Gallipoli campaign. The original plan was to take the peninsula in 11 days. It dragged out to 240 days of fighting and ended in stalemate. The Anzacs never penetrated more than 1.2 kilometres inland from their landings: Lone Pine marks the point of maximum advance. The British gained a maximum of 5.5 kilometres penetration at Cape Helles and 3.2 kilometres at Suvla Bay. The entire campaign captured less than 1 per cent of the peninsula. An additional 420,000 Allied troops joined the original invasion force of about 80,000 during the campaign. The Turkish defenders more than matched that number and, by the end, had 253,000 killed or wounded. The Allies' casualty list totalled 251,000 killed or wounded – a daily average of almost 1000 from each side for the entire campaign. These young men had an average age of less than 23 years.

The Allies' withdrawal from the peninsula was perhaps the most efficiently organised operation of the entire campaign. It was achieved without a single casualty on the night of 19/20 December 1915 when the Anzacs were evacuated from North Beach, on the northern side of Anzac Cove, where they had landed 240 days earlier. Even here, Captain Ali challenges the traditional view that the Turks were hoodwinked into allowing the invaders to slip away:

'From the Turkish point of view, the withdrawal was exactly what they wanted. What was the point of shooting the retreating troops in the back as they left our shores. The Turkish survivors always claimed they realised the withdrawal was occurring but they were content to let it happen and stop the killing.

'They were soldiers, the Australians and the Turks. They had to do what they had been taught to do. And they tried their best. But it's interesting that the result on the battleground was that neither side lost or gained even one metre, except at Lone Pine. At Lone Pine only, at the cost of 2,200 Australians' lives, they gained an area not bigger than two tennis courts.

'Why? Not only the Turks, but also the Anzacs, were country men. They were not soft city people, they were equal in strength. That's the reason neither side gained the upper hand and that

created a very important result: the Turks couldn't defeat the Anzacs; the Anzacs couldn't defeat the Turks. They were equal in their strength, their power and their courage.'

Today the sacred sands of Anzac Cove attract Australians in ever growing numbers – so many, in fact, that Anzac Day 2003 was celebrated over two days. These Aussies, young and old, are drawn by the spirit of Anzac. They are trying to understand its origins and the impact it has had on their nation. They are looking for their roots while paying homage to the men of Anzac who shed their blood in helping to establish our national identity.

Walking along the beach, you can still see the concrete remains of Watson's Pier, named after Lieutenant Watson, the engineer responsible for building four piers on the beach to receive supplies. You can see where the Anzacs came to swim off the beach – during their brief respites from the tensions of the front lines, a time for washing and relaxation. Even then, they faced the constant danger of shelling from the Turkish artillery raining death on them from their hidden emplacements behind the high ground. The road that runs above the beach was also built by the Anzacs and is still used today. On the northern headland of the beach, Ari Burnu cemetery holds the remains of some of the first casualties of the campaign, and includes some of men of the 8th and 10th Light Horse Regiments, the heroes of The Nek, who fell in that futile action.

It is here you will find a remarkable memorial – a rarity in the history of warfare – where one country has honoured the soldiers of another country that came to invade it. In 1985 the Turkish government unveiled a monument to the Anzacs and officially named the place Anzac Koyu, or Anzac Cove. The monument immortalises the words that Mustapha Kemal, by then the president of his nation and known as Kemal Ataturk, spoke to the first Australians, New Zealanders and British to visit the battlefields after the war in 1934:

'Those heroes that shed their blood and lost their lives . . . you are now lying in the soil of a friendly country. Therefore rest in peace, there is no difference between the Johnnies and the Mehmets to us where they lie side by side here in this country of ours . . . You, the mothers, who sent their sons from far away countries, wipe away your tears; your sons are now living in our bosom and are in peace. After having lost their lives on this land they have become our sons as well.'

Ari Burnu cemetery was where the Anzac Day dawn services were held until the 85th anniversary of the landings in 2000, when the service was moved to the specially built Anzac Commemorative Site at North Beach because of the vast increase in numbers of people attending. Now the service is conducted on a beautiful, open grassed area in front of the landmark the Anzacs nicknamed The Sphinx (after the real one they'd seen during their training in Egypt). The Gallipoli Sphinx stares impassively down as you look up from the beach, just as it did when those young soldiers first looked up at it, their eyes filled with a mixture of fear, hope and awe as they realised the massive task before them. The sloping face of Plugge's Plateau, once full of dugouts used as casualty clearing stations, dressing stations, depots and headquarters, is now shrouded in a cloak of hardy bushes, which hug it tightly as they shelter from the powerful sea winds.

All around, the ghosts of the men who died here are present. In the stillness of the crisp winter morning at Anzac Cove, in the ravines of Shrapnel Gully, in the hallowed battlegrounds of Lone Pine and The Nek, their spirits remain. They seem to call on those who visit here to remember their sacrifices and make sure they were not in vain.

Charles Bean, who saw it first-hand, reflected on the special meaning of Gallipoli to the Anzacs and their fledgling nations. It was not simply the sacrifice of the 8141 Australians and 2500 New Zealanders who perished there, or the 18,000 Aussies and 5000 Kiwis wounded . . .

'But the standard set by the first companies at the first call – by

the stretcher bearers, the medical officers, the staffs, the company leaders, the privates, the defaulters on the water barges, the Light Horse at The Nek – this was already part of the tradition not only of Anzac but of the Australian and New Zealand peoples.

'By dawn on December 20th Anzac had faded into a dim blue line lost amid other hills on the horizon as the ships took their human freight to Imbros, Lemnos and Egypt. But Anzac stood, and still stands, for reckless valour in a good cause, for enterprise, resourcefulness, fidelity, comradeship, and endurance that will never own defeat.'

FIVE

Shelled to hell

After Gallipoli it was clear the Australian Army had a character and a style of its own. Although many Diggers were of British origin (almost 30 per cent were actually born in Britain), it was evident after Gallipoli that our Army was quite different from the British Army. Notwithstanding the fact that the campaign had been lost, it was also clear that Australians had developed an immense pride in their performance at Gallipoli.

Our national characteristics were clearly identifiable in the Diggers – mateship, endurance, ingenuity, teamwork, courage, resilience and the like. Clearly these didn't emerge overnight. They were honed by the challenges our forebears faced in surviving in our remarkable country, with its vast distances, harsh terrain and unpredictable climate. Australians in almost every sector, overcoming obstacles to build our nation – from pioneering in the outback to getting a telegraph line to Darwin, creating the School of the Air, the Flying Doctor Service, mapping and building roads, national education and health services – required a practical, pragmatic approach built up over long periods of hardship. The spirit needed to survive and grow was constantly tested by droughts, bushfires and floods. It produced generations of Australians capable of heroic struggles in their daily lives.

Gallipoli provided a focal point for our Diggers to show that spirit. In some ways it served as our symbolic rite of passage to nationhood. We didn't have to fight a civil war or a war of independence to become a nation. That was a miracle of compromise. We marched to nationhood at Gallipoli just 14 years after our independence, and the Diggers paid for our right to that independence with their blood.

It was evident to Charles Bean and other observers that the Australians and New Zealanders who returned to Egypt from Gallipoli were an entirely different body of men from those who had landed at Anzac Cove eight months earlier:

They were a military force with strongly established, definite traditions. Not for anything, if he could avoid it, would an Australian now change his loose, faded tunic or battered hat for the smartest cloth or headgear of any other army. Men clung to their Australian uniforms till they were tattered to the limit of decency.

The crucial attribute of the AIF was its discipline – or, perhaps, the compatibility of its discipline with the initiative and readiness to take risks that marked its men. As in every army, its discipline, to be effective, had to be based on the conditions and outlook of the nation.

In their way, the critics from the colonial days were right: a people with Australian outlook and standards could not have produced an efficient army of the kind those critics envisaged – that is, one imbued with the automatism of the old-time grenadier. But the Australian commanders and the troops themselves, from highest to lowest, as a result of their outlook and of the natural relations between them, developed a system of discipline which, though outwardly that of the British Army, was in spirit more akin to that of the French. It aimed at the best and most reasonable use of the national material for the purpose in view. It succeeded because the troops wanted the object, and understood the methods, almost as thoroughly as their leaders.'

Our Diggers' reputation, earned at Gallipoli, was consolidated by their subsequent actions on the Western Front in France after they were moved there in March 1916. The trench warfare in France was conflict at its most diabolical. Nothing, not even the worst privations of Gallipoli, could have prepared the Diggers for what lay ahead.

In the aftermath of Gallipoli, the Anzac forces were reinforced and divided into two Army corps: One Anzac Corps, under the command of General Birdwood, comprised the 1st and 2nd Australian Divisions and the NZ Divisions; and Two Anzac Corps, commanded by General Godley, was made up of the 4th and 5th Australian Divisions. Both Anzac corps were initially held by Kitchener in Egypt because he feared that the Turks, now freed from their defence of the Dardanelles, would turn their attention to the Suez. However, the Turks were distracted by the Russian invasion of Armenia, and a far more immediate threat emerged for Kitchener.

On 21 February 1916, the Germans set the Western Front alight when they launched a massive attack on Verdun, a strategically important French bastion on the Meuse River. The Germans had a brutally simple aim: bleed the French white! They reasoned that if they could concentrate a massive assault on the heart of the French Army, they could knock the French out of the war. That would leave the British with the virtually impossible task of countering the enormous German Army on its own. For their part the French resisted mightily, under the battle cry 'Ils ne passeront pas!' ('They shall not pass!'). Kitchener realised he had to act to ease the load borne by the French. Just eight days after the Verdun assaults began, he ordered General Birdwood to bring One Anzac Corps to France as soon as possible and General Godley to follow with Two Anzac Corps as soon as it had completed the building of its artillery units.

The Anzacs would reinforce the British Expeditionary Force, which had more than trebled in size since the start of the war to have 49 divisions in France. The British forces there, including those of the supporting Commonwealth countries, now totalled 1.2 million men, of which almost 100,000 were Australians. Another 90,000 Aussies waited in England and a further 25,000 were deployed in the Middle East. The French could call on 111 divisions, giving the Allies a grand total of 160 divisions to defend against the 120 German divisions facing them.

The Anzacs were greatly disappointed when their troop trains bypassed Paris on the way to the front. Once at the front they were first sent to a generally quiet sector where the British allowed new arrivals to acclimatise, 'The Nursery', southeast of Armentières. From their arrival, in April 1916, the Aussies realised they were facing a far more sophisticated enemy than they had faced at Gallipoli. The German Army was state-of-the-art, with much better-equipped and better-trained troops than the Turks.

The fighting on the Western Front by this stage had degenerated into a massive siege, with both sides suffering unheard-of casualties in the previous clashes as waves of men were decimated by artillery and massed heavy machine-gun fire. Each side was now hunkered down in an intricate web of defensive trenches as they daily pounded each other's lines with an ever-increasing storm of artillery bombardment. Attempts by both sides to break the deadlock by driving a wedge through their opponent's defensive line had proven disastrous.

The Somme campaign began east of Amiens on 1 July after an extraordinary bombardment that lasted a week and sent 1.7 million shells onto the German defences. The British and the French planned to pierce the German line and then exploit the gap with British cavalry, which would take the German from the rear. The Allied artillery barrage was ineffective, and Britain lost an astonishing 60,000 soldiers in a single day.

It was against this background that the Australian 5th Division, which had only just moved into The Nursery, was thrust into a quick but vicious battle at Fromelles, a village in northern France just south of Armentières. The 5th Division fought alongside the British 61st Division in a feint to help

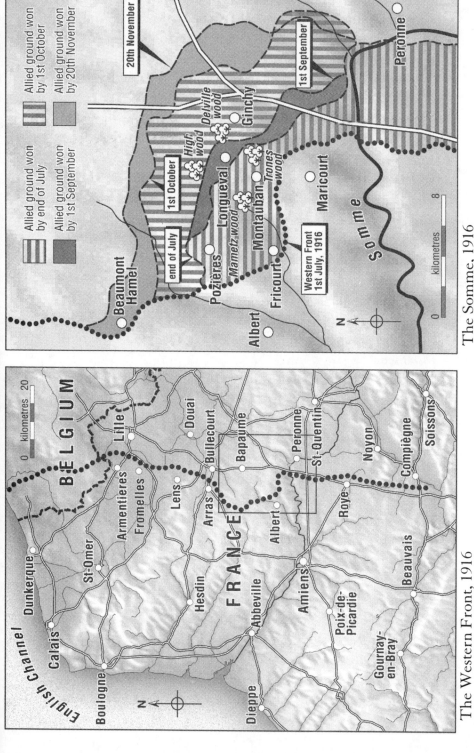

The Somme, 1916

The Western Front, 1916

take pressure off the main British offensive, about 80 kilometres south along the Somme River. The inexperienced Australians were sent to assault a salient in front of the Aubers Ridge called the 'Sugar Loaf'. They were ordered into battle while there were still more than two hours of daylight after a seven-hour artillery bombardment.

Sergeant Clair Whiteside wrote to his mother as he recovered in England after being wounded at Fromelles (from *A Valley In France* by Elizabeth Whiteside):

'Well, we hugged the trenches for a few hours while the curtain raiser, the artillery duel was on. When its chief job was done, viz wire-cutting, the hour was up. The first thin line of heroes get on the parapet and make off for the opposing lines. The first lines fare the best – for the terrible machine gun is deadly once he sees the game is properly on. It looked like putting up cardboard nine-pins in a hurricane – only it was human beings who were facing up to it. A good number were wounded before the charge, but a short distance into No-Man's Land and the grass was thick with them.'

The Diggers advanced on three fronts, the 8th Brigade on the left, the 14th in the centre and the 15th on the right. The first two made good ground and captured a kilometre of German trenches but the 15th Brigade, on the right, found the artillery barrage had missed its mark and the enemy had been able to reman the trenches immediately the firing stopped. Sergeant Whiteside continued:

'A machine-gun was rat ta tat tat tapping in the grass a few yards to my left and it was while trying to learn something about its crew that a sniper caught me. Got a nasty one on the head and, of course, for a minute, thought I was done for. Had the sensation poor old rabbit gets when you hit him on the ears. Did not go round in a circle like poor old raw bunny but I can tell you it seemed to lift me bodily. However I had a heaven-sent vision of beef tea and chicken and thinking Fritz might not have too many chooks on hand, or not feeling disposed to give them out to the fighting "kangaroos", I made towards our own base and the

ticklish part of the game had just started.'

The men of the 15th Brigade were cut down as soon as they charged from the old orchard where they had formed up. The British attack on the Australians' right also met with heavy resistance from the entrenched Germans, suffered heavy casualties and made little headway. This meant that the other two Australian brigades, which had advanced about a kilometre ahead, were then exposed to the full brunt of the German fire and counterattacks from the Sugar Loaf salient along their right flank. The Aussies withstood the first major counterattack but a second followed, and first the 8th Brigade and then the 14th, had to withdraw. In that disastrous day and night of fighting, the 5th Division lost 5553 dead and wounded, including 400 captured. Worse still, the Germans had quickly realised the attacks were only a feint and their purpose of preventing German forces in the area from being deployed to the Somme was not even achieved.

In his book *Digger*, John Laffin pointed to Fromelles as a graphic illustration of mateship in its purest form:

'Many wounded lay in front of the 5th Division's lines, appar-
ently without hope of rescue. Major A.W. Murdoch of the 29th
Battalion, disobeying standing orders imposed by Haig himself,
fashioned a Red Cross flag and with one soldier crossed no-
man's-land, distributing water bottles on the way. At the
German wire he arranged a truce with a Bavarian lieutenant so
that the wounded could be collected. Murdoch offered himself as
a hostage until the collection was finished. It ended prematurely
when General McCay, under pressure from Haking, ordered
stretcher bearers not to go out.

'Ending of the truce did not end the rescue work. For three
days and nights small groups of Australians – sometimes even
one man – went out and brought in wounded, despite the great
risk under fire. More than 300 men, who would otherwise have
certainly perished, were saved. It was a remarkable demonstra-
tion of the creed of mateship.'

Nevertheless, once again an Australian fighting force had been dashed against a brick wall to little ultimate effect. Charles Bean said: *'The value of the result, if any, was tragically disproportionate to the cost.'* The Diggers had been given a foretaste of the grim fighting that lay ahead of them – static, set-piece battles on a scale they could never have imagined when they enthusiastically joined up in that sunny land that now seemed a world away.

Worse was to come when the Anzacs' 1st, 2nd and 4th Divisions were committed to the battle of the Somme. This was to be the bloodiest fighting in the entire war. The artillery barrages to which they were subjected were so massive they could often be heard in England. The Germans and the Allies were deadlocked in the trenches, with each trying to outlast the other in a war of attrition. The endless tit-for-tat artillery bombardments reduced towns, countryside and soldiers to piles of pulverised waste. This was an Armageddon where men were no match for the modern weapons of warfare. In addition to the high explosives that tore apart the beautiful French countryside, blasting men and buildings into atoms, both sides resorted to gas attacks as they desperately tried to gain an advantage. In his book *Warrior Race*, Lawrence James puts the changes in warfare that were occurring into perspective:

> *'Technology now dominated the battlefield. This was clear from the calculus of death: the infantry suffered one casualty for every 0.5 they inflicted, the artillery one for every ten, and gas units one for every forty. Most of the technology was relatively new; telephones, bicycles, motor cars and lorries, wireless telegraphy and aircraft had all appeared and been developed during the thirty years before the war.*

> *'Other inventions were a direct response to the war. Armoured cars appeared in the autumn of 1914; chlorine gas was first used by the Germans at Ypres in April 1915; flamethrowers were*

introduced (again by the Germans) at Hooge the following July; and a British invention, the tank, made its debut at the batlle of Fleurs-Courcelette in September 1916.'

The Australian 1st Division was ordered to attack Pozières, a vital area north of the Somme, which had held firm after four earlier British attacks. The Australians stormed towards Pozières and, fighting with confidence and determination, drove the Germans before them. The Aussie flair was swiftly being recognised by friend and foe as the men of the 1st celebrated by smoking captured German cigars and wearing their spiked helmets as they dug in to consolidate their gains. The Australians repulsed a German counterattack the next morning. The Germans, realising they had a new and worthy opponent, resolved to force the newcomers back with a methodical bombardment of the position, which reduced the land to a mudpile and cut the Australians to shreds. Charles Bean quotes this description by Lieutenant J.A. Raws of the 23rd Battalion:

'. . . we lay down terror-stricken on a bank. The shelling was awful . . . we eventually found our way to the right spot out in no man's land. Our leader was shot before we arrived and the strain had sent two officers mad. I and another new officer took charge and dug the trench. We were shot at all the time . . . the wounded and the killed had to be thrown to one side. I refused to let any sound man help a wounded man; the sound man had to dig . . . we dug on and we finished amid a tornado of bursting shells.

'I was buried with dead and dying. The ground was covered with bodies in all stages of decay and mutilation and I would, after struggling from the earth, pick up a body by me to try and lift him out with me and find him a decayed corpse . . . I went up again the next night and stayed there.

'We were shelled to hell ceaselessly. X went mad and disappeared . . . there remained nothing but a charred mass of debris with bricks, stones, girders and bodies pounded to nothing . . . we are lousy, stinking, unshaven, sleepless . . . I have one puttee, a

dead man's helmet, another dead man's protector, a dead man's bayonet. My tunic is rotten with other men's blood and partly spattered with a comrade's brains . . .'

Sadly, Lieutenant Raws and his brother were both killed later in the battle.

This was warfare on a scale never before contemplated, let alone seen. In a single day at the start of the Somme offensive, the British Army suffered 57,000 casualties with more than a third of them killed. The battle dragged on for four months as small-arms fire gave way to artillery and the Allies' casualties climbed to half a million men. The static nature of the fighting can be seen in the fact that both sides produced maps showing the front lines and entrenchments in minute detail.

The psychological impact of the artillery pounding soon became a major weapon wielded by each side. Brave men who had survived countless bombardments were often pushed beyond their capacity to withstand the constant concussion and apprehension. Many were sent 'over the top' of their trenches time and again into the 'meat grinder', where they threw themselves against heavily protected enemy defensive positions in futile attempts to gain a few metres of bombed-out mud. Many soldiers survived with lifelong nightmares centred on the images of their mates being mutilated or blown to pieces before their eyes. Others spoke of having to leave their wounded friends to die in 'no-man's land' between the two front lines. When the winter rain turned the battlefields into quagmires, troops edged their way through the slush along wooden duckboards. Horses often became bogged and some men actually drowned, held down by their heavy equipment, after slipping off the duckboards into holes more than 2 metres deep.

Over the next months and years, a series of names would enter the Australian consciousness – Pozières, Mouquet Farm, Bapaume, Bullecourt, Messines, Ypres, Menin Road, Polygon Wood, Broodseinde, Poelcapelle, Passchendaele, Amiens, Hazebrouck, Mont St Quentin, Albert and Villers-

Bretonneux. They came to symbolise the sacrifices of thousands of young Diggers who would find their final resting places in these battlegrounds, far from their homeland.

The Australians maintained a constant strength on the Western Front of about 120,000 troops over the three years of trench warfare there. During that time they suffered 181,000 casualties, with 46,000 deaths, 114,000 wounded, 16,000 gassed and 4000 taken prisoners of war. But the Diggers made their presence felt in ways far in excess of their numbers. Measured in terms of total deaths for each 1000 men mobilised, the Australians lost 145 – the highest rate of all the Commonwealth armies. Diggers also won a remarkable 53 Victoria Crosses on the Western Front (compared with a total of 20 throughout the entire World War II). Ironically, the Anzacs' performance under fire meant they were often placed in the most dangerous positions, because they were so often effective in creating breakthroughs. This, of course, exposed them to even more casualties. Yet it still failed to break their fighting spirit.

Despite the undeniable valour displayed by so many, the horrors of trench warfare took an enormous mental as well as physical toll, and a new form of battle injury began to be observed by the frazzled medical staffs – 'battle fatigue' or 'shell shock'. In his fascinating book *A War of Nerves*, Ben Shephard writes of the experience of the Australians at the Somme:

> *'They were good, strong soldiers, many of them Gallipoli veterans, and they swept their way into the village of Pozières – which had eluded the British earlier in July – "like a pack of hungry dogs that had tasted blood".*
>
> *'But there was no comparable advance elsewhere and for the next seven weeks the Australians were "shelled to bits" in the inevitable counter attack. In the end 22,826 Australians fell to win a "few yards of ground". On 24 July an Anzac counted some 75 shells, 9.2s and larger, landing within five minutes in an area of some four acres.'*

Just think about it. That's a massive deadly explosion every four seconds in an area about the size of two soccer fields. Imagine the feelings of those soldiers as they prayed the next one wouldn't have their name written on it. Imagine what they witnessed as those shells dealt their random destruction. How often could you take that? How many mates could you see being maimed or blown to pieces before your eyes? Shephard quotes Charles Bean from the official Australian war history, who observed that the shelling at Pozières:

'... did not merely probe character and nerve; it laid them stark naked ... The strain eventually became so great that what is rightly known as courage – the will to persist – would not suffice since, however keen his will, the machinery of the man's self control might become deranged.'

Shephard also cites another letter, quoted by Bean, from the same Lieutenant J.A. Raws:

'I have had much luck and kept my nerve so far. The awful difficulty is to keep it. The bravest of all often lose it – one becomes a gibbering maniac ... Only the men you have trusted and believed in before proved equal to it. One or two of my friends stood splendidly, like granite rocks round which the seas raged in vain. They were all junior officers; but many other fine men broke to pieces. Everyone called it shell-shock but shell-shock (i.e. shell concussion) is very rare. What 90% get is justifiable funk due to the collapse of the helm of self-control.'

The battles of Fromelles, Pozières and another at Mouquet Farm tested the Diggers to the limit. In seven weeks they lost 28,000 officers and men. As always, Charles Bean put it beautifully, calling the area 'more densely sown with Australian sacrifice than any other place on earth'. But somehow the Australians were able to sustain these massive losses and bounce back. Their outstanding performances in the light of such losses gave the lie to earlier British criticisms of a lack of discipline. In fact, the distinctly Australian system of discipline worked exceptionally well, particularly as so many officers and NCOs were among the casualties.

Australia's most decorated soldier, the remarkable Henry William 'Harry' Murray, a former miner and timber-cutter from Tasmania, was consistently outstanding during this period in France, just as he had been at Gallipoli where he won the first of his two Distinguished Service Orders. He fought at the Somme, Pozières, Mouquet Farm and Stormy Trench, where he won his VC.

Murray was a 33-year-old when he joined up, and immediately distinguished himself in combat because of a seemingly complete lack of fear. His rise through the ranks was meteoric: from private at the start of World War I to Lieutenant Colonel by war's end. During his service he won the Distinguished Service Order twice and a Distinguished Conduct Medal, in addition to his Victoria Cross. King George V made him a Commander of the Order of St Michael and St George and the French awarded him a Croix De Guerre. Charles Bean recorded his role during the battle of Mouquet Farm:

'The bombardment became so heavy that on August 14th Lt-Colonel Ross, a British officer commanding the 51st Battalion, wrote to his brigadier (General Glasgow): "It is my genuine (not depressed) opinion that it would be a mistake to press the offensive further locally in this salient".

'The attack, however, was made. A quarry near the Farm was captured and a company under Captain Harry Murray seized part of the German "Fabeck Trench", north-east of the Farm. Here Murray and his men were outflanked by the Germans, who had been ordered by their corps commander not to permit the British plan to develop. But this former miner, who was to become known as a most famous fighting leader, fought his way back with his men in one of the most ably conducted actions in Australian experience.'

The 4th Australian Division was recalled and its 4th Brigade, after a series of desperate assaults, each of which won some small gains, gradually began to surround Mouquet Farm itself. But, as Bean reported, the Australians lacked the numbers to consolidate their position:

'After fierce fighting above ground and in the deep passages below the Farm, it was thrown out of the Farm itself; but north-east of the Farm it clung to part of Fabeck Trench and other posts. Lieutenant Duncan Maxwell – whose fine company commander, Captain Littler of Anzac fame, was killed in this attack – held on to the most exposed corner under a bombardment that shattered most of his troops, and with the rest was still in position when the Canadian Corps, which had been relieving I Anzac on the Pozières front, got a full company under Captain J.H. Lovett through to reinforce him.

'After fighting beside the Canadians for two more terrible days Maxwell (afterwards a Brigadier of the Second AIF), and the Australians surviving in these positions, came out. One who saw them come through Pozières wrote at the time in his diary: "The way was absolutely open (to shellfire), and others were bending low and running hurriedly. Our men were walking as if they were in Pitt Street, erect, not hurrying, each man carrying himself as proudly and carelessly as a British officer".

'This was how the tradition of Anzac Beach, then only 16 months old, worked at Mouquet Farm.'

At Stormy Trench, one of the many assaults during the bitter fighting of the spring offensive around Bullecourt, in February 1917, Harry Murray again showed the way:

'As a preparatory measure, the corps was ordered to place the enemy under strain by small assaults. One of these, at Stormy Trench, completely succeeded at the second attempt on February 4th, largely through the bold, untiring leadership of the same Captain Harry Murray who had distinguished himself at Mouquet Farm (and who now won the Victoria Cross). The ground here gained was being much extended by constant nibbling, when the month of bright freezing weather ended in thaw.'

The citation for Harry Murray's VC says it all:

'For most conspicuous bravery when in command of the right flank company I attack. He led his company to the assault with great skill and courage, and the position was quickly captured.

*Fighting of a very severe nature followed, and three heavy
counter-attacks were beaten back, these successes being due to
captain Murray's wonderful work.*

*'Throughout the night his company suffered heavy casualties
through concentrated enemy shell fire, and on one occasion gave
ground for a short way. This gallant officer raised his command
and saved the situation to sheer valour.*

*'He made his presence felt throughout the line, encouraging
his men, heading bombing parties, leading bayonet charges, and
carrying wounded to places of safety. His magnificent example
inspired his men throughout.'*

At Stormy Trench the Australian 13th Battalion won one
Victoria Cross (Murray's), three Military Crosses, three Distinguished Conduct Medals and 14 Military Medals.

Bean put down the underlying success of the distinctly
Australian style of discipline shown during the fighting
largely to the selection of the Australian officers. Where the
British officers' selections were dependent on their social
standing and school background, the Australian system was
based on commanders choosing leaders from the men in their
units: *'. . . those whom they themselves would most desire to have
under them in action; and, contrary to the old British rule, the
general practice was for these, when promoted, to serve in their old
battalions, commanding comrades whom they knew, and
commanded by the seniors who knew them and had selected them.'*

There was therefore a natural succession of leadership built
into the Australian units, which came to the fore when
commanders fell in action and were almost seamlessly
replaced by the logical next in line. There have been some
remarkable instances of this transfer of leadership, including
one notable occasion when a sergeant took command of a
battalion. In May 1918, the Australian 6th Brigade was attacking the German stronghold at Ville-sur-Ancre, north of
Morlancourt, trying to win the high ground to the south. The
22nd Battalion was given the task of capturing two sunken
roads, known as 'Big Caterpillar' and 'Little Caterpillar'. After

the attack began at 2 am, the battalion was caught in heavy fire and suffered massive casualties, including all its officers. Sergeant William Ruthven rose to the occasion and took command. He led the surviving men in attacks which captured their objectives. He won the Victoria Cross for his gallantry and inspiring leadership.

Bean credits the Anzac's Gallipoli Commander General Birdwood with instilling in his officers an unbreakable rule that they must look after their men's interests before their own. He acknowledges General Monash as having introduced the principle that 'the staff was the servant of the troops':

'It was a point of honour that, at any rate when in the line, officers should receive the same food as the troops, and the platoon commander should take his meal in the trenches, among his men.'

This was demonstrably different from the British habit, where officers always had a separate mess from the other ranks and this mess provided substantially better food than that available to the troops. Lawrence James in *Warrior Race* illustrates the chasm between the approaches of the Australian and British officers with his reference to the British Brigadier General Crozier, who compared his troops to retrievers:

' "Your troops are like dogs", Crozier advised. "They require careful handling before being gradually shot over, and led up to the point of more serious work". There were other, equally effective techniques and Crozier approvingly singled out a colonel in his brigade who enforced "public school discipline" in his battalion. In the heat of battle, Crozier resorted to draconian measures; he once threatened to shoot a "funker" on the spot and actually shot dead a subaltern who was running away during a German attack in April 1918. Reports of Crozier's quirks filtered back to his superiors, for his divisional commander vetoed his promotion "owing to his roughness and the ruthless way he handled his men". Unperturbed by criticism, Crozier boasted that his brigade always held the line.'

James also points out that while the junior officers largely shared the same dangers as their troops, they had such compensations as servants and far better access to alcohol. James summarised the difference between the British and Australian approaches:

'If he was to lead effectively, the [British] *officer had to isolate himself from his men, for familiarity would undermine his authority. It was different in the Australian army where egalitarian traditions of "mateship" were strong. On the eve of an inspection, an Australian officer told his men: "Now boys, these English officers are coming to size us up today. So look smart . . . And look here, for the love of Heaven, don't call me Alf".'*

Many believe that the connection between the Diggers and their officers which grew from their shared life and battle experience created an essential point of difference between the Australian Army and many others. The high casualty rate among the Australian junior officers is testament to this bond.

Put simply, an Australian officer had to earn the respect of his Diggers. Respect did not pass automatically with the rank. It was attached to the individual who wore the badge, not to the badge itself. This trait has passed the test of time. It was so during World War II and in every conflict since. The relationship that is subsequently built up between the respected officer and his men fosters the initiative for which the Digger is justly famed. For to motivate the Digger to take responsibility for his own welfare and that of his mates, and to actively contribute to the achievements of his unit, there must be an underlying trust.

It was this trust which enabled Lieutenant F.P. Bethune, a Tasmanian section commander, to write this famous order to his men after he had been ordered to hold his machine-gun post at all costs against the German offensive in March 1918:

'Special Orders of No 1 Section 13/3/18
1 *This position will be held and the section will remain here until relieved.*
2 *The enemy cannot be allowed to interfere with this programme.*

3 *If the Section cannot remain here alive, it will remain here
   dead, but in any case it will remain here.*

4 *Should any man, through shell-shock or other causes attempt
   to surrender, he will remain here dead.*

5 *Should all guns be blown out, the Section will use Mills
   grenades and other novelties.*

6 *Finally, the position, as stated, will be held.'*

Lieutenant Bethune and his section survived 18 days in their
position without loss.

Away from the Western Front battlefields, other Australian
units gained fame for their part in a strikingly different kind
of war in the Middle East. This was mobile warfare, and the
Australian Light Horse and their hardy bush mounts shone in
their fight against the Ottoman Empire, the same Turkish
troops that had prevailed against the Anzacs at Gallipoli. The
Light Horsemen overcame the heat, the lack of water, the
desert and their enemy to secure the Sinai Peninsula, Palestine
and Syria. During this campaign the Light Horse rode into
history when they carried out the last great cavalry charge in
capturing Beersheba.

By this stage the Australians were recognised as having a
separate character from the other soldiers fighting in France.
The Australians' straightforward approach and larrikin
humour soon won over the French locals, who called them 'les
bon soldats' ('the good soldiers'). The Anzacs also established
a tradition that has been followed faithfully by Diggers in
subsequent wars by casting a glad eye over any local madem-
oiselle who passed their way.

But the Diggers also caused their share of problems during
their time in France, winning a reputation for unruly behaviour out of the front line. Their well-documented dislike of
regimentation culminated in riots at the Etaples base camp on
the outskirts of Paris in the summer of 1917, as Lawrence
James notes in *Warrior Race*:

*'Australian and New Zealand troops were prominent in the
disturbances, as was to be expected. All were volunteers and*

aggressively democratic in the attitude to officers (their own were appointed from the ranks) and notoriously indifferent to saluting. These soldiers closed ranks in the face of the military police, whom they regularly defied; a week before the Etaples ructions, an Australian pioneers had appeared outside an assistant provost-marshal's office and sung the "Marseillaise".

'The victim of this revolutionary serenade later complained that Australian personnel were automatically blamed for nearly all crimes committed by soldiers in France. At Etaples, Aussies and Kiwis lived up to their reputation and confirmed Haig's fear that their insubordinate attitudes might lead British soldiers astray. This did not occur, nor was there anything to suggest that the restlessness at Etaples was an expression of political grievances or pacifism.'

The Australians' reputation developed in line with their newly acquired collective nickname. Charles Bean reported the word 'Digger' for an Aussie soldier as common among the Anzac troops in France by 1917, and suggested that it originated with New Zealand's gum-diggers. Many WWI veterans believe the name simply arose from their trench digging in France. John Laffin also suggests that Western Australian soldiers, who were originally goldminers, brought the word with them. Certainly, by the close of 1917 in France, the Anzacs were calling each other 'Digger' or, as happens so often to words in Australia, shortening it to 'Dig'.

The Diggers' greatest commitment and greatest sacrifices were made in France, and nowhere in that land is there a better example of the impact made by the Diggers during World War I than in the small village of Villers-Bretonneux, about 16 kilometres down the road from the regional centre of Amiens on the way to the town of St Quentin. It was here on Anzac Day 1918 that the Australians recaptured the village and, in doing so, halted the German advance. Three weeks earlier, the village had been captured from British troops who had taken over its defence from the Australians. The Germans had used tanks, leading their infantry, for the first time in battle, to overwhelm the British defenders. The British then borrowed two Australian brigades to try to retake the village.

As the Diggers of the 15th Brigade attacked from the northeast of the village, they could see Villers-Bretonneux, or what was left of it, to their right. It was lit by the glow of a burning house. Bean describes the scene when Captain Young of the 59th Battalion gave the order to charge:

'There went up from the unleashed line a shout – a savage, eager yell of which every narrative speaks – and the Australians made straight for the enemy. From that instant there was no holding the attack. The bloodthirsty cry was caught up again and again along the line, and the whole force was off at the run.'

The 13th Brigade drove up from the south and the two Australian units swept past the township on either flank and then dispatched the trapped German garrison. During the fighting, Lieutenant Sadlier of the Australian 51st Battalion won the Victoria Cross for his part in destroying six machine-gun posts in a wood near the township. Villers-Bretonneux was liberated. The German Army had had its last throw of the dice. It went on the defensive after this reverse and the Digger had played a substantial role in turning the tide.

The people of Villers-Bretonneux have never forgotten the Australians' role in saving their town. Even today, the town is redolent of the men who came from the other side of the world to help free it. A plaque outside the Town Hall sums it up:

'In 1916, the Australian Army entered the Western Front with a force of 180,000 men, three times the number that had served in Gallipoli in 1915. 46,000 of the 60,000 killed in the War died on the Western Front. From a population of just 4.5 million people, 313,000 volunteered to serve during the War. 65% of these became casualties.'

Down the road from the Town Hall you'll find Rue Victoria, where the local primary school stands. It's named the Victoria Primary School in honour of the schoolchildren of the Australian state of Victoria, who donated their pennies to help rebuild it after it was completely destroyed in March and April of 1918. The school was eventually rebuilt in 1927.

As you walk inside the main gate you're greeted by the universal sound of kids at play. But this playground has a message not seen anywhere else. The children swarm after a soccer ball under a large sign across the eaves of their shelter. The blue letters are half a metre high against a yellow background. They are in capitals, in English, and they read: 'DO NOT FORGET AUSTRALIA'. On the front wall of the school hangs this plaque:

'This school building is the gift of the school children of Victoria, Australia to the children of Villers-Bretonneux as a proof of their love and good-will towards France. Twelve hundred Australian soldiers, the fathers and brothers of these children, gave their lives in the heroic recapture of this town from the invader on 24th April 1918 and are buried near this spot. May the memory of great sacrifices in a common cause keep France and Australia together forever in bonds of friendship and mutual esteem.'

Above the classrooms the school treasures an Anzac museum, which contains a fine collection of memorabilia, artefacts and photos commemorating Australia's role in the liberation of their town.

Away from the town centre, along the main road to Amiens, you'll be stunned by a vision that has stood unchanged since the guns fell silent in November 1918. The proud skeletal ruins of the Villers-Bretonneux Chateau are silhouetted against the grey skyline. Even without its roof and much of its rear external walls, it gives an impression of the grand life it must have presided over before the war. Occupancy of the chateau changed with control of Villers-Bretonneux. The Germans used it for their local headquarters until they were driven out by the Australians, who then moved in. It was subsequently used by the senior Australian officers as they planned the great offensive by the Australian Corps on 8 August 1918. It was later handed over to the Australian

Graves Unit, which was left with the heartrending job of building the Villers-Bretonneux and Adelaide cemeteries nearby.

The Adelaide cemetery, just outside Villers-Bretonneux, past the railway crossing on the Amiens Road, was started in June 1918 by Diggers from South Australia. It contains 519 Australians, all killed between March and September 1918, including four unknown soldiers, of a total of 864 soldiers interred there. Most of these Diggers were killed in the street fighting in Villers-Bretonneux on Anzac Day 1918. Among these graves is one with the following inscription:

'The remains of an unknown Australian soldier lay in this grave for 75 years. On November 2 1993 they were exhumed and now rest in the tomb of the Unknown Soldier at the Australian War Memorial in Canberra.'

Villers-Bretonneux is twinned with the Victorian town of Robinvale. The link is Flight Lieutenant Robin George Cuttle, one of the early heroes of the Royal Flying Corps, who was killed near Villers-Bretonneux. He was a member of the Cuttle family, whose property was subdivided to create the town under a Soldiers' Settlement Scheme after World War II. The name Robinvale (from *vale*, Latin for 'farewell') commemorates him. It was officially twinned with Villers-Bretonneux with ceremonies in France and Australia in 1984 and 1985.

Head back out now through the Villers-Bretonneux town centre onto the road to Fouilloy and you'll reach the impressive Australian National Memorial. It forms part of the Villers-Bretonneux cemetery where 779 Diggers rest, including 47 unknown soldiers. Long, neat lines of graves face each other on either side of a large 'Cross of Sacrifice'. Seven rows on each side of the cross traverse a gentle slope on the high ground overlooking the surrounding countryside, where most of those resting here died. Watching over these graves is the tall stone tower of the memorial, which records on its walls the names of 10,982 Australians killed in France who have no known grave. Climb the tower and you can see much of the wide, lush but featureless Somme battlefield. Here a million soldiers from the two contending sides endured unspeakable horrors as a constant flow of men were fed into the charnel house. Images from black-and-white photos and jerky films hint at the torment played out on this now silent countryside. It's difficult to imagine a more powerful anti-war experience than spending some time reflecting on the hell on earth that visited here.

A little further ahead, on the road to the village of Corbie, with its expansive view of the Somme Valley, near where the Statue of Saint Colette stands, another notable event in the war occurred. In late April 1918 an Australian, Sergeant Cedric Popkin of the 24th Machine-Gun Company of the 4th Division, is credited with firing the burst that brought down Baron Manfred von Richthofen, the famous German flying ace, known as the 'Red Baron', who collected 80 Allied aircraft 'kills' during his domination of the skies from 1914.

It was also in this area, as the Germans turned their attention to their offensive against the French Army to the south, that the Australian soldiers' penchant for ingenuity re-emerged. The Diggers called their tactics 'peaceful penetration'; Charles Bean called it a 'private war'. It was a form of guerilla fighting in which the Diggers attacked the Germans whenever they let down their guard. The Aussies would send small patrols into the German lines to sneak up on their exhausted opposition. In a perfect example, Lieutenant Irvine of the 18th Battalion realised that the Germans manning a post in front of him were asleep in broad daylight. He and his scouts sneaked across no-man's land and captured the entire garrison of 21 soldiers without alerting the rest of the German line to their sortie.

The Australians brought great pressure to bear on the German lines, preventing them from getting desperately needed rest and fraying their nerves. Charles Bean quoted a German prisoner on the impact of the tactics:

'You bloody Australians, when you are in the line you keep us on pins and needles; we never know when you are coming over.'

This approach exemplified the Australians' attitude of maintaining aggression and, wherever possible, freedom of movement, despite the static nature of the fighting. It was consistent with the philosophy espoused by the commander of the Australian Corps, General Sir John Monash:

'The role of the infantry was not to expend itself upon heroic physical effort, not to wither away under merciless machine-gun fire, not to impale itself on hostile bayonets, but, on the contrary, to advance under the maximum array of mechanical resources in the form of guns, machine-guns, tanks, mortars and aeroplanes.'

In May 1918 Monash succeeded the Briton, General Sir William Birdwood, as commander of the Australian Corps after Birdwood was promoted to lead the 5th Army. This was another important step in the 'Australianisation' of the Australian Corps. The appointment was symptomatic of the capacity of the Australian Army to embrace multicultural diversity: Monash was the Australian-born son of Polish-Jewish migrants. He had excelled at Melbourne's Scotch College, where he was dux, before becoming a brilliant engineering student at Melbourne University and a successful civilian-soldier. He had, of course, played a leading role at Gallipoli and was highly regarded by the Diggers and his fellow officers.

Monash was recognised as a brilliant planner. His attention to detail in the preparation of operations was prodigious, as was his ability to juggle the various elements at his disposal once hostilities had commenced. He had a keen understanding of the needs of his men and the extent to which they could be pushed. Because of his background he approached his tasks untrammelled by the strictures of the British military system. This allowed him greater freedom intellectually. He appreciated the special qualities of his men and used them wisely. He realised the Diggers were in many ways a different breed from the other armies fighting in France: their origins, upbringing, attitudes, even their physical appearance, set them apart. The Australian fighting spirit had impressed British commanders, generous in their praise of the Australians' contributions at Gallipoli and in France. Charles Bean tried in his reports from the various fronts to make the Australian public aware of the high esteem in which their Diggers were held. But those at home generally did not fully appreciate the Diggers' achievements until some time after the war.

The following month, the Australians undertook their first action as a corps when they successfully captured the German front-line defences at Morlancourt and Sailly-Laurette, taking 325 prisoners and effectively eliminating an entire German battalion. Bean quotes the German divisional commander as reporting to his superiors that in a few minutes 'a complete battalion had been wiped out as with a sponge'.

In July, Monash set new standards of planning for the Australian forces. Bean called him 'a master of lucid explanation'. In preparing for what was to become known as the Battle of Le Hamel, Monash and his staff choreographed a precise operation involving British tanks and Australian infantry. As Bean reports, the planning was well worth the effort:

'The attack was a brilliant success. The Australian infantry had been hurriedly trained with the tanks, and though at several points – one of them vital – the machines were late and the infantry had to go through without them, the general perform-ance fulfilled the Diggers' highest expectations.

'The new tanks were slightly faster than the infantry, and could reverse, turn and manoeuvre quickly, and their crews never failed to take them where required. In addition, the few carrier tanks, bringing up supplies behind the advancing line, did in a few minutes the work then ordinarily done by hundreds of infantrymen.

'The tank crews on their part particularly noted (to quote their commander) "the superb morale of the Australian troops, who never considered that the presence of tanks exonerated them

from fighting, and took instant advantage of any opportunity created by the tanks". The infantry walked enthusiastically behind machines marked with the infantry's own battalion colours.

'Within two hours the impression left by Bullecourt was reversed [when the tanks had been an abject failure and 1170 Diggers had been taken prisoner]. *From this time the British Tank Corps looked to the Australian Diggers above all other infantry in France, and the Diggers never ceased to welcome the chance of working with the tanks. Their only complaint, on this occasion, as constantly before, was: "Why did we stop before reaching his guns?"'*

Thus, on 4 July 1918, in just over and hour and a half, three Australian brigades, the 6th, 11th and 4th, advanced 2 kilometres to reclaim the town of Hamel and capture the German positions on the ridge overlooking the village, 1600 prisoners, and substantial amounts of enemy equipment and supplies. Also in this battle, for the first time, American troops fought alongside the Diggers. Four companies from the US 33rd Division (about 500 troops) were sprinkled among the Australians to give them combat experience. Another first – one that was to have vast ramifications in the future – was the dropping of ammunition to the troops by parachute. This was a concept developed by Captain L.J. Wackett of the 3rd Squadron, Australian Flying Corps, which worked in tandem with the Australian infantry.

The success at Hamel was replicated, using similar preparation, artillery and tank support, at the Battle of Amiens on 8 August 1918. For the first time all five Australian divisions fought together. Together with the Canadian Corps, they formed the spearhead of the attack mounted by the 4th British Army. The attacks took place under a dense fog, made even thicker by white smoke-shell in the creeping barrages preceding them. The plan involved concealing the noise of the preliminary positioning of the supporting tanks by planes consistently flying over the Germans under cover of the fog. It worked to perfection: many panicked German units were bypassed in the fog and overwhelmed when attacked from the rear. The attack overall smashed through the German defences, inflicting 27,000 casualties including 16,000 prisoners. General Ludendorff called it Germany's 'Black Day' (in *No Man's Land – The Story of 1918* by John Toland):

> *'Our fighting machine was no longer of real value. Our capacity for war suffered harm even if the far greater majority of our divisions fought bravely. August 8 marked the decline of our military power and took from me the hope that . . . we could restore the situation in our favour . . . The war had to be ended.'*

But the Germans fought on, and the Diggers spent the next two months in almost continuous combat. Amazingly, they still had the dash and courage to perform one of their most outstanding actions in the war. In late August about 1200 Diggers (around 300 from each of four heavily depleted battalions) charged a superior German defensive force and took Mont St Quentin, the high ground overlooking the old town of Peronne on the Somme. Bean notes that the Australian company leaders knew they were well short on the desirable numbers, so they 'decided that the best chance lay in making a noise as they attacked, "yelling", as Captain E.T. Manefield urged, "like a lot of bushrangers" ':

> *'The cheering platoon at once ran into crowds of Germans, who seemed bewildered and quickly surrendered – indeed in many cases they were simply pushed to the rear with their hands up, leaving their machine-guns lying on the ground. They were from one of the best divisions of the German Army, the 2nd Guard, which had just been sent to relieve the over-strained garrison. "It all happened like lightning," says the history of the Guard Alexander Regiment, "and before we had fired a shot we were taken unawares".'*

Once again, Monash had planned the assault meticulously and the Diggers had shown extraordinary spirit:

> *'This brilliant action, in which, without tanks or creeping barrage, the Australians at a cost of 3000 casualties dealt a*

stunning blow to five German divisions, coincided in time with a thrust by the 3rd Army and the Canadians towards Cambrai and gave Ludendorff additional cause for retiring from the line of the Somme below Peronne, where he had previously intended to hold on.

'He could now only retreat to the Hindenburg Line, which, however, also had been pierced by the British northern thrust (not far from Bullecourt).'

Bean summed up the Diggers' contribution to the Western Front campaign by referring to the growing reputation of the Australian flyers who had risen, like their infantry brothers, to claim the honour of leading most of the engagements in which they participated. He quotes Lieutenant Colonial L.A. Strange, one of the originals flying in France, in his memoirs, *Recollections of an Airman*, on the Australian flyers:

'Their records show that they were the finest material as an attacking force in the air, just as their infantry divisions on the ground were the best that the war produced on either side. It became the practice for our Australian squadrons to lead the 80th Wing's bombing raids. When later in the year over a hundred machines set out on one of them, the spearpoint was always formed of Australian airmen led by an Australian.'

Bean concludes:

'Such was the reputation attained after two and a half years of intense warfare on the Western front by the force whose first trial was the equally intense struggle on Gallipoli.

'There is no question – although their own home folk in Australia at first found this difficult to believe – that the spirit and skill of the Australian Imperial Force, and particularly of the infantry, in the final year's fighting in France materially affected the course of the campaign there, as did that of the other Dominion forces.'

On 11 November troops across the front were relieved to receive the following official communiqué:

'Eleven o'clock today, November 11, troops will stand fast on the positions reached at the hour named. The line of outposts will be

established, and reported to Army Headquarters. The remainder of the troops will be collected to meet any emergency. All military precautions will be preserved, there will be no communication with the enemy. Further instructions will be issued. Acknowledge.'

When the clock struck eleven, on that eleventh day of that eleventh month of 1918, and all the guns fell silent after four years, the Digger had established his niche in history. The Armistice was welcomed with relief, rather than joy, by most of the troops who had survived, as Bean recalls:

'For the troops there the change went too deep for outward rejoicing; on the surface, life continued as usual except for the cessation of actual fighting. But, in the back areas, as in London and Paris, the people and servicemen burst into demonstrations increasing in exuberance with the distance from the front.

'In Australia a false report from America set fire to public enthusiasm four days earlier, but that did not damp the genuine outburst of public relief when the true news arrived on November 12; as in England, people flooded into the streets; flags broke out, bonfires blazed, bells rang, bands played, and for that day serious work was at an end.'

Many recalled the words of the English poet and writer Laurence Binyon, from his poem 'For The Fallen', some of which forms the 'Ode' played out in RSL clubs across Australia and at cenotaphs every Anzac Day:

They went with songs to the battle, they were young,
Straight of limb, true of eyes, steady and aglow,
They were staunch to the end against odds uncounted,
They fell with their faces to the foe.
They shall grow not old, as we that are left grow old:
Age shall not weary them, nor the years condemn
At the going down of the sun and in the morning
We will remember them.

SIX

Between the wars

It would be more than a year before the last of the Diggers returned home. At war's end they were dispersed in almost all the theatres of the conflict: 92,000 in France; 60,000 in England; 17,000 in Egypt, Palestine and Syria; and smaller groups scattered in Mesopotamia, Persia and Kurdistan.

Sensibly, the Anzac leaders adopted a policy of 'first come, first go' in repatriating the Diggers. In spite of the Diggers' lingering reputation for poor discipline when not on operations, the process was achieved without any drama. The men were sent home in groups of 1000 – a manageable trainload and shipload. Generally, each of these 'battalions' was accompanied by its own staff officers, band, education and recreation staff, and facilities. They all passed through camps on England's Salisbury Plain on their journey to the transport ships that would ultimately deliver them to their waiting loved ones.

For some unlucky Diggers, fate had one more blow in store. They came in contact with the then raging Spanish flu, and most of the 143 Australian graves in the cemetery at Sutton Veny, near Salisbury, contain Diggers who succumbed to influenza. Still more got even closer to home before dying in transit and being buried in Sierra Leone in Western Africa.

Today, on that same Salisbury Plain, you can visit the Fovant Badges – regimental badges evocatively carved in the soft, chalky hills by the soldiers who camped there. They are lovingly tended by a dedicated group of locals, who maintain them as a memorial to the thousands of men who passed through this beautiful land.

The repatriation of the Australian forces was achieved with admirable efficiency. But that was just the start. The Diggers, in the main, were able to put aside their slouch hats and uniforms and merge back into the Australian heartland. But things were never quite the same. Barely a family escaped loss, and thousands welcomed home a severely wounded loved one. There was great dislocation as Diggers found their wives or sweethearts had taken up with others. Many waiting women found it hard to come to terms with the changes the war had wrought on their men. Some widows and bereaved fiancées would never find another partner, and some mothers and fathers would never recover from their broken hearts. Then there were the wounded. Gassed and mutilated Diggers would linger on for years, requiring constant treatment. The 'repat' hospitals became a fixture in the community, and most families knew a long-suffering veteran or one whose life was cut short by injury or impaired health.

Out of a population of about five million, 60,000 of our finest sons had been killed. This loss would echo throughout the nation for a generation. Like the other countries involved, we had lost the cream of the crop. The balance of male to female had been disturbed. Then there were the psychological legacies. For some, the war never ended: they wasted away in a mad netherworld. Some walked on eggshells, fearful of any sudden noise, which would send them diving for cover. Some became unpredictably violent or withdrew into bouts of depression. Others managed to cope with their nightmares and feelings of guilt but these often remained just below the surface, ready to be triggered by sights, sounds or smells that would bring the horrors flooding back. Some families broke under the strain. Many marriages shattered or hung on by a thread, often simply because divorce was still a socially unacceptable option.

There were few medicines and virtually no counselling to ease the psychological damage. Many families found it hard to understand the Diggers' need to be with their mates. But the Diggers knew that only those who had shared the horrors could understand their sense of doubt, loss, guilt and helplessness, their mood swings and periods of restlessness. The great majority of returned Diggers avoided talking about their wartime experiences. This reticence became a typical Digger response down the years, through World War II and down to Vietnam, and caused considerable damage to both veterans and their loved ones.

On the positive side, the Australian government established a system of pensions and health services for injured veterans, paid war gratuities to all who served, and made home loans available to them under the War Service Homes Act. The government also oversaw a 'soldiers' land settlement' scheme, managed by the states, which aimed at resettling veterans in selected rural areas. The war prompted the formation of the RSL (originally the Returned Soldiers' and Sailors' Imperial League of Australia) and Legacy, which continues today to provide for the children of dead or disabled veterans.

Charles Bean believed our Diggers' performance in World War I enabled Australia to secure a seat on the League of Nations and brought 'a new confidence into Australian national undertakings'. Bean had little doubt about the real basis for the success of the Diggers:

'Actually it was discipline – firmly based on the national habit of facing facts and going straight for the objective – that was responsible for the astonishing success which first gave other nations confidence in Australia, and to the Australian nation confidence in itself.'

Sadly, the 'Great War' was not, in the hopeful words of American President Woodrow Wilson, 'the war to end all wars'. Around eight million died in the conflict and another 20 million or more were wounded or disabled, but even that grievous toll was not sufficient disincentive to provoke another global conflict just 20 years later.

Much of the credit for immortalising the Digger rests with Charles Bean. He personally wrote six of the 12 volumes of the *Official History of Australia in the War of 1914–18*. Bean worked for 23 years to complete this work and wrote more than two million words. The most admirable aspect of his beautifully crafted reporting is that it was gathered first-hand. In addition, Bean witnessed many of the battles and travelled incessantly to find out 'what actually happened at the cutting edge of the military machine, where the intention and effort of one side grated on that of its opponents'. Bean set out to go behind the official records and reports to examine the impact of the conflict on those in the front lines, to find 'the hopes, fears, ambitions, resolutions, enthusiasms and sufferings of ordinary men'.

Charles Bean established himself in the highest echelon of war correspondents, not only for his monumental effort in chronicling the exploits of the Australian forces but also for his great vision – both in recognising the importance of recording our history for future generations and in his push to establish a national war memorial. (Luckily, he lived to play an important role in making the War Memorial in Canberra a reality as chairman of the board of management.)

For some years after the war ended there was an understandable abhorrence of war and anything associated with it. In Australia this even extended to many schoolteachers, who resisted the study of our contribution in World War I as an endorsement of war. Bean took the longer, wider view as he wrote in the Foreword to his summary volume *Anzac to Amiens*, originally published in 1946 when Bean was 67:

> *There is little fear that a short history, written largely for teachers and school libraries, will meet today among teachers the disapproval which it would have met for many years after*

the First World War. Not that the detestation of war was greater than now; but there was a widespread feeling, not merely that military operations bulked too largely in history – which is true, despite the immense influence of wars on almost every phase of human development – but that, sustaining a pride in the military efforts of our countrymen, the history of war encouraged war.'

Bean here has incisively summed up the importance of our learning of the achievements and sacrifices of our Diggers, not just in World War I but in subsequent conflicts. We should do it to honour those who sacrificed their lives, their health, their futures, so we could enjoy freedom. As the original introduction to the guide to the Australian War Memorial states:

'The collection consists of the documentary records of the Australian fighting forces, and the pictures, photographs, dioramas and other models, as well as the material relics, of their campaigns. The gathering of these relics began on the battlefields of World War I, and the decision that they should become part of the nation's war memorial was made by the Commonwealth on a suggestion from the battlefield in 1917.

'Conceived at Anzac on Gallipoli, born amid the thunder of the guns at Bullecourt in France, the Memorial has been raised by the living members of the Australian forces to their fallen mates. It constitutes not a general museum portraying war, much less one glorifying it, but a memorial conceived, founded and, from first to last, worked for by Australia's soldiers, sailors and airmen.'

It's the spiritual element that sets the Australian War Memorial apart. Right from your first step inside you feel a sense of reverence. This is missing in many other war museums, which cater first for material relics, weapons and examples of battles. The Memorial is a shrine, an exhibition and a research centre.

The cloisters of the sacred Assembly, which leads across to the Hall of Memory and features the names of all those who gave their lives for the liberty we enjoy, set the tone. The

Shrine, or the Hall of Memory, honours the ideals for which the fallen sacrificed their lives. The various stained-glass windows represent the qualities we value in our soldiers: comradeship, patriotism, chivalry, loyalty, endurance, audacity, coolness under fire, resourcefulness, devotion, and independence. It's a fitting tribute to all those who didn't return home, and it's the centrepiece which gives meaning to the superb displays and collections that form the rest of the Memorial.

The popularity of the Australian War Memorial is one of the heartening indicators of our national maturity. It is in fact our most popular tourist destination, with more than a million visitors each year, many of them schoolchildren who come from all around the nation. Indeed, the growing interest of young Australians in visiting the Memorial, attending Anzac Day dawn services and marches, making pilgrimages to Gallipoli and trekking the Kokoda Track sets us apart from many other nations, where it's usually the older brigade who take an interest in their history. Many young Aussies are searching for their roots and for an understanding of what it means to be an Australian. Understanding the spirit of the Digger is an essential step in their quest.

Virtually every suburb and town across Australia has some memorial to those who served and died in the Great War. The creation and subsequent growth of Anzac Day as a day of national reflection shows the depth of the respect for our veterans.

As with so many great traditions, the Anzac Day dawn service started almost by accident. The late Reverend Arthur Ernest White, a Church of England padré to the 44th Battalion of the First AIF, had conducted a 4 am service before the embarkation of the early Anzac forces from Albany, Western Australia. Albany was the departure point for the Anzacs' epic journey into history. By coincidence, on his return after the war, his first parish appointment was back in Albany. To commemorate Anzac Day in 1923, he decided to repeat his service:

'Albany was the last sight of land these Anzac troops saw after leaving Australian shores and some of them never returned. We should hold a service here at the first light of dawn each Anzac Day to commemorate them.'

The dawn service was so powerful it was soon emulated and quickly spread through the country.

Recently, there have been calls for further memorials in Albany to commemorate its role in the Anzac legend. A Perth public servant, Stan Crombie, is trying to raise funds for a column of bronze statues of Diggers, a memorial wall incorporating the names of the 60,000 Diggers who died on the battlefields of World War I, and a nightly sounding of the *Last Post*, just as it's played every night at 8 pm in the Belgian city of Ypres.

It's significant that while Britain and other European nations commemorate the end of World War I on the day it officially ended, Remembrance Day, 11 November, with a minute's silence at exactly 11 am, Australia and New Zealand chose a day with completely different connotations. Instead of celebrating a day of victory, we commemorate the courage and the sacrifices of our veterans on the anniversary of the day our Anzacs landed on Gallipoli.

While the general population in Australia began the long process of returning to normality, the AIF was officially disbanded on 1 April 1921. Two days earlier, the Royal Australian Air Force was created, largely from those who had flown with the Australian Flying Corps in France, Palestine and Egypt.

By the mid-1920s all the lessons we had learnt from our lack of preparation prior to World War I had been forgotten. The government of the day decided to switch the emphasis for our defensive core from the Army to the Navy. In 1928 our permanent naval strength was about 5000, while the permanent military force had dwindled to a mere 1750 men.

The Great Depression saw this situation deteriorate even further, and in October 1929 the newly elected Scullin Labor government honoured its election promise to abolish compulsory military training. The plan now was for a volunteer army of 35,000 plus 7000 senior cadets. This was the Militia, and it replaced the Citizen Military Forces. The size of the Army reached a new low when Duntroon was closed down and moved to Sydney's Victoria Barracks, with a total of 30 cadets in training there. But the decline continued even further so that by 1932 the permanent army force had dropped to 1536 – lower than it had been when the federal government took over control of the defence forces from the states 29 years earlier! The Citizen Military Forces' level of 46,000 in 1929 fell to 28,000 by 1932.

Much of the reduction was justified at the time by the global push for disarmament, which continued even in the face of some clear signs of trouble brewing when Japan invaded Manchuria in 1931, showing up the ineffectiveness of the League of Nations in the process. Japan withdrew from the League as it set its course for expansion in Asia. In 1933, Adolf Hitler seized power in Germany and later that year pulled his country out of the League. Two years later, the other main player in the coming conflict revealed his hand. Under its dictator, Benito Mussolini, Italy invaded Ethiopia. It ignored the subsequent economic sanctions applied this time by the League of Nations and proceeded to conquer Ethiopia, only then withdrawing from the League.

The threats were growing. The stage was set. Yet the Australian government continued its reliance on London for global strategic intelligence and planning. In essence, we relied on Britain to maintain our security against the growing Japanese threat to our region. The understanding was that Britain would use its naval base at Singapore to protect us.

A growing number of our experienced defence personnel had grave misgivings about this plan. Many had first-hand experience of the exigencies of war, and knew that if Britain were caught up in a conflict that threatened its own security it would relegate our needs to the bottom of the pile. They called for our Army to be beefed up urgently so we could protect ourselves long enough for our Allies to come to our aid in a worst-case scenario. Our government eventually acted in 1938, prompted by Hitler's invasion of Austria. But although spending on our armed forces was doubled, it was too little and came from too small a base. Events in Europe were gathering pace, and by 1939 British Prime Minister Neville Chamberlain's response to a query from his Australian counterpart, Joe Lyons, showed a worrying lack of conviction:

> 'In the event of war with Germany and Italy, should Japan join against us, it would still be His Majesty's Government's full intention to despatch a fleet to Singapore. If we were fighting against such a combination never envisaged in our earlier plans, the size of that fleet would necessarily be dependent of (a) the moment when Japan entered the war and (b) what losses, if any, our opponents or ourselves had previously sustained. It would however be our intention to achieve three main objectives:
>
> (i)   the prevention of any major operations against Australia, New Zealand or India.
>
> (ii) to keep open our sea communications.
>
> (iii) to prevent the fall of Singapore.'

Towards the end of 1938, many Australians were joining the Army and the Militia in response to a government campaign to attract recruits. The Militia numbers jumped from 35,000 in September 1938 to 43,000 by the end of the year and to 80,000 by mid-1939. But there was of course no equipment for these new recruits because we'd left it too late, and the hasty orders we'd placed with British suppliers were overtaken by their own army's urgent demands.

Noted military historian David Horner did not pull any punches in his book *Crisis of Command*:

> 'It is now generally agreed that the Australian defence policy between the wars and up to the fall of Singapore was at the best, naively optimistic, and at the worst, some might say, close to treason.'

SEVEN

World War II

Australia's direct involvement in World War II was inevitable once Hitler unleashed his forces against Poland early on 1 September 1939. Most Australians already knew that their government had committed itself to supporting Britain's stance against Germany. The policy of trying to appease Germany and Italy in their aggressive expansion plans had failed. Britain and France jointly warned Hitler that if he invaded Poland they would declare war. On the evening of 3 September at 9.15 pm, without consulting Parliament, Prime Minister Robert Menzies announced on radio that we were at war, just 20 years and ten months after the last one ended:

'It is my melancholy duty to inform you officially that in consequence of the persistence by Germany in her invasion of Poland, Great Britain has declared war upon her and that as a result, Australia is also at war . . .'

Hitler's non-aggression pact with Russia sealed Poland's fate. It eliminated the threat of a double front for Hitler and it split Polish territory between Germany and Russia, which moved into eastern Poland on 17 September.

The day after Australia entered the war, the Chief of Staff's Committee was created, made up of the chiefs of the Army, the RAN and the RAAF, to give advice to the War Cabinet. But, unlike World War I, when the Australian government immediately offered Britain an expeditionary force (the First

AIF), this time the government was aware of a wildcard in the game – Japan. And, more realistically, we were probably even less prepared than we had been in 1914.

In late November the government said it would send the newly raised 6th Division to Palestine for training, then to join the British Expeditionary Force in France. This division had been formed from volunteers outside the existing Militia structure. There were echoes of 1914 as loved ones farewelled the men of the 2nd AIF on 20 January 1940 and 11 transport ships, carrying the 16th Brigade of the 6th Division, sailed from Fremantle. By February they were camped in Palestine but it would be almost a year later before they first saw action, a successful capture of the Italian stronghold at Bardia. The 6th Division was led by a Gallipoli and Western Front veteran, Lieutenant General Sir Thomas Blamey.

David Horner sums up the situation in *Crisis of Command*: *'In March 1940 there were 4000 permanent soldiers, 3000 militia permanently called up and some 5000 in garrison units. The militia numbered 62,300. Half had done three months training and the second half were about to begin; after that they were to revert to the pre-war system – that is a 12-day camp plus home training. With 20,000 national servicemen also being trained, the defence of Australia rested on about 75,000 men.'*

(We can put this into perspective by recalling that we sent 300,000 troops overseas in World War I, of whom 60,000 were killed.) Around this time, the government decided to form another division, the 7th, which would join the 6th to form the 1st Australian Corps of the 2nd AIF. Blamey was given command of the Corps, with Major General Lavarack leading the 7th and Major General Iven Mackay taking over as CO of the 6th.

Germany's early successes were chilling. Australians learned the meaning of a new and frightening word – '*Blitzkrieg*', or 'lightning war', as Hitler's panzer divisions overran Denmark

Kilitbahir Fortress at Eceabat on the Gallipoli Peninsula guards The Narrows – a strait 1500 metres wide at the entrance to the Dardanelles – just as it has done since it was built in the 18th century. (Lisa Cotton)

Anzac Cove and the steep hills that confronted the Anzacs on 25 April 1915. Visible in the centre of the shoreline are the remains of Watson's Pier, one of the jetties built by Australian engineers to offload supplies. (Lisa Cotton)

Looking down at the difficult terrain of Ari Burnu from Malone's Gully. At the top left is The Sphinx, and directly behind it is Anzac Cove. (Patrick Lindsay)

Above left: Captain Ali Efe examines bone fragments uncovered by rain storms at Lone Pine, Gallipoli. (Patrick Lindsay)

Above right: Bone fragments at Lone Pine. (Patrick Lindsay)

An Australian bullet at Lone Pine. (Patrick Lindsay)

"THOSE HEROES THAT SHED THEIR BLOOD
AND LOST THEIR LIVES...
YOU ARE NOW LYING IN THE SOIL OF A FRIENDLY COUNTRY.
THEREFORE REST IN PEACE.
THERE IS NO DIFFERENCE BETWEEN THE JOHNNIES
AND THE MEHMETS TO US WHERE THEY LIE SIDE BY SIDE
HERE IN THIS COUNTRY OF OURS...
YOU, THE MOTHERS
WHO SENT THEIR SONS FROM FAR AWAY COUNTRIES
WIPE AWAY YOUR TEARS;
YOUR SONS ARE NOW LYING IN OUR BOSOM
AND ARE IN PEACE.
AFTER HAVING LOST THEIR LIVES ON THIS LAND THEY HAVE
BECOME OUR SONS AS WELL."
ATATÜRK 1934

The monument at Anzac Cove built by the Turkish Government in 1985 immortalises the words Ataturk used in his address to the first Australian, New Zealander and British veterans to visit the Gallipoli battlefields in 1934. (Lisa Cotton)

Right: Private Reginald Rutherford Waters, 23rd Battalion, of Carlton, Victoria. Private Waters embarked the HMAS *Euripides* from Melbourne on 8 May 1915. He died of wounds received at Lone Pine on 30 November 1915.
(AWM, DA08755)

Below left: Lieutenant Arthur Rafferty, who lost his arm after being wounded on Hill 60 at Gallipoli, recuperating in London in late 1915.
(Murray family collection)

Below right: The author making notes at Lone Pine.
(Lisa Cotton)

Lone Pine today. Australian trenches were located where the graves in the foreground now stand. Turkish trenches were located near the monument. (Lisa Cotton)

The author and Captain Ali Efe at the Lone Pine monument, under which Turkish and Australian soldiers died together in the Turkish trenches. (Lisa Cotton)

Ari Burnu cemetery, Anzac Cove. Some of the first Anzacs to die on the Peninsula are buried here. The cemetery also contains the remains of some of the Light Horse heroes of the gallant but futile charge at The Nek. (Lisa Cotton)

Some of the scores of gun emplacements near Eceabat on the Gallipoli Peninsula. Turkish artillery, firing from these positions, bombarded the British fleet when it tried to storm the Dardanelles on 18 March 1915. The direct result of the failure of the naval attack was the attack by land on 25 April 1915. (Patrick Lindsay)

A padre reads the burial service beside the grave of a fallen Australian, in a cemetery near a casualty clearing station on the Western Front in 1916. His mates stand around the newly-dug grave. (AWM P00077.011)

The Menin Gate, Ypres, Belgium, is a monument to the Allied soldiers who died in World War I in France with no known grave. (Lisa Cotton)

Buglers from Ypres Fire Brigade play the Last Post every night at 8 pm at the Menin Gate Memorial. (Lisa Cotton)

The names of some of the 10 000 Australian Diggers honoured on the walls of the Menin Gate. (Lisa Cotton)

The remains of Villers-Bretonneux chateau today. During World War I it was used as a headquarters by the French, then the Germans, and then by Australians after they liberated the town on 24 April 1918. (Lisa Cotton)

THEIR NAME LIVETH
FOR EVERMORE

The magnificent Australian National Memorial outside Villers-Bretonneux. The cemetery contains the graves of 779 Diggers, and the stone tower records the names of the 10 982 Diggers killed in France who have no known grave. (Lisa Cotton)

THIS SCHOOL BUILDING IS THE GIFT OF THE SCHOOL CHILDREN OF VICTORIA, AUSTRALIA, TO THE CHILDREN OF VILLERS-BRETONNEUX, AS A PROOF OF THEIR LOVE AND GOOD-WILL TOWARDS FRANCE. TWELVE HUNDRED AUSTRALIAN SOLDIERS, THE FATHERS AND BROTHERS OF THESE CHILDREN, GAVE THEIR LIVES IN THE HEROIC RECAPTURE OF THIS TOWN FROM THE INVADER ON 24TH APRIL 1918, AND ARE BURIED NEAR THIS SPOT. MAY THE MEMORY OF GREAT SACRIFICES IN A COMMON CAUSE KEEP FRANCE AND AUSTRALIA TOGETHER FOREVER IN BONDS OF FRIEND-SHIP AND MUTUAL ESTEEM.

The plaque commemorating the generosity of the schoolchildren of Victoria who collected money after World War I to enable Villers-Bretonneux to rebuild its school. (Patrick Lindsay)

DO NOT FORGET AUSTRALIA

The playground of Victoria Public School in Villers-Bretonneux, with its message to students in gratitude to the Diggers who liberated the town in April 1918, and the Australian children who raised money to help rebuild the school. (Patrick Lindsay)

Adelaide Cemetery in Villers-Bretonneux contains the graves of 519 Diggers, all killed between March and September 1918. The soldier who now rests in the Tomb of the Unknown Soldier at the Australian War Memorial in Canberra was taken from a grave here. (Patrick Lindsay)

The Australian soldier in the foreground was wounded in both arms and captured by the Germans in the Western Desert in 1942. The dressing station was later captured by British troops and the prisoner returned to his mates. (AWM 042076)

Above left: Captain Ralph Honner in Derna during World War II. (AWM 005638)
Above right: Corporal Vic Murray was captured in one of the early battles fought by Diggers in Libya during World War II. He was one of many who endured four years of captivity in Italy and Germany. (Murray family collection)

A wounded Australian soldier, Lieutenant Valentine G. Gardner, has his cigarette lit by a Salvation Army chaplain, 22 September 1942. Behind them is a Papuan stretcher bearer, popularly known as a Fuzzy Wuzzy Angel. (AWM 013287)

Above left: Private H. R. Nash was wounded during a jungle clash with the Japanese in the Kokoda area, New Guinea, in May 1942. Nash made his way back to the base in the Owen Stanley Ranges on foot, taking seven days to cover the distance. (AWM 013259)

Above right: Australians who advanced along the New Guinea coast to link up with the Americans at Saidor staged an impromptu surf carnival on their first free day, 28 February 1944. (AWM 016614)

A hospital ward in Changi, Singapore, shows members of the 8th Division released from the Changi POW camp on 15 September 1945. All were suffering from malnutrition. (AWM 019199)

Above left: Lieutenant Colonel Phil Rhoden in Balikpapan, Borneo, in 1945.
(AWM 116221)

Above right: With the billy on the fire, a British soldier and two Australians warm themselves while waiting for their tea to brew during the Korean War, 1950.
(AWM HOBJ1886)

The No. 4 Platoon, B Company, 3rd Battalion, the Royal Australian Regiment (RAR), which distinguished itself in the Battle of Kapyong in Korea in April 1951.
(AWM 147350)

Back on the Long Tan battlefield after the heroic action by Delta Company of the 6th Battalion, RAR, in which more than 200 Viet Cong were killed. Second Lieutenant David Sabben advances cautiously through the rubber plantation, past the bodies of dead Viet Cong, on 19 August 1966. (AWM FOR/66/0658/VN)

Lance Corporal Georgie Richardson and Sergeant Bob Buick apply first aid to Private Jim Richmond, who was found twelve hours after the Long Tan battle. He was shot twice through the chest and lay all night, face down, at his section post. (AWM FOR/66/0664/VN)

Above right: Captain Barry Petersen (left) in Montagnard tribal dress in Vietnam in 1965 with a local chieftain and another member of the Australian Training Team Vietnam, WO2 Jock Roy. Many believe Petersen was the inspiration for the central character in the movie *Apocalypse Now*. (AWN DNE/65/0428/VN)

Above left: Corporal Brett Woodward leads Section Two Three Bravo, of 5/7th Battalion, RAR, on patrol in Bobonaro Province, East Timor, in 2003. (Patrick Lindsay)

Above left: The men of Section Two Three Bravo, 5/7th Battalion, RAR, at Junction Point Charlie near the border with West Timor, 2003. Back row: Brent Thomson, Joshua Nicholas. Centre: Wayne Griggs, Scott Dudley. Front: Brett Woodward, Billy Boulton, Matthew McMahon, Clint Holdsworth. (Patrick Lindsay)

Above right: The control tower at Junction Point Charlie overlooking the Tactical Coordination Line on the border between East and West Timor. (Patrick Lindsay) and Norway, then turned west and south to take Belgium, Luxembourg and the Netherlands. Then they swept into northern France and trapped the British Expeditionary Force at Dunkirk.

Mussolini saw his chance and declared war on 10 June as Germany entered Paris. By 22 June France had capitulated. Hitler was at his peak: he had Britain in his sights. But Churchill had been appointed Prime Minister on 10 May and was using his extraordinarily inspirational oratory to rally his people for the expected invasion.

By this stage the seriousness of Australia's situation was also clear. Britain was under siege, on the brink of the 'Battle of Britain' – the desperate four-month air campaign fought over its skies – and was asking us to provide a division for the defence of Singapore:

'... we can no longer concentrate upon the defence of Singapore Island entirely, but must consider the defence of Malaya as a whole, particularly the security of up-country landing grounds. For this reason, and because we cannot spare a fleet for the Far East at present, it is all the more important that we should do what we can to improve our land and air defences in Malaya.'

With the 6th Division already in the Middle East and the 7th still in training, the Australian government could not comply. There were many at home who thought Australia should start seriously considering its own security as the intelligence of the Japanese threat increased. David Horner's assessment of the situation is as frightening in retrospect as it must have been to those in the know at the time:

'There was no co-ordinated plan for the defence of Australia. General Jackson of Northern Command, which at that time included New Guinea, described the situation:

"No plans for the defence of Northern Command were in existence when I took over command in May 1940. Approximately half of the troops to be raised in Queensland were to leave the State, and proceed to New South Wales, in the event of an invasion of Australia in accordance with long-standing *plans.* [Presumably he meant plans similar to the 1931 plan]. *The main activity in the command was the raising and reinforcing of the Australian Imperial Force.*

"Up to the end of 1940 Government Policy did not permit of consideration by the military authority of defence against raids. Authority was then given to consider defence against invasion without increase of forces. In November 1940, General Sir Brudenell White, then Chief of the General Staff, impressed on me while down in Melbourne, that in the event of anything happening in this country of ours, I was the fighting commander of the north. I proceeded on those lines but unfortunately for Australia, Sir Brudenell was killed shortly afterwards [in a plane crash which also killed three Government Ministers near Canberra], *and complacency ruled in his stead."*

'The latter comment was unfair to Sturdee, the new CGS [Chief of General Staff], *and was probably the result of a long-standing feud between Jackson and Sturdee. But the problem of the continental defence of Australia does not appear to have been discussed by the Government until early 1941.'*

As Britain's position darkened, recruiting numbers soared in Australia. In three months more than 100,000 men enlisted, which was one in six of all men in their twenties – so many, in fact, that in early July 1940 the government was forced to temporarily suspend the intake because of the lack of equipment for them and because of the impact the rush had had on essential employment and in depleting the Militia. What was interesting was that, of those 100,000 enlistments, two-thirds applied to join the RAAF.

By the beginning of 1941 the government had given the green light to an armoured division, which brought our overseas volunteer force to five divisions. Our Militia, which was restricted to the defence of Australia, also had five divisions, plus two cavalry divisions. That meant our forces totalled 12 divisions.

The government had already made one strange decision.

The RAAF 10 Squadron had been in Britain when war was declared. It was placed under RAF command and the Australian government added six more squadrons to serve with the RAF – about 3000 personnel. When you took out the squadron then being formed to be based out of Port Moresby, it left nothing to defend Australia.

But while 100 or so Aussie pilots took part in the Battle of Britain, our first substantial contribution to World War II happened largely by accident or, more accurately, because of the enemy's manoeuvring rather than by our planning.

Italy had massed half a million troops in Libya and Ethiopia, more than the Allied forces there. After both British and Indian units had engaged the Italians in Egypt, the Australian 6th Division was introduced and attacked Bardia, then Benghazi in Libya. The Diggers proved themselves worthy of their predecessors from the 1st AIF, capturing Bardia on 3 January, Tobruk on 22 January and Benghazi on 7 February 1940. The Aussies captured more than 40,000 prisoners at Bardia and another 25,000 in Tobruk, along with a large swag of equipment.

Ralph Honner was a company commander in Libya. He had been convinced a war was inevitable and made his commitment early, as his service number shows – WX15. (That means he was the 15th to join the AIF from Western Australia: each recruit's state was signified by the first letter – N=NSW, V=Victoria etc. – while the X signified the AIF. Militia recruits simply had the state initial then their service number.) Ralph Honner's company had remarkable success in Bardia:

'My 100 men took 25,000 prisoners at Bardia, running all the time through the attacks, taking half of Bardia. We did have the only six tanks left in Libya in the British Army and they were a great help. We didn't think we had many casualties but they mounted up.'

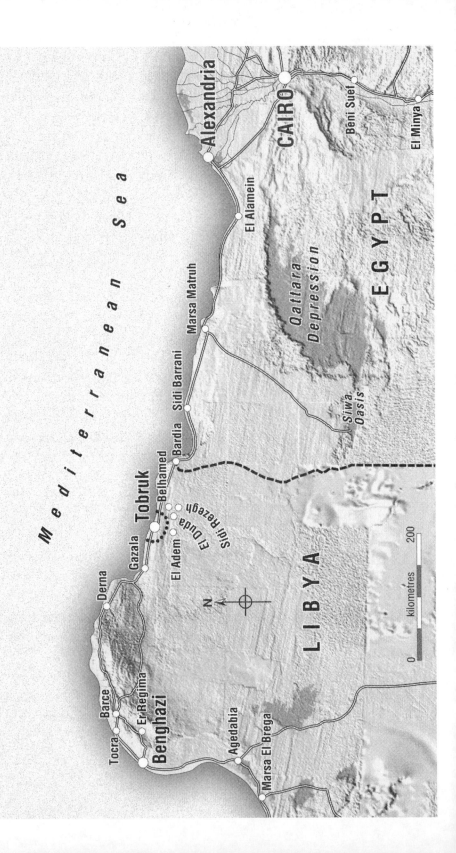

The total of 40,000 prisoners taken at Bardia included four Italian generals. The 6th Division lost 130 killed and 326 wounded. Its performance had given the Diggers great heart as they confirmed themselves the equals of their fathers who had fought in France in 1918. At home the victory brought forth celebrations and relief, which grew after the Diggers' successes at Tobruk, Derna and Benghazi. But it proved a false dawn.

The Allies realised that Hitler could not abandon Mussolini's embattled troops, and expected the Germans to reinforce the Italians. At the same time they decided they must support their last surviving ally in Europe that was still resisting the German advance, Greece. In a move still debated by historians, Churchill demanded that Australian troops be moved from Libya to Greece. In so doing he took advantage of the confusion between Menzies and General Blamey, each of whom expressed misgivings but were told the other had approved. (Inexplicably, they apparently didn't confer directly.) The 6th Division, together with substantial British forces, was withdrawn from Libya and sent to Greece. The Australian 9th Division took over from the 6th in Libya. At the same time the Germans' Afrika Korps, under the legendary Lieutenant General Erwin Rommel, arrived in Libya. The balance of power had shifted.

The German fight-back was powerful, enhanced by tanks, artillery and air support. The Diggers were forced to withdraw from Benghazi and fall back on Tobruk. By early April the Australians had established defensive positions in the ancient fortress there and were under siege.

From the start, the Germans exhibited their traditional confidence. Despite suffering some costly rebuffs when they unwisely came too close to the Aussies' perimeter, they dropped leaflets calling on the Diggers to surrender:

AUSSIES

After Crete disaster Anzac troops are now being ruthlessly sacrificed by England in Tobruch and Syria. Turkey has just concluded a pact of friendship with Germany. England will shortly be driven out of the Mediterranean. Offensive from Egypt to relieve you totally smashed.

YOU CANNOT ESCAPE

Our dive bombers are waiting to sink your transports. Think of your future and your people at home. Come forward. Show white flags and you will be out of danger!

SURRENDER

The Diggers' response, as mentioned in the history of the 2/13th Battalion, *Bayonets Abroad*, typified their attitude:

'To the eternal regret of everybody very few floated into the Battalion area as they were to command a high price as souvenirs. If the German Intelligence could have seen and heard the efforts expended to procure even one of these pamphlets to read and keep they would have been extremely flattered.'

There was never any chance of the German propaganda leaflets working. From the start the Australian commander, General Morshead, gave this message to his brigade commanders:

'There'll be no Dunkirk here. If we have to get out, we shall fight our way out. There is to be no surrender and no retreat.'

When the Afrika Korps tried to take Tobruk they were in for a surprise:

'The Germans were quite unprepared for the resistance they met. They had been fed on victories in Europe, a triumphant passage across North Africa, and hopes of rich prizes in Egypt. They had been told that the defenders of Tobruk were little better than a rabble, imperfectly armed and lacking the heart to oppose the armoured might of the Afrika Korps. Never before had they experienced troops who would crouch under the assault of the tanks to rise and savage the infantry bereft of the accustomed support. Never before had they encountered the formidable barrier of 25-pounders fought to point-blank

range by indomitable gunners. This was the first significant demonstration that the tank was not the final answer.'

The Diggers at Tobruk also surprised the Germans with their aggressive patrolling. In the tradition of their forebears in World War I in France and their 'peaceful penetration' they harassed the attackers, often moving a few kilometres out from their perimeter as they used the swirling sandstorms (or the khamsin, as it was known locally) as camouflage:

'Far from proving a deterrent, the enemy tanks patrolling the front provided a target, and it became an ambition to "bag" a tank under cover of the sandstorm. It was on one of these daring patrols that we had the misfortune to lose Sgt Rod Cutts, who, with one of his five men, was surprised at close quarters by his quarry when the dust "lifted". These clear periods in a perfectly good sandstorm were something of an enigma and caused a great deal of embarrassment to those depending on the swirling dust for concealment.'

The Germans began night patrolling to try to find weaknesses in the Diggers' defences. But the Aussies countered this tactic by sending out their own standing patrol as soon as darkness fell. They would then shadow the incoming Germans and attack them to great effect on their way out. This effectively denied the Germans access to no-man's land and to the vital intelligence they were seeking about the defensive position:

'The pattern that life was to follow for the weary months to come was being established – digging and sleep during the day; digging and patrolling during the night. The enemy, for his part, was confining his activity to shelling the forward posts and gun positions while the Luftwaffe, with high level and dive bombing, sought to destroy dumps and guns.'

The Diggers were becoming accustomed to the desert heat. In fact, it was the least of their worries:

'The dust caused them the most discomfort. When a wind blew it covered the odd variety of holes in which they lived, matted their hair, covered the blankets in which they slept, formed a

*powdery scum on the food which they ate, gave them bloodshot
eyes and seized the mechanisms of their rifles and machine guns.*

'*Nor was an ample water ration forthcoming to alleviate their
lot. The ration at first was half a gallon per man per day, but
after June 19th it was increased to three-quarters of a gallon.
The greater part of this ration, however, did not get beyond the
various B echelons. The quartermasters made it into tea and
used it liberally (we suspect) to make the monotonous bully-beef
stews go further than they should have.*

'*The man in the front line usually got his water-bottle filled
each day. From it he was expected to quench his thirst, wash his
body and his clothes, shave himself daily and, if he had any left
over, he was quite welcome to brew a cup of tea!*

'*In these early days the other major discomfort manifested
itself in the form of fleas (prolific breeders in the dust) and other
forms of vermin with which the Italian posts abounded. Taken
by and large, however, no-one was complaining.*'

It was in the early fighting at Tobruk that Corporal Jack
Edmondson gave an example of the highest peaks to which any
Digger could aspire. The Germans had broken through the
southern perimeter during the night and had taken a position
which Lieutenant Austin Mackell realised could be used as
a bridgehead that enemy tanks could penetrate. He took six of
his men and, under the covering fire of his neighbouring
platoon, attacked the Germans, aiming at driving them back
before they could establish themselves. Jack Edmondson was
wounded in the fighting but pushed on, bayoneting at least five
of the enemy, including two who were attacking Lieutenant
Mackell. Edmondson continued fighting until he could no
longer stand. The Germans fled, leaving 12 dead and one
prisoner. Jack Edmondson died of his wounds the following
day. He was awarded the Victoria Cross for his remarkable
bravery and selflessness – the first for an Australian in World
War II. That fine war correspondent Chester Wilmot reported
in his book *Tobruk 1941* on Lieutenant Mackell's return from
the action:

*'"We've been into 'em, and they're running like ——!"
Mackell reported to his CO in classically laconic Digger style.'*

Time and again the Australians' patrolling kept the
Germans off-balance, and their steadiness in the face of tank
attacks astounded the enemy. When Rommel threw his tanks
against the Tobruk defences these met with British and Australian artillery and anti-tank guns. The 1st Royal Horse
Artillery duelled with the tanks with its field guns firing 'over
open sights' (or at point-blank range), knocking out seven
tanks and sending the others retreating into the fire of the anti-
tank weapons. The final result saw the Germans withdrawing, leaving 17 destroyed tanks, 150 dead and 250 wounded.
The defenders lost 26 killed and 64 wounded.

On another occasion, on the night of 16 April, patrols from
the 2/48th Battalion stunned the attackers by capturing 803
prisoners, including virtually an entire battalion of the Italian
62nd Regiment, while suffering just two casualties themselves.

Rommel simply underestimated the spirit of the Diggers
(and the British soldiers with them) when he began his assault
on Tobruk. He was to stretch them to their limits but he never
broke them, as Chester Wilmot explained:

*'The German makes a very good soldier but a very poor psychol-
ogist. In this war, as in the last, his most costly errors have sprung
from an inability to appreciate the character of the men he is
fighting. When the Germans pushed the Tommies and the
Diggers back into Tobruk, they little realised that they were
packing in dynamite and that the harder they thrust, the more
explosive it became.'*

The Germans' persistent attempts to break down the
defenders' morale by calls for their surrender and by mocking
them in Goebbels-inspired radio broadcasts by the Nazi
stooge, 'Lord Haw Haw', had the opposite effect of that
desired. Lord Haw Haw dubbed the defenders 'rats caught in
a trap'. The Diggers grabbed it as a badge of honour, calling
themselves the 'Rats of Tobruk':

'The longer the odds Lord Haw Haw offered against the Diggers'

chance of getting out, the more heavily the Digger backed himself. He and his father before him had gambled on the outcome of a drought or a strike. They had defied the bullying of man and nature and had gambled with their livelihood. It was a small step from this to gamble now with their lives. Tho' odds would be long, the fight would be hard, but they knew what was at stake.'

The fortitude of the Diggers was exemplified by Private Jenkins of the 2/13th Battalion. He had been cut off from his mates during the first skirmishes of the Diggers' withdrawal at Er Rejima. Jenkins had evaded the Germans, then, with two British soldiers, set out for Tobruk, which friendly locals had told him was held by the Allies. It took them 41 days to travel more than 400 kilometres on foot, avoiding both German and Italian patrols before finally making it through the perimeter at Tobruk to rejoin their comrades.

By August of 1941 Blamey had persuaded his government, and his military superiors, that the Australians, who had been in constant combat since March, should be relieved. Blamey wanted to consolidate his Australian Corps and he believed the Rats of Tobruk needed a chance to recharge their batteries. His request was granted, despite Churchill's resistance, and the Australian units were replaced gradually from early August. The 2/13th was the last out on 16 December, about a week after Rommel had finally accepted that his task was impossible and withdrawn his forces to the west.

The Rats of Tobruk showed that the Germans were far from invincible – but at a cost: the 9th Division lost 832 killed and 2177 wounded, with 941 taken prisoner. The commander of the British Eighth Army, General Sir Claude Auchinleck, described the Rats' efforts:

'Our freedom from embarrassment on the [Egyptian] frontier area for four and a half months is to be ascribed largely to the defender of Tobruk. Behaving not as a hardly pressed garrison but as a spirited force ready at any moment to launch an attack, they contained an enemy force twice their strength. By keeping the enemy continually in a high state of tension they held back four

Italian divisions and three German battalions from the frontier area from April until November.'

The feats of the Rats of Tobruk turned the tide of war in the Middle East. They stand with great feats of arms of the Australian Digger. The Rats' endurance, courage, resilience and ingenuity have earned them an honoured place in our history.

Chester Wilmot always believed Tobruk to be a crucial element in the eventual defeat of Hitler:

'The belief that Germany's power was irresistible had been disproved at Tobruk, and Hitler's crack troops had been defeated and driven back in both Russia and Libya. But in April and May of 1941, between Hitler and a great politico-military triumph in the Middle East there stood little but Tobruk.'

While the Rats held on grimly at Tobruk, much was happening elsewhere in the world. The Australian troops committed to defend Greece had fought staunchly, but had been overwhelmed by German numbers and firepower. Many were withdrawn to Crete, although 2000 were left behind as POWs. Those who were hurriedly moved to Crete had little time to establish their defences and very few heavy weapons with which to combat the rampant German forces. But the Diggers once again drew on their inner reserves of strength. Ralph Honner remembered the remarkable fortitude of two of his men on Crete:

'They were in an exposed position and, of course, the Germans had all the air power and although their bombing didn't hurt us because you can always see the bombs dropping from low level and you can always dodge them but their strafing was very telling and lost a high proportion of our men there.

'I remember these two men on a Bren gun. They stayed on throughout the day to stop any German advance and the German advance was thrown back. But one of them died before he could be relieved on the gun and the other one was severely wounded.

One died in the evening and the other was wounded but they wouldn't leave the gun all that time. You couldn't pull them off it.

'Now people like that were dying all the time. I never heard anyone screaming. I remember one at Derna beside me. He said quietly: "I'm hit . . . I'm hit again . . . They've got me again". That's all. He died.'

Crete was eventually surrendered to the Germans, but they paid dearly for it. At least 4000 of their elite forces were killed and more than 200 planes lost. The Australians lost 204 killed, 507 wounded and 3102 taken prisoner.

In December 1941, just as Rommel was leaving Tobruk, half a world away the Japanese struck at Pearl Harbor. Australia's approach to the war changed abruptly. So did the role of our Diggers. Our only battle-tested forces – the 6th, 7th and 9th Divisions – were in the Middle East. Two brigades of the 8th Division were awaiting their baptism of fire in Malaya.

Suddenly, Australia itself was vulnerable. This was more evident by the hour as reports poured in of the extent of the Japanese attacks. They had not only bombed Pearl Harbor but simultaneously attacked Malaya and southern Thailand, the Philippines, Guam, Hong Kong and Wake Island. Not only was Australia in peril but, despite the warnings and the time since the war in Europe began, it was not prepared to defend itself.

EIGHT

The bloody track

Isurava battle site, Kokoda Track, Papua New Guinea

The first thing you notice is the darkness: it's almost beyond dark. The tree canopy in the deep jungle of the Kokoda Track blots out the stars and the moon and brings a nightfall straight out of a horror movie. One Digger said it was as black as the inside of a cow.

We are at the site of the old village of Isurava, about a day's march south of Kokoda Township, towards Port Moresby along the Kokoda Track. This is where one of the critical battles that saved Australia from possible Japanese invasion in World War II was played out. The Track itself is an ill-defined, meandering native walking pad, which winds its way from the swampy north coast, near Buna and Gona, to the south coast at Port Moresby. In doing so it traverses the Owen Stanley Range, the mountainous spine running east–west across Papua New Guinea. The Track exists in most places only because of the constant use of the local people, who chip back rampant vines and undergrowth with their jungle knives as they walk from village to village. In this way the Track is a living thing, which shifts according to the demands of the terrain and the people who have inhabited it for 30,000 years – diverting around fallen trees, swollen rivers, rock-slides, and changing direction to accommodate movements by

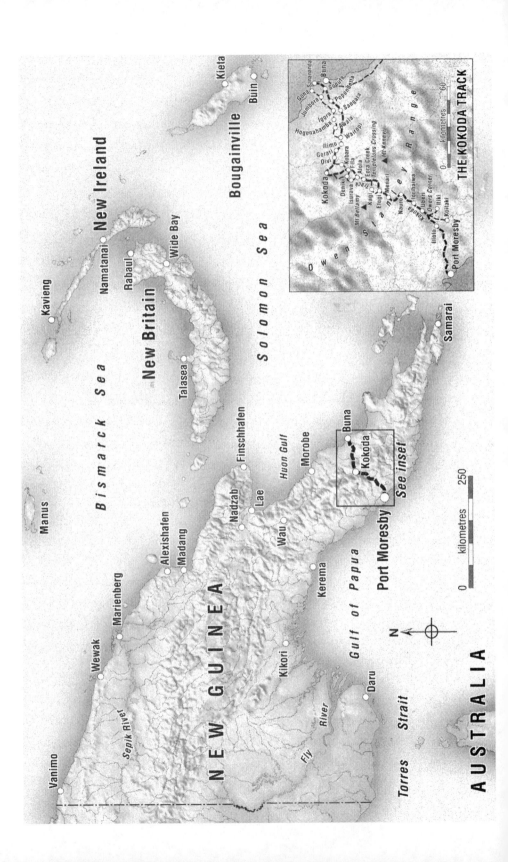

THE KOKODA TRACK

Kieta
Buin
Bougainville

New Ireland

Namatanai
Rabaul
Wide Bay
New Britain

Kavieng

Talasea

Bismarck Sea

Solomon Sea

Samarai

Finschhafen
Morobe
Huon Gulf

Buna
Kokoda
See inset

Nadzab
Lae
Wau

Manus

Alexishafen
Madang

Port Moresby

Marienberg

Kerema

Gulf of Papua

NEW GUINEA

Wewak

Kikori

Vanimo

Daru

Sepik River

Fly River

Torres Strait

AUSTRALIA

N

0   kilometres   250

Inset — The Kokoda Track:

Gona
Sanananda
Buna
Soputa
Jumbora
Popondetta
Igora
Sangara
Awala
Hagenahamba
Wairopi
Ilimo
Kobara
Templeton's Crossing
Mt Kenevi
Gorari
Eora Creek
Oivi
Fila
Alola
Kokoda
Deniki
Isurava
Kaile
Menari
Efogi
Mt Bellamy
Nauro
Ioribaiwa
Uberi
Owers Corner
Itiki
Koitaki
Bilolo
Port Moresby

Owen Stanley Range

0   kilometres   60

villages and their gardens. This is some of the toughest terrain in the world. When people say they've walked the Track, they really mean they've climbed it – up and down shark-toothed ridges, valleys and watercourses, across raging whitewater rivers and streams and through dense rainforest jungle.

At Isurava, the eerie darkness that falls like a curtain each night hints at what it must have been like during the titanic battle fought here six decades ago. Then, rather than bringing relief to the Diggers, night brought heightened tension and the need for constant vigilance against Japanese insurgency. The Japanese were skilled jungle fighters and caused many casualties by creeping through the Australian defences after dark. Many Diggers had no idea what hit them. That's not surprising, as you can't see your hand in front of your eyes.

Dawn reveals that little has changed in the years since the tumultuous four-day battle was fought here. Although the jungle has continued its relentless cycle of growth and decay, there are many clues that point to the event. The remnants of weapons pits are still scattered throughout the area. These were desperately scraped out of the jungle floor with bayonet and tin hat (the Diggers had no entrenching tools), and served the Diggers as their only shelter from Japanese mortar, field guns, machine-gun and rifle fire, and the torrential rain that drenched them every day and left them huddled together and shivering each night.

In August 1942, in this remote stretch of jungle, a band of young Diggers stood as our last line of defence against a massive Japanese invasion force, some 14,400 strong. By that stage the Diggers numbered about 400 men. They were Militia troops: average age 18 and a half years. They had joined up in October and November 1941 and, before Christmas that year, were on the steamship *Aquitania* headed for Papua New Guinea. They had never fired a shot in anger before being thrust into the jungle. This was their baptism of fire. (In

1942 there were two sides to the Australian Army: the Militia, who volunteered to defend Australia, and the AIF troops, who had volunteered to go wherever necessary in the world to fight. The AIF troops initially looked askance at the Militia. They called them 'chockos' – short for 'chocolate soldiers' – because they reckoned they'd melt in the sun, or 'koalas', because they were a protected species. Until Isurava, the two sides of the Army had never fought alongside each other.)

By the time they had fallen back on Isurava, the Militia troops of the 39th Battalion had been in the jungle for almost six weeks, during which time they'd been savaged by the first waves of the Japanese invaders around the village of Kokoda, about halfway between Buna and Gona – where the Japanese had landed – and Port Moresby. The troops had been sent to Kokoda Township to secure what was the only decent airstrip on the Track. But they'd lost their two most experienced leaders, their commanding officer, Lieutenant Colonel Owen, and company commander, Captain Sam Templeton, during the battle at Kokoda. By the time they regrouped at Isurava they were short of food, their clothing was rotting on their bodies, many were already malarial and some had dysentery or dengue fever. They had little ammunition, no artillery, mortars, or heavy machine guns. Japan had air superiority, so they had little prospect of being resupplied. They made their stand at Isurava because the area around the tiny hamlet here formed a natural citadel. Because of the nature of the Track, they knew the Japanese couldn't bypass them. The alternative of bush-bashing around them, through impenet-rable jungle, was simply not an option. So these young men waited – hungry, frightened and exhausted – to challenge an undefeated Japanese invasion force which had been virtually in constant action since it first invaded Manchuria in 1937. It's difficult to imagine a more one-sided scenario.

The Japanese invaders, the Nankai Shitai (or South Seas Force), had been hiding in the Bonin Islands, about 800 kilo-metres south of Tokyo, waiting for the signal that Japan's attack on Pearl Harbor had been successful. Then, under the command of General Tomitaro Horii, it attacked and captured the US base on Guam before heading for New Guinea.

On 23 January 1942, the South Seas Force overwhelmed the 1400-strong Australian garrison at Rabaul. (The massacre of the surviving Diggers from the Rabaul garrison at Tol Plantation, where they were tied with wire and used for bayonet practice to 'blood' young Japanese troops, set the tone for the subsequent combat on the Track and elsewhere in New Guinea. It was a grim reality check for our young Diggers.) For the first time in our short history our territory had been invaded (Papua New Guinea was then an Australian Protectorate under the League of Nations), and mainland Australia was under direct threat. And, as we have already seen, we were not prepared.

With our most experienced troops fighting in the Middle East, the sudden entry of Japan into the war and her remarkable run of conquests, culminating in the fall of Singapore and the capture of virtually our entire 8th Division there, sent shockwaves through the Australian population. Our harbours, beaches, public buildings and streets soon sprouted concrete and sandbagged defences and gun sites. Families hurriedly dug trenches and bomb shelters in their backyards and sent children off to the relative safety of the country. Blackouts, rationing and a general air of panic saw property prices plunge and recruitment numbers soar. Prime Minister John Curtin called for 'total commitment' to the war and said that, for the first time, Australia was 'inside the fighting line'. Having seen the abject failure of Britain's 'Singapore Plan' for the defence of the region, Curtin had no qualms about turning to the United States for assistance:

'Without any inhibitions of any kind, I make it quite clear, that Australia looks to America, free of any pangs as to our traditional links of kinship with the United Kingdom. We know the problems the United Kingdom faces. We know the constant

threat of invasion. We know the dangers of dispersal of strength. But we know that Australia can fall and that Britain can hang on.'

Once Rabaul fell and the Japanese were on our doorstep, few disagreed with Curtin's approach. While Curtin's government tried to extricate our AIF troops from the Middle East to bring them home to defend Australia, and until the Americans could be persuaded to commit troops to help defend us, it was forced to rely on untried Militia troops as our only defenders.

Two Militia battalions had been rushed to Port Moresby immediately after Pearl Harbor. The 39th Battalion was largely drawn from Victorian volunteers and the 53rd Battalion comprised young men from New South Wales. Their training was virtually non-existent. Because of the shortage of weapons and ammunition, they drilled with wooden 'rifles'. They were denied any chance of proper training as jungle fighters, or indeed as infantrymen, because as soon as they arrived at Moresby they were set to work unloading ships on the docks and preparing the defences around Moresby's airfield. This lack of training made the young Diggers' later achievements even more praiseworthy.

The dramatic difference in the experiences of these two Militia battalions on the Track is a powerful example of the critical importance of training and leadership in combat. The young men of the 39th Battalion had the great fortune to have Lieutenant Colonel Ralph Honner assigned to them as their new CO. He was one of our finest company and battalion leaders during World War II and, by the time he was posted to Isurava, had already shown outstanding leadership as a company commander with the 2/11th AIF Battalion in Libya, Greece and Crete. His inspirational guiding hand would prove critical during the battle of Isurava and in subsequent battles down the Track. The 53rd Battalion, on the other hand, had suffered an unfortunate start. They had been given very little proper training before they were almost shanghaied onto the *Aquitania*, many without even the chance to say a final farewell to their loved ones. Then in the first contacts with the Japanese they lost two key leaders, their CO and his adjutant, before they could gain confidence under fire. This disastrous beginning was to have serious later consequences.

Ralph Honner arrived at Isurava after the 39th had begun digging in there. He immediately reorganised their defensive positions and began to work on their teamwork:

> *War is largely a matter of confidence. If the troops have confidence in their mates, confidence in their weapons, confidence in their leadership and sufficient confidence in their numbers – in that they've got a fair chance and are not hopelessly outnumbered – they'll fight well. When that confidence goes, then something snaps and the force can be dissipated.'*

Without the chance to build combat confidence, the 53rd Battalion suffered a series of setbacks in its initial contacts with the enemy. With the loss of their CO and some key officers and NCOs, the unit struggled to regroup and suffered a crisis of morale. This was observed by the medical officer of one of the AIF units that later fought alongside the 53rd, the 2/16th Battalion's Captain H.D. 'Blue' Steward, in his memoirs *Recollections of a Regimental Medical Officer*:

> *The problems of our companies at Abuari* [across the valley from Isurava] *were aggravated by the poor state of the Militia 53rd Battalion whom they were supposed to be supporting. Many of these lads, mostly from Sydney, were only eighteen. They had been dragooned into service, given a hurried medical examination and pushed through their embarkation procedure in 24 hours. They had no chance to arrange their affairs nor even farewell their families. It all savoured of the press gangs sweeping the London streets to shanghai men into the Royal Navy. Their training was abysmal, and in Port Moresby they had been . . . employed more as labourers than prepared as soldiers for a fighting role. Many of them resented the harsh manner of their conscription, their patent lack of training, their inferior weapons and the uncertain quality of some of their officers.'*

Ralph Honner also observed the problems:

'With the 53rd they had good blokes and bad blokes. They must have had some good leaders and some poor ones. It's a combination of factors. I think what counted against them is that they weren't all volunteers and a lot of them were unwilling soldiers. The 39th were all volunteers although they were a Militia unit. They had had time to breed confidence in each other and it's your own mates you stand by first and next your own section and next your own company, next beyond is the battalion, possibly beyond that, the brigade. But beyond that, who cares?'

Ralph Honner set about trying to make up for one of the key elements denied the 39th Battalion – sound training. He immediately began establishing patterns of defence. He created interdependence between the various positions and tried desperately to boost the confidence levels of his charges:

'We rehearsed what we could do. See, we were holding a perimeter at Isurava where we didn't have enough troops to hold it. We couldn't have a reserve. We could only post battalion localities where the enemy could get through between them. We could only rehearse counter attacks by planning that if the enemy get into this territory and wipe it out, it's already being forced back by a counter attack from a company on the other side.

'We rehearsed the counter attacks and we rehearsed the co-operative fire between neighbouring companies. And when the troops could see these working and could see that something was being done to give them the greatest possible security against loss, I think they began to grow confidence in each other. They saw a battalion working as a battalion and being prepared to use its best efforts to save them if they were in trouble. They weren't alone. I think that sense of reliance on your mates is the most important thing.'

Ralph Honner could do little more. His patrols told him the Japanese were preparing their advance. The 39th were hopelessly outnumbered, by at least ten to one, even allowing for the restrictions the Track placed on the numbers that the invaders could bring to bear against the Australians. But, despite their youth and lack of combat experience, the men of the 39th drew on some inner strength. They knew they were fighting as the last line between the Japanese and their homes and their families. They were hoping that the AIF units rushed back from the Middle East would reach them in time. They resolved to stay and fight, as Private Kevin 'Spud' Whelan recalled:

'We got a message from Port Moresby that the 2/14th were on the way and we had to fight to the finish. There was no give in at all. We had to stay there – fight till death. And that was a bit horrifying. I thought well I won't see my family again. I won't see Australia again. But I was prepared, like the rest of us, to stay there and fight to the finish.'

Ralph Honner was gratified at the transformation he observed in his young soldiers despite their rapidly deteriorating physical condition:

'Indeed, the strangest feature of their story is that the weaker they became the stronger and fiercer waxed their resolution to hold on at all costs until the long-promised relief should become a reality. In the testing crucible of conflict, out of a welter of defeats and disasters, of mistakes and misfortunes, of isolated successes and precipitate withdrawals, they were transformed by some strong catalyst of the spirit into a devoted band wherein every man's failing strength was fortified and magnified by a burning resolve to stick by his mates.'

Much of the credit for this transformation must go to Ralph Honner and his dynamic leadership. He understood the essence of the Digger and what motivated him. One example of his decision making exemplified his approach. Shortly after he assumed command of the 39th at Isurava, the temporary CO told him he believed B Company was 'unreliable' and 'finished as a fighting force', and that it should be taken out of the line. Some of the men from this company had been separated from the main body and had taken to the jungle after the chaotic early skirmishes with the Japanese advance parties around Kokoda. Although they had struggled back to the 39th's lines after a few days' wandering in the jungle, they were regarded with suspicion.

Ralph Honner had a different attitude and took a completely different action. Far from shunning them, he gave B Company the most important position to defend – the high ground on the left flank, where the Japanese were most likely to attack. Many years later, he explained his reasoning:

'Should I leave the key to our stronghold in such frail hands? I felt that to replace these unfortunates with another company could be the lethal act of contempt, destroying where I should be building. I appointed Lieutenant French to command and made it clear to him and his men they now had the most dangerous sector to hold – the post of honour. When the testing hour did come, B Company bore the heaviest burden and held on doggedly.'

It was classic leadership. Ralph Honner gave his support and confidence to the men of B Company and they reciprocated. Through his leadership he was able to turn a group of young men riddled with self-doubt into a cohesive force, which played a vital role in the defence of Isurava. He gave them the chance to show they possessed the spirit of the Digger, and they repaid him handsomely.

The battle of Isurava raged for four days and nights, from 26 to 29 August 1942. The Japanese bravely attacked up the steep gullies in waves of 100 and 200 men. The defenders hurled them back, first with grenades, then rifles and machine guns, and finally in ferocious hand-to-hand combat. When you walk around the battle site you can imagine the intensity of the fighting. Because of the nature of the terrain, this was combat at its most basic – man against man in a terrifying collision of noise and chaotic action, all played out along razor-back ridges and sheer gullies. In his inimitable style, Ralph Honner recorded the scene:

'Mortar bombs and mountain gun shells burst among the tree tops or slashed through to the quaking earth where the thunder

of their explosion was magnified in the close confines of the jungle thickets. Heavy machine-guns – the dread "woodpeckers" – chopped through the tress, cleaving their own lanes of fire to tear at the defences. And while bombs and bullets crashed and rattled in an unceasing clamour that re-echoed from the affrighted hills, the enveloping forest erupted into violent action as Nippon's screaming warriors streamed out of its shadows to the assault. No pygmy figures of fun these, but hardy men of war – tall veterans of unflinching valour and powerful physique, trained in the mountains of their homeland and the jungles of the East for just such desperate warfare and they waged this day.'

There were countless acts of unrecognised courage as the young Diggers held on grimly. They ignored their lack of sleep, their hunger and their fear as they waited for the next assault. Some positions rebuffed as many as ten human-wave assaults in a day. The Japanese dead piled up around their perimeters like sacks of grain. But they kept on coming. And the pattern was always the same, as Ralph Honner recalled:

'A platoon or company attack was heralded by a shouted order from the rear, echoed by subordinate commanders farther forward, and then succeeded by a wave of noisy chattering right along the front, almost as if the men were assuring each other that they were all starting out together to die. And as the chatter ceased they crashed from their concealment, leaping to the attack in a co-ordinated line.'

The more the Japanese attacked, the more determined the defence of the young Diggers. But by sunset of the second day of constant fighting, Ralph Honner knew their time was almost up. Then, just in the nick of time, relief arrived. Honner and his desperate defenders watched in awe as the first of the AIF troops surged in:

'. . . I do not remember anything more heartening than the sight of their confident deployment. Their splendid physique and bearing, and their cool automatic efficiency – even the assembly-line touch as two platoon mortar-men stepped one on

either side of the track to pluck bombs from the haversacks of the riflemen filing past them without checking their pace – made a lasting impression on me. And they were to prove even better than they looked.

'We would've been wiped out that morning or the next evening or the next morning if we'd stayed there. And I was going to stay there because the reinforcement was promised and I was just hoping like hell it was coming because if it hadn't come, we'd have been done. I couldn't implement a plan of withdrawal in the face of an incoming reinforcement. We had to stay. They had to get to us. I think the 39th were pretty happy that they were just holding on by the skin of their teeth at that moment.'

The hardened AIF veterans took their places alongside their 'chocko' brothers and they seamlessly fought as one – AIF and the Militia side by side. The Militia troops were buoyed by the professionalism and the courage under fire displayed by the 2/14th Diggers. They were also impressed by their demeanour and their presence as, being generally four or five years older than the 39th troops, they were bigger and stronger. One of Ralph Honner's youngsters later told him: 'I thought they were Gods!'

But the 'chockos' showed they too were made of stern stuff. A group of 30 sick and wounded men from the 39th Battalion, who had been sent to the rear by Ralph Honner, showed their courage and devotion to their mates when they heard the battalion was in trouble. On hearing the news, 27 of them immediately turned around and headed back into the maelstrom at Isurava. Of the three who couldn't return, one had lost his foot, one had lost his forearm and the other had a bullet in the throat. Like their fathers before them and their fellow Diggers in the AIF alongside them, the 'chockos' of the 39th Battalion showed the mateship, courage, endurance and selfless sacrifice so often exhibited by the Digger. Even their enemy recognised the courage of the Aussies at Isurava. One of the Japanese 144th Regiment, Shigenori Doi, recalled:

'During the battle we had advanced about 200 metres and I remember that an Australian soldier, wearing just a pair of shorts, came running towards us throwing hand grenades. I remember thinking at the time this was something that would be very hard for a Japanese soldier to do. Even now, when I think about it, I'm affected by the memory of this, this warrior. I suppose the Australians had a different motivation for fighting, but this soldier, this warrior, was far braver than any in Japan. When I think about it now, it still affects me.'

The late Alan Avery, a 2/14th veteran, who had already been wounded and won a Military Medal in Syria, recalled Isurava as the fiercest fighting in which his battalion had ever engaged:

'Everyone should have got a gong [a medal] *up there you know. They really should have. There were so many acts of bravery there. A fellow there – a Jap, he jumped into a foxhole and he bit a big lump out of a bloke's jaw. The combat was that close you see.*

'These actions don't last forever. They last for a very short space of time but if you're there you're thinking it's a long, long time. You couldn't see anything and you went by the noise. They rattled tins and things to try to upset you. And we knew they were getting closer and closer. I think that in their previous warfare, this noise factor could have upset a lot of people but we held our ground and waited until we saw the whites of their eyes and it was on.'

Alan was involved in one of the critical actions at the height of the battle. The Japanese had broken through the Australian's defence on the northeastern perimeter and directly threatened battalion headquarters. Alan and his lifelong mate, Bruce Kingsbury, volunteered to join a counterattack to try to block the hole in their defensive shell. Sergeant Bob Thompson led the group, and it included Corporal Lindsay 'Teddy' Bear, who had been wounded in earlier fighting. Teddy Bear wielded the Bren machine gun in the initial stages and fired until its barrel glowed red. But gradually the loss of blood from his wounds took its toll and he was forced to hand the gun to Bruce Kingsbury. The fire was so intense it pulverised the soft jungle foliage they were using as cover and exposed both sides. The Japanese were massing in preparation for a final death thrust to the Australian HQ when Kingsbury saw his chance. In an inspired act of selfless courage, he charged directly at the Japanese, firing the Bren gun from the hip and cutting a swathe through the attackers. Alan Avery was at his shoulder:

'He came forward with this Bren and he just mowed them down. He was an inspiration to everyone else around him. There were clumps of Japs here and there and he just mowed them down. He just went straight into 'em as if . . . as if bullets didn't mean anything. And we all . . . we all got a bit of the action you see. When we saw him, when you see a thing like that you sort of follow the leader, don't you?'

Kingsbury accounted for at least 30 of the enemy himself and his mates carried on the attack, putting the attackers to flight and securing their position once again. Sadly, at the height of his glory, Bruce Kingsbury was struck down by a sniper firing from the top of a nearby rock. Immediately after he fired, the Japanese melted into the jungle and everything fell quiet. Alan Avery followed the sniper with a burst of furious Tommy-gun fire but it was too late. Bruce Kingsbury was posthumously awarded the Victoria Cross for his superb gallantry – the first won on Australian territory and the first in the southwest Pacific.

In war, one man's actions can have repercussions far in excess of their obvious immediate impact. Kingsbury's commanding officer, Lieutenant Colonel Phil Rhoden, always maintained that Bruce's action was far more than a remarkable act of bravery; he saw it as the turning point of the Kokoda campaign:

'Nobody knew its importance until later. But it gave us time to consider action, gave us options. If he hadn't stopped them it would have been like water pouring through a hole in the dam

wall. They would have come through and it would have been a domino effect. You can argue his action saved Australia because, at the time, the 25th Brigade was on the water and the 16th Brigade was still in Australia. Without Kingsbury, the Japanese could have been waiting for them in Moresby when they arrived.'

Early in 2002, Ivan Nitua and the villagers from Isurava located Kingsbury's rock and cleared away six decades of jungle growth to expose it. Today the rock stands as a permanent memorial to Bruce Kingsbury's sacrifice and that of his fellow Diggers, who put their lives on the line at Isurava to save their country. The rock is just metres from the four impressive black granite pillars that now form the Isurava Memorial, jointly dedicated in August 2002 by the prime ministers of Papua New Guinea and Australia. The pillars are set in a clearing on the hallowed ground at Isurava, looking down the rugged Eora Valley to the Kokoda plateau. Carved into each pillar is an attribute of the Diggers of Isurava which, when combined, allowed them to prevail against all odds: 'Courage', 'Endurance', 'Mateship', 'Sacrifice'. These are attributes all Diggers aspire to attain, and those who fought at Isurava have set the standard just as their fathers did before them at Gallipoli.

Visit the Isurava battlefield and you will feel the same timelessness you feel at Gallipoli, or the Somme. You will experience that same sense of frustration at the young lives cut short. In the stillness of the morning, wander around the positions. Move from one foxhole to another and imagine them occupied by frightened but determined young men, brimming with potential. Here they risked all they had to safeguard their families and loved ones in Australia. Here they fought with desperate courage to hold off an equally determined and brave enemy intent on their destruction. And here they shed their blood in the mud and slush as they refused to give ground.

In so many ways, Isurava represents the spirit of the Digger. It was where the 2/14th's intelligence officer, Captain Stan Bisset, lost his beloved elder brother Butch. Stan turned 30 during the battle. Lieutenant Harold 'Butch' Bisset, aged 32, was commander of 10 Platoon of the 2/14th, which at Isurava took over 'the position of honour' from Ralph Honner's B Company, 39th Battalion. Butch and his 29 men withstood the most furious assaults launched on the position. In one 24-hour period, they repelled between 30 and 40 charges by waves of between 100 and 200 enemy troops all through the day and into the night. Stan was about to head off to reconnoitre a fallback position when he got word that Butch had been hit, caught by a burst of machine-gun fire across his abdomen as he distributed ammunition to his men. This was a death sentence on the Track. If you couldn't walk out or survive being carried out – an excruciatingly painful journey of between 10 and 15 days on a stretcher carried by up to eight local natives (the famous 'Fuzzy Wuzzy Angels') – you died. One of the medical officers on the Track, Major Rupert Magarey, summed it up:

> 'If you got an abdominal wound on the Kokoda Trail you might as well have given up. You never told the troops that, but you knew bloody well that that was what would happen. To deal with an abdominal wound you have to have an operating theatre, an anaesthetist, a surgeon, possible an assistant surgeon and a good deal of gear. So you gave them a shot of morphine . . .'

When Butch Bisset was hit he insisted that his men leave him to die. He even pulled his revolver on them and de-manded they give him some grenades so he could take some of the enemy with him. His men ignored his orders. They made a makeshift stretcher from saplings and a groundsheet and began carrying Butch back for treatment, with the enemy close on their tail. As they carried the stretcher with one hand, Butch's men fired at their pursuers with the other until they got him safely to their medical officer, Captain Don Duffy, one of Stan and Butch's old friends:

'His condition was pretty bad and he was in pain so I gave him a morphia injection to relieve it. He would not have been able to stand any attempt to move him further and was already in shock and likely to die soon. We just sat by him as the minutes passed, Stan deeply moved and not trusting himself to speak while I brooded, as one does at these times, on the terrible wastage of good young lives of one's friends. He died about two thirty in the morning.'

Nearby, Corporal Charlie McCallum, from B Company of the 2/14th Battalion, a gentle but powerfully built farmer from Gippsland, rose to superhuman heights. Charlie had already been wounded three times when his platoon was ordered to withdraw just as the Japanese were about to swamp their position on the high ground at Isurava. Despite his wounds, Charlie held off the charging enemy, allowing his mates to pull back to another position down the Track. Charlie held and fired his Bren gun with his right hand and carried a Thompson submachine gun in the other hand. When his magazine ran out on the Bren, he swung up the Tommy gun with his left hand and continued to cut down the surging Japanese as he changed magazines on the Bren. When the Tommy gun was empty he used the Bren again, and continued his one-man assault until all his comrades were clear. At least 25 Japanese lay around him. One got so close he actually ripped a utility pouch from Charlie's belt before falling dead at his feet. When he knew his mates were safe, Charlie fired a final burst and calmly moved off back down the Track. He was recommended for a Victoria Cross – a recommendation endorsed by brigade and division – but this was inexplicably downgraded to the second-highest award for gallantry, the Distinguished Service Medal. His citation read, in part:

'At all times in action, McCallum was admirably calm and steady. On this occasion his utter disregard for his own safety and his example of devotion to duty and magnificent courage was an inspiration to all our troops in the area. His gallant stand and the number of casualties he alone inflicted checked the

enemy's advance and allowed the withdrawal to proceed unhindered and without loss.'

Sadly, Charlie would die only a week or so later in the next major battle down the Track at Brigade Hill.

The magnificent performances by the 39th Battalion, the 2/14th Battalion and, shortly afterwards, its sister unit, the 2/16th Battalion, at Isurava and in subsequent actions nearby, was sadly in contrast to that of the 53rd Battalion, which never recovered from the loss of its leaders and the early setbacks. The unit's brigade commander, Selwyn Porter, wrote later:

'As a whole they [the 53rd] *had received more collective training than the 39th Battalion and, although leadership was lamentably weak, in some cases, it is felt that the conditions surrounding their initial tactical use resulted in the creation of a state of bewilderment which was understandable. After the death of their CO, there was no one to undertake a deliberate policy of marshalling and repairing their impaired morale. Some AIF units have suffered similarly; but there has always been someone sufficiently interested to smother the stigma attached to such until time and effort repaired the unit concerned. The 53rd Bn's execution was completed when it arrived back in Moresby.'*

The 53rd Battalion disappeared as an entity, combined into the 55th/53rd Battalion. Many of its veterans believe the 53rd was made a scapegoat. No unit wants the 'unreliable' tag that has often been given to the 53rd. In Army terms this means it lacked 'fighting spirit' and could not be committed to combat because of the unacceptable risks that would flow to other units fighting alongside it. There is strong debate as to whether the tag was justified in the case of the 53rd. But the bottom line is clear: the system let down the men of the 53rd Battalion.

Undoubtedly the 53rd's fate would have been different without the chaotic pressures of war, but the treatment meted out to the young men at the time has left lasting scars. Their feelings of frustration have been magnified by the fact that many of the survivors of the 53rd's initial setbacks went on to perform admirably in other units. This was especially so at Buna, Gona and Sanananda, where so many Kokoda veterans were thrown needlessly against the entrenched beachhead positions of the remnants of the Japanese South Seas Force, who were determined to fight to the death and take as many of their enemy as possible with them.

Isurava proved a turning point in the Japanese advance on Port Moresby. The casualties suffered by the Japanese there, and the psychological impact of the mauling on their confidence, meant they were forced to reconsider their tactics and the timetable for their advance. Their overconfident commander, Major General Tomitaro Horii, had allowed only ten days for his force to travel down the Track and take Moresby. More importantly, he had issued them with only sufficient rations to achieve their goal within that time. He had expected little resistance and had planned to replenish his supplies from stores captured from the enemy, just as previous Japanese advances had done during their virtually unchecked surge through Asia and the Pacific. Isurava not only fatally damaged Horii's timetable, it (along with the concurrent Australian victory at Milne Bay) shattered the air of invincibility that had hitherto accompanied the Japanese war effort. At the Battle of the Coral Sea, the US Fleet and the RAN closed off the Japanese option of a naval landing at Port Moresby. The Japanese leadership had gambled instead on the land approach across the Track. Now that was in jeopardy.

After withdrawing successfully from Isurava, the Australians fought a courageous hit-and-run guerilla campaign down the Track. At Brigade Hill and Mission Ridge, the 2/14th and 2/16th were joined by the 2/27th Battalion and they made another stand. Here General Horii threw the full force at his disposal against the Australian defences, who were outnumbered again by about ten to one. Afterwards, the Diggers renamed it Butcher's Hill. Gallant Charlie McCallum, one of the heroes of Isurava, died in the furious fighting as the Diggers lost almost half their numbers before once again withdrawing, all the while aggressively harrying the Japanese and maintaining a force between them and Moresby.

One of the most remarkable feats of endurance and courage on the Track came in the aftermath of Isurava. During the withdrawal, a group of 50 men of the 2/14th troops was separated from the main force during a Japanese ambush. Captain Sydney Hamilton 'Ben' Buckler took command of the three officers and 47 other ranks as they took to the jungle and tried to circle the enemy to return to their own lines. It was the beginning of a six-week odyssey. The party was slowed down by eight wounded members – four stretcher cases, three walking wounded and Corporal John Metson. He'd been shot in both ankles but he refused to let his mates carry him. He knew how much energy was needed to carry stretchers through the thick jungle, a task made even more onerous because Buckler's party had to avoid the Track and travel through the jungle for fear of running into the enemy. So John Metson wrapped a torn blanket around his knees and hands and he crawled. For three weeks he cheerfully crawled through the jungle, ignoring the growing pain in his shattered ankles and the damage to his hands, knees and legs as he kept up with his mates through the cloying mud and the torrential rain. He was a constant inspiration to the others in the party as they lived off the land and avoided Japanese patrols before reaching a friendly village called Sangai on 20 September 1942. By this stage the party was exhausted and extremely weak from lack of food. The stretcher bearers' hands were so badly lacerated from their work that they could barely hold onto their charges. The wounded men were in constant pain from the movement and their maggot-ridden wounds, for which the party had no medicine. Ben Buckler decided their best chance of survival was to leave the wounded in the care of the villagers at Sangai, then to try to make it back to Australian lines and send back help for the wounded. Before leaving, Buckler ordered his party to 'present arms' in a salute to their wounded comrades. He then led the others back to safety after another three weeks' trekking down a parallel track to the Kokoda Track and, finally, by raft down the Kemp-Welsh River.

Tragically, when a rescue party eventually made its way back to Sangai village, they found the wounded Diggers had been betrayed to the Japanese and massacred. The perpetrator was never found. John Metson's selfless action won him the British Empire Medal – and a place in the annals of the finest traditions of the Digger.

By the time the main force of the Australians had battled their way back down the Track to Ioribaiwa, a steep ridge about 30 kilometres from Moresby, it was the Japanese who were in trouble. By then, desperately short of food and ammunition, they had lost the initiative. They saw the lights of Port Moresby in the distance, but they had run their race. Now the Australians had the advantage, with manageable supply lines and fresh troops. Nevertheless, as Phil Rhoden recalled, the Australians too had paid a heavy price for derailing the Japanese advance. Even when at the end of their tether, the Japanese inflicted grievous casualties with their mountain guns at Ioribaiwa. With amazing determination and ingenuity they had broken the guns down into man-sized components, which they had then lugged across the Track before reassembling them on the slope facing Ioribaiwa Ridge. Then, for days, they pounded the exhausted Australian defenders across the valley. The casualties suffered by the 2/14th were typical, as Phil Rhoden recalled:

> 'By the time we got back to Ioribaiwa we were down from 550 to about 200 men. By the last days at Ioribaiwa we were five and 86 – five officers and 86 other ranks – the rest were either killed, wounded, sick or missing.'

At Ioribaiwa the reality of the Japanese situation struck home. Abandoned by his superiors, who were concentrating their forces and supplies elsewhere to combat the American entry into the war, South Seas Force Commander General Horii ordered his men to 'advance to the rear' (there was no word for 'retreat' in the Japanese Army lexicon), and their journey to oblivion began. The Australian 7th Division pursued them back along the Track, demoralising them and inflicting heavy casualties in a series of fierce battles as they forced them back over the ground they had so recently won at such heavy cost.

By early November the Australians had retaken Kokoda and raised the Australian flag over the plateau there. The Japanese withdrew to the beachheads at Buna and Gona where they had landed three and a half months earlier. On the way there, they suffered a body blow. General Horii and some of his top staff officers were drowned while crossing the swollen Kumusi River, about a third of the way between Kokoda and the beachheads. Despite the loss and a chronic lack of food and ammunition, the dwindling South Seas Force kept its resolve and was soon bunkered down at Buna, Gona and Sanananda, determined to fight to the last man.

Clearly, the invaders were no longer an offensive threat. But, instead of quarantining them at the beachheads and effectively starving them into submission, General Douglas MacArthur, for his own reasons, was determined to force a swift conclusion. He insisted that the Australians, many exhausted from their long campaign up and back along the Track, attack the Japanese in their strong defensive positions, without giving them time for the necessary reconnaissances. Corporal Col Blume of the 2/14th Battalion, having fought at Isurava and Brigade Hill, was thrown straight into battle at Gona:

> 'Gona was hell. We got straight off a plane and we were ordered straight in. We didn't get time to recce. We were sent in and walked straight into a Japanese firing line. Quite a few of my platoon were killed and wounded. I was lucky.

'Charlie Butler came past. He had his eye blown out. I had to feel for his eye. I patched him up. Another chap came through, Bill Bryant, big chap, he was on a stretcher with a badly wounded leg and he said: "Can you do anything for me Col?" and I said: "I can only tie it up Bill" and I tied it up. They carried him out, following the signal wire, because that was the only way they could get out of the swamp. Later on, I heard he lost his leg."'

Driven on by General MacArthur's constant urgings, many veterans of the Track lost their lives because of the haste with which they were thrown in against the Japanese defenders at the beachheads, in frontal assaults across open beaches. Ralph Honner felt the losses there keenly:

'As we were never in great numbers in the Australian Army, you were always protective of the ones we had. You couldn't afford to lose lives if you could possibly save them. You couldn't afford to put in a frontal attack across open ground at an enemy that's going to kill us all because we've got nothing left.'

But, once again, ingenuity was born of necessity:

'You've got to devise some means of surprising them by man-oeuvre, by outflanking them, by coming from the rear, by using darkness or smoke if you can, by using what I did at Gona which is firing on them with our own artillery to keep their heads down while the infantry get in amongst them with the artillery still firing. If you have any losses they'll be peanuts compared to the losses if you don't have their heads kept down. Anything to keep down the losses.'

At the beachheads the Diggers were joined by American troops for the first time and the differences between the two forces was stark. MacArthur had spent the Kokoda campaign belittling the Australians' performance, at one stage writing:

'The Australians have proven themselves unable to match the enemy in jungle fighting. Aggressive leadership is lacking. The enemy's defeat at Milne Bay must not be accepted as a measure of relative fighting capacity of the troops involved. The decisive factor was the complete surprise obtained over him by our preliminary concentration of superior forces.'

This disparaging nonsense was typical of MacArthur's approach, which some observers called 'megalomaniacal'. In *The Odd Couple: Blamey and MacArthur at War*, Jack Gallaway called MacArthur's press releases 'ripping yarns', so far were they removed from reality. Any success under his command was trumpeted in a release which implied – and sometimes openly stated – that MacArthur himself was leading the troops from the front. Successes were invariably credited as 'Allied' successes, while any setbacks were sheeted home to the Australian troops taking part.

During the Kokoda campaign, MacArthur went on record saying the Australians actually outnumbered the enemy on the Track, and he attacked General Blamey over what he claimed was unsatisfactory progress by his troops there:

'Operational reports show that progress on the trail is NOT, repeat NOT, satisfactory. The tactical handling of our troops in my opinion is faulty. With forces superior to the enemy we are bringing to bear in actual combat only a small fraction of available strength enabling the enemy at the point of actual combat to oppose us with apparently comparable forces.'

Ironically, the very first US Army unit to try to join in the action during the final stages of the Kokoda campaign reflected just how successfully the Diggers had handled their task. One battalion of the US 126th Regiment was sent in a classic American 'cut 'em off at the pass' manoeuvre up the Kapa Kapa Track, a native path that ran roughly parallel to the Kokoda Track. The Americans hoped to outflank the retreating Japanese and cut off their retreat. After 42 days (compared to an average of ten days by the Australians along the Track) the Americans eventually stumbled out of the jungle on the other side, but they were completely unfit for combat operations for some months. They had not encountered a single enemy soldier. They became known as the 'Ghost Battalion'.

This reality check had little impact on MacArthur's attitude or self-aggrandising approach. His obsession with personal publicity is legendary and well documented. *The Pacific War Encyclopedia* notes that between December 1941 and March 1942, the US Army Forces Headquarters in the Far East issued 142 dispatches. Of these, 109 mentioned just one name: the theatre's commander, General Douglas MacArthur. MacArthur's dispatches reveal that he never embraced the concept of an 'Allied' command. Rather, he saw the Australian contribution as a tool to be used as he saw fit, all under the triumphant MacArthur standard.

During the battles for the beachheads, MacArthur's persistent clamouring for a quick victory resulted in needless Australian and American casualties. It also highlighted the difference in combat performance between the Diggers and their American Allies as they fought alongside each other for the first time. The American forces at Buna were listless. The Australian General Vasey reported to Blamey that the US 126th Regiment had 'maintained a masterly inactivity'. The comparisons between the two armies moved Blamey to write to MacArthur (no doubt with some relish, after MacArthur's earlier unjustified slurs against the Diggers):

'It's a very sorry story. It has revealed the fact that the American troops cannot be classified as attack troops. They are definitely not equal to the Australian Militia and from the moment they met opposition they sat down and have hardly gone forward a yard.'

Once again, in the pestilent swamps and beaches of Buna, Gona and Sanananda, the Diggers proved themselves courageous and resourceful warriors, who adapted to the dangerous and difficult task of defeating a heavily entrenched enemy with little concern for its ultimate fate. The Australians bore the brunt of the bitter fighting there, instinctively understanding the need for committed close-quarter fighting, as distinct from the Americans who, according to the Australian General Herring's report to Blamey, failed to come to grips with the situation:

'I think it is fair to say that 32 US Div has still not realised that

the enemy will only be beaten by hard fighting, and that while bombing, strafing, mortars and artillery may soften his resistance to some extent, the men who are left will fight it out and will have to be taken out and killed in hard fighting.'

MacArthur reacted according to type. He called in his top general, Robert Eichelberger, and ordered him to head to Buna with the following line, straight out of Hollywood: 'Bob I want you to take Buna, or not come back alive!'

This, at least in a limited way, addressed the root cause of many of the problems at the beachheads – the simple fact that the top brass had never been there and had little appreciation of the immense problems facing the troops there. In fact, despite his penchant for press releases that stated he was leading the assaults, MacArthur never saw the battlefield. This rankled with Bob Eichelberger, who was quoted by MacArthur biographer William Manchester as saying:

'The great hero went home without seeing Buna, before during or after the fight while permitting press articles from his G.H.Q. to say he was leading his troops in battle. MacArthur . . . just stayed over at Moresby 40 minutes away and walked the floor. I know this to be a fact.'

(To understand the forces generating the incessant pressure from MacArthur which so dominated the battles for the beachheads, we must look at the wider picture. At the time, General Dwight Eisenhower, for whom MacArthur entertained a long-standing jealousy, was enjoying great success in North Africa, while the great American Admiral 'Bull' Halsey was winning fame at Guadalcanal. MacArthur could see himself being forced into a backwater and out of the limelight.)

Eichelberger sacked many of the commanders on the ground within days of arriving at Buna. But this changed very little. The Japanese were still fighting to the death in concealed bunkers, many with log roofs and good fields of fire across open ground. They had to be taken one by one. The cost was high. Ralph Honner recalled that the CO of the 2/16th

Battalion, Colonel Albert Caro, a veteran with his men of the Track, objected to the needless carnage at Gona:

> *'Charlie White, whom I taught at school, led an attack along the beach. He was hit and wounded but he got up and went on until he was killed. There was no point in doing it. They couldn't take anything. They couldn't capture anything. They couldn't get through. But higher command ordered that they do this along the open beach. Caro protested – his battalion commander – and was sacked because he protested against useless slaughter. The battalion commander shouldn't have to bear the burden of carrying out stupid orders.'*

Ralph Honner believed that many casualties at the beach-heads resulted from the Diggers' reactions to a bizarre incident that had occurred on 7 November at Koitaki Planta-tion near Port Moresby. Here, General Blamey addressed the veterans of the 21st Brigade, the troops that had fought the bloody withdrawal down the Track from Kokoda to Iorib-aiwa. No exact recording of Blamey's speech was made, but the Diggers who heard it have never forgotten it. Blamey told them they had been beaten by inferior troops in inferior numbers. He then made a comment that haunted him for the rest of his days. David Horner quotes Blamey's personal assis-tant, Major Carlyon, who was present at the parade:

> *'He told the men that they had been defeated, that he had been defeated, and that Australia had been defeated. He said this was simply not good enough. Every soldier there had to remember that he was worth three Japanese. In future, he expected no further retirements, but advance at all costs. He concluded with a remark which I think was particularly ill-chosen and unfair . . . "Remember," he said, "it's not the man with the guns that gets shot; it's the rabbit that is running away."'*

Ralph Honner always maintained that this unjustified slur against the Kokoda veterans, from a commander who clearly had no understanding of what they had endured and what they had achieved, left deep psychological scars. These resur-faced when the same troops were thrown in against the entrenched Japanese at the beachheads. The result was an attitude by many that, no matter what, they would leave no doubt as to their courage. In doing so, many exposed themselves to far greater risks than were necessary, and many paid the price. On 8 December the 39th Battalion broke through into what was, by then, the shell of the village at Gona and Colonel Ralph Honner sent back his famous signal: 'Gona's gone!'

At Buna the Americans were stymied, as David Horner writes in *Crisis of Command*:

'In Urbana Force Eichelberger continued to urge his troops, and they pushed their way between the Japanese defences, but by 24 December they had been held up. Caught between [the Australian commander, Brigadier] Wootten's successes and MacArthur's demands, Eichelberger was beginning to feel the burden of command. The next day he wrote to MacArthur: "I think that the all-time low of my life occurred yesterday. We had seven line companies available. I had given five of them to Grose to make the attack . . . [He] took counsel of his fears and . . . delayed the advance".

'During the preceding month the pressure on all commanders had been extreme. The constant exhortations from MacArthur, who knew his own career was balanced on a knife edge, placed the division commanders in a position where they were forced to accept heavy casualties yet achieve little.'

With Brigadier George Wooten, the commander of the Australian 18th Brigade, leading a combined force of Australian and US troops, Buna eventually fell on the evening of 2 January 1943. The cost was 2870 battle casualties, 913 of them Australian. MacArthur sent out his customary press release, claiming the Americans had taken Buna and had now defeated the Japanese at the beachheads. He ignored the fact that the Japanese were still holding out strongly at Sanananda (which would not fall until 22 January) and he omitted any mention of his faithful commander, General Bob Eichelberger. For his part, Eichelberger was generous in his praise of the

Diggers of the 18th Brigade. He wrote in his memoirs, quoted by David Horner:

> 'One cannot compare the Australians who made the frontal attack at Cape Endaiadere with their American comrades two miles away fighting the water before Buna Mission. The Australians were fresh; they were veterans, they were not sick; they were well fed and well clothed. They fought with courage and tenacity and won a brilliant victory taking tremendous losses.'

Later he added of the 18th Brigade: 'I would say no finer soldiers ever fought on a desperate field'.

This generosity was not always reciprocated by the Australians. Private Gryff Spragg recalled one Australian brigadier called on to report first on his own situation at Sanananda and then on that of the units fighting alongside him:

> 'On one of his flanks was this American brigade and, after making a complete and detailed report of his own situation, he merely, under the heading of the "Right Flank", put: "Hebrews 13, verse 8" and if you look that up, it says: "Jesus Christ, the same, yesterday, today and forever".'

By the time Sanananda fell, the 39th Battalion, the Militia battalion that had borne the brunt of the initial Japanese assaults at Kokoda and Isurava, had been reduced from about 550 troops to little more than a platoon (32 men). With little thought of the magnificent heritage the unit had created in its short history of around 18 months, Higher Command disbanded rather than reinforced it. Its remnants were scattered into other units.

The official war historian, Dudley McCarthy, made special mention of the remarkable record of the 39th Battalion in the Gona campaign – the battalion that had done so much to elevate the status of the Militia. Ironically, he also praised men from the maligned 53rd Militia Battalion, who had joined the 39th as reinforcements:

> 'Although, therefore, undoubtedly much of the dash and devotion (perhaps the major part) of the men of this battalion

could be attributed directly or indirectly to their AIF leaders, just as obviously this could not have been the whole explanation. Perhaps the key lies in the fact that the 39th had already acquitted itself well in battle with the Japanese before its arrival at Gona. Had enough battle wisdom come from that experience to make the battalion the fighting force it proved itself to be?

'Again, a positive answer must surely be sharply qualified for the reinforcements who had built the battalion's shattered strength could, at the best, have been only vicariously battle-wise. Most significant, too, in this connection, is the fact that about 100 of those had come from the 53rd Battalion whose record had not been good. And high praise was given these men after Gona by the original members of the 39th!

'Surely the final element in the complex answer must be found in the pride with which the battalion remembered its earlier experiences and that it had been the first Australian unit to meet the invaders. From that recollection moral strength must have flooded in like a tide bearing with it a high purpose, a will to endure greatly, and a contagious inspiration for newcomers.

'So it was that this militia battalion became the pivot on which the capture of Gona finally swung, pressed to a successful conclusion a difficult and costly action after the fall of the main Gona bastion, and accepted losses which were remarkably high even for the type of warfare that developed in Papua.'

But, as Ralph Honner wrote, the 39th retained their spirit right to the end:

'Although instances of heroism and fortitude in battle are more memorable and more inspiring, I would mention one less dramatic episode as typifying the spirit that still permeated the battalion as its remnants marched out of its final campaign into history.

'When the last Japanese beachhead at Sanananda fell in January 1943, the 39th mustered only 7 officers and 25 other ranks. The RMO [Regimental Medical Officer] *considered some of these unfit for the next day's march to Dobodura Airfield. Higher authority refused a vehicle for them, providing*

transport only for stragglers who should fall out on the march.

'But in the 39th marchers didn't fall out, so they all marched, all the way — for some a long torture on the verge of uncon-sciousness that only pride and the solicitous support of their mates made endurable. Pale, silent and sweating under the fierce sun, they toiled in the wake of truck loads of cheering, fresh-looking "stragglers"; and as last they straightened up to march at attention across the airfield. When an amazed bystander exclaimed "What mob's this?" he was ignored except by my second-in-command at the end of the line who barked: "This is not a mob! This is the 39th!"'

The Kokoda campaign (from the initial battles along the Track through to the final annihilation of the Japanese South Seas Force at the beachheads) was one of the most gruelling in Australian military history. It was a total disaster for the Japanese – less than 10 per cent of the original invasion force of 14,000 ever returned to their homeland. It was a major triumph for the Australians (and the Americans who joined them at the beachheads). Yet it has never received its due credit.

A comparison between the Americans' campaign at Guadalcanal and Kokoda illustrates the point. Guadalcanal attracted strong publicity at the time and was highlighted in many Hollywood blockbusters. Because of MacArthur's media manipulations, Kokoda received scant coverage. Worse than that, its coverage was inaccurate and left an impression that has taken years to correct. But the facts stack up differently. The Americans threw 60,000 troops against the Japanese on Guadalcanal. Of these, 1600 were killed and another 4200 wounded. In total, the Australians committed less than half that number during the entire Kokoda campaign, yet they (and the Americans at the beachheads) lost more than 3000 killed and another 5500 wounded. And that does not take account of the huge casualties suffered on the Track and the beachheads from disease, estimated at three times the number of casualties. Overall, during the Papuan campaign 2165 Diggers were killed and 3533 wounded, while the Americans had around 3000 casualties in total.

The Kokoda campaign has had long-lasting impact on the Australian Army. One of the other major differences between the earlier fighting by Australians in World War II and the Kokoda campaign was that the Diggers heading to New Guinea knew they were defending their homeland. Phil Rhoden believed this was a crucial motivating factor in the development of their determination to prevail against over-whelming odds:

'We were fighting for Australia on Australian soil. It was impor-tant that we won because if we didn't win who knows what would have happened.

'We didn't know their numbers but we certainly knew that there were a hell of a lot more than us. We certainly knew they had more ammunition and firepower than we had. Those mountain guns, when they cracked in the trees above you, were not only damaging physically but they were terrifying as well with the noise they made. It was a new conception, a new thing for us – no place you could get into a dugout or into a hole. We were all one. No place where the commander could get away and study his maps. You were just all in there together.'

Kokoda was the first time that both sides of the Army, the AIF and the Militia, fought together. Along with the simulta-neous action at Milne Bay, it was the first time the rampant Japanese had been defeated on land. It was the first time that Australians had been called on to directly defend their homeland from the threat of invasion. The lessons that were learned on the Track by bitter experience were passed on for subsequent use in New Guinea and Borneo, and later still in Vietnam.

As they had in World War I, the subunit structure of the Australian Army, the leadership of the field officers and the NCOs, and the initiative of the individual soldier proved to be key elements in their eventual triumph. Ralph Honner had a slightly different take:

'We do give high praise to the ingenuity and individualism and there was a great deal of it but there was also a great deal of looking to the platoon commander and the company commander. He's got the job. He leads. That's his job and they followed him and they looked to him. So, when a company went into attack, the individual soldier wasn't taking over on his own initiative, he was seeing that the leader was doing the leading and he would back him to the hilt but he wasn't taking over.'

But it was leadership that in the end made the crucial difference: the instinctive leadership of the Digger, where each man, when needed, steps up and carries his share of the load. One photograph taken before the 2/14th Battalion started their march up the Track shows the need for this depth in leadership. It shows five of the battalion's officers standing in a line before the camera, smiling, full of hope and promise: Lieutenant Moore was killed at Isurava; so was Stan Bisset's brother, Lieutenant Butch Bisset; Captain Claude Nye died at Brigade Hill; Lieutenant 'Mocca' Treacy survived Isurava and the remarkable 42-day journey with Buckler's party, only to die at Gona; of the five, only Lieutenant Lindsay Mason survived, after being wounded in late September 1942 in the final stages of the withdrawal down the Track. This photo illustrates the extent of losses in officers that many units suffered. In each case, when an officer went down, the next in command took his place. This continued through the ranks. Many Diggers started the campaign as privates and emerged as officers during the subsequent battles in New Guinea and Borneo.

Teddy Bear, one of the 2/14th's heroes at Isurava, was an excellent example. A private in the Middle East, where he won a Military Medal for bravery in action, he had been promoted to corporal by the battle of Isurava. He was a sergeant in the following campaign in the Ramu Valley, where he won the

Distinguished Conduct Medal for valour at Shaggy Ridge. He was wounded again there and then sent home to the officer training course in 1944 when, not surprisingly, he won the Baton of Honour and ended the war as a highly respected officer.

NINE

Alamein and after

While the 7th Division Diggers were embroiled in the Papuan campaign, the Australian 9th Division was playing a leading role in one of the great battles of World War II, the Alamein offensive in Egypt, where it suffered nearly 6000 casualties.

The Australians formed part of the Eighth Army, under Britain's Lieutenant General Bernard Montgomery, which faced off against Field Marshal Erwin Rommel's Afrika Corps.

It's hard to imagine a greater contrast in scale and terrain than those between the battles in the Papuan jungles and that of El Alamein. That Diggers could excel in both theatres, under such diverse conditions, is testament to their adaptability and skills as warriors. Dudley McCarthy, in his official history, *South-West Pacific Area – First Year*, summed up the warfare in the jungle:

> 'In it there is none of the wild, heart-thrilling drama of great bodies of men meeting on wide battlefields in the shocks of massed encounter. Instead, for the most part, it is the story of small groups of men, infinitesimally small against the mountains in which they fought, who killed one another in stealthy and isolated encounters beside the tracks which were life to all of them; of warfare in which men first conquered the country and then allied themselves with it and then killed or died in the midst of a great loneliness.'

On the other hand, the battle for El Alamein, about 110 kilometres from Alexandria in Western Egypt, was warfare on a vast scale: massed troops, thundering bombardments, and huge movements of armoured weapons and aircraft. Montgomery called on 220,000 men, more than 1000 tanks and almost as many artillery pieces. Rommel had 180,000 troops, 600 tanks and 500 guns.

The AIF Diggers who had been rushed back from the Middle East to fight in the Kokoda campaign had shown remarkable versatility as they switched from their recently learned desert fighting skills to learn a completely different method of fighting in the jungle. CO of the 2/14th Battalion, Lieutenant Colonel Phil Rhoden:

'In the Middle East, of course, you could see where you were going. That was a great advantage. There was room to man-oeuvre. There was room to make plans during the course of a battle. If things were not going right you could send people round on the flanks and you could influence things by having fire-power, artillery, airplanes. There were so many ways you could influence the course of a battle. It was like coaches in football moving people off the bench; you could have an influence. But in New Guinea, you were stuck, stuck on the Track.

'There was just that Track. There was a bit of measure off the side but not much and if you got into that you were in real trouble. The Japs had the idea of coming up front, accepting many casualties, then spreading out to the flanks and they outflanked us sometimes but they didn't get far.

'Of course we were so outnumbered that we couldn't extend to prevent them. In fact, they didn't have to go far out. I likened it to a couple of Melbourne Cricket Grounds – the space in which we were operating. And they were almost down the end of the cricket pitch sometimes.

'In New Guinea it was that close but in the Middle East things were wide open. In the jungle, for example at Isurava, we had rifles, grenades and Tommy guns and Bren guns but that's all. No mortars, no heavy stuff, no artillery, no airplanes to call

*in. You just had to take it and like it. That's the difference
between arms, space and numbers.'*

The 9th Division of the AIF who had stayed in the Middle
East were seasoned desert fighters by the time of the El
Alamein offensive, but even they were astonished by the ferocious artillery barrages that marked the start of the battle
against Rommel's men at 9.40 pm on 23 October 1942 and ran
for 12 furious days. Tom Roberts of the 2/7th Australian Field
Regiment was there. He recorded his thoughts in his war
diary, *Will We be Disappointed – After?* (privately published by
his widow Pat Roberts after Tom's death):

*'She's on . . . As I write the terrific roar of gunfire and bursting
shells continues a din that has lasted an hour or more. At 21.30
hrs we had delivered the last of between 6000 and 7000 rounds
and were back to fill up again when it began. All traffic had
stopped. All noise had stopped. Not a gun was to be heard
anywhere . . .*

*'Then one gun spoke – a Pommy 4.5 gun-howitzer was
guessed by the sound. And almost before the sound reached us the
whole skyline and ground was a mass of light from the flash of
hundreds of guns: the initial crash was tremendous. From then
on the roar was continuous as each gun fired at top speed for its
own particular target. Jets of flame burst out on every side . . .
shells screamed over our heads from the guns behind us and tore
through the air at all angles and elevations. In a few seconds
we could hear the reports from some of the bursts and in a few
cases could see the flash of their explosions.*

*'Big fires started in a few seconds and we knew men were
dying terribly, and are still doing as I write. None of us spoke.
Each man was busy with his own thoughts.'*

Tom Roberts had fought in the British Royal Field Artillery
in World War I, enlisting as a 14-year-old in 1914. After the
war he came to Australia, working as a jackaroo and eventually
becoming a world authority on horses and equine training.
Although he was within months of the upper age limit of 40,
he joined up again in 1940 because he felt his World War I

experience would be invaluable. His mature observations in his (illegal, of course) diary paint vivid pictures of the stresses of the fighting the Diggers experienced at Alamein:

'I don't think I'll ever forget this experience. The loud cutting report of our guns and their blinding flashes, the deeper duller "Woof" and the blinding light of Jerry's shells as they landed and the "phut" and whine of the fragments; the darkness and not knowing when you were going to fall into a shell hole. The air was full of death and worse.

'Frightened? I was frightened beyond all description. It's the uncertainty and the inability to do anything about it that gets you. You think: "I'm still alive. I'm unhurt." And you know that even before the thought is formed almost, you may be blown to fragments or perhaps have one nice little chunk blown off you, an arm, a leg or your jaw. . . . You are filled with an extraordinary feeling of excitement.'

In the initial 15-minute barrage, the British guns poured 900 artillery rounds a minute on the German positions, then paused, and followed with another even more intense barrage which heralded the advance of the Allied troops. Within two hours they had taken their first objectives.

Despite the huge scale of the El Alamein offensive, as always the real drama was played out by individuals. One, Private Percy Gratwick of the 2/48th Battalion, turned the tide with an inspired burst of leadership, individual courage and initiative. His platoon had been attacking one of the critical strongpoints, the ground around a hill called Trig 29, when they were pinned down and savaged by German fire. The platoon's original 30-odd men had by that stage been reduced to just seven. Percy Gratwick summed up the situation and suddenly leapt up to charge the two dominant enemy machine-gun posts. He captured one post, destroyed a mortar gun and killed several of the enemy before he was killed. Nevertheless, his extraordinary courage opened the way for his comrades to finish his work and capture the position. He was awarded a posthumous Victoria Cross.

Tom Roberts was on hand when his Forward Operations Post found itself caught in the middle of a tank battle in a Bren carrier:

They turned to get clear of them but took a direct hit through the carrier. Bill [Captain Bill Ligertwood] *had his right leg blown off above the hip and Tom* [Private Lewis] *had a very severe injury to his back. The other two* [Jack Flanagan and Keith Farr] *were knocked out. After a while Jack came round and sat up – the Captain told him to "Attend to Lewis who is badly hurt".*

Jack went over to Tom and went to turn him over to look at his back but it looked as though he would break in two. The fight had moved away and things were quiet by this time: "Drag me over and I'll give you a hand," said Bill Ligertwood. "Drag me over?" thinks Jack and then had a good look at the skipper for the first time. His right leg and hip had been completely torn away. Nevertheless he made Jack drag him over to Tom and lying down, he assisted in turning him over.'

After the two wounded men had been put on stretchers, Tom Roberts recalled that, despite his terrible injuries, Captain Ligertwood's primary concern was that his men return for their radio.

'He insisted they come back and salvage the equipment – which they did. All this in no man's land with a tank and infantry battle going like hell. Guts. Neither Tom nor Bill are expected to live.'

A week later, Tom made the following entry:

'Capt. Bill Ligertwood has died from his wounds. Exit "Twinkletoes". I only hope I can show as much courage if it is asked of me.'

Tom Roberts noted that many of his mates had adopted a fatalistic approach to their chances in the chaos of battle:

'It's no use worrying or stirring about your future; what will happen will happen, they say. And, of course, so many things have happened while we have been in action that make one think that way.

'The two brothers in the 14th Battery who, realising that

being together on the same gun increased their chances of both being killed, split up on two guns: a bomb dropped between the guns and singled out one man from each gun. The two brothers were killed, each the only one in the crew. "Fate" say the boys.'

During the fighting the Diggers developed a respect for their German foes because of their attitude to such things as the building the Diggers knew as the Blockhouse, a prewar gangers' hut near the railway line. The Germans had used it as a field hospital and, when the Australian 2/32nd Battalion captured the area, they used it as their Regimental Aid Post. There, the 2/32nd's medical officer, Captain Bill Campbell, worked tirelessly with three captured German medical officers and nine orderlies, tending to the wounded from both sides. The German artillery honoured the Red Cross marked on the building and, aside from a few stray shells, it was left untouched in the middle of the maelstrom that continued around it.

In the heat of the raging battle, Tom Roberts was caught in a dive-bombing attack by the screaming German Stuka bombers, and in his diary he gives a vivid description of the terrors of those deadly minutes:

'Some fellows say they lie there and pray. I never do, although this is by far the closest thing I've struck so far. I find myself with racing thoughts: "What is the best thing to do?" . . . "I'm all right so far." I keep thinking this: "I'm all right so far".

'I lie there and I'm astonished that I'm still unhurt. Great rushes of air pass above me, pieces of iron and steel sing in every possible key as they spin and pass over me. The sound of the explosions is not a short report but more like a long rroarrr . . . I am conscious of every part of my body: I feel my heart throbbing against the earth; I let my mind rush over my arms, my legs, my back and every part of me and think that the next second they may be burning or smashed to pulp.

'I feel I want to do something. I think "What can I do?" and make myself lie still, if wriggling against the side of the trench and pushing my head into the corner is keeping still. "There is

nothing you CAN do: you've got to take what's coming," I tell myself . . .

'A momentary pause and I think "It's over" when CRASH, CRASH, Crash, Crash, each one closer than the other, makes me think this time I CAN'T be missed. This swine adds the rattle of his machine guns to the fury . . .

'It seems to have been on for hours yet afterwards I know it must have happened in a few seconds. At last . . . quiet. I listen, for perhaps five seconds, for the sound of engines. I think I must have had my eyes shut, for I didn't get any sand in them.'

Tom Roberts' mates weren't so lucky. They were caught in the open when the Stuka bombers struck. Bill Jury managed to dive into a slit trench. But, in one of those deadly random accidents of war, a bomb perforated a nearby truck's petrol tank. The flaming fuel spewed over Bill Jury's trench:

'Bill's face is black, the skin blistered and the lips cracked. In places, his hair is completely burned off to the scalp, in others it is untouched. "Oh Robbie," he said as he saw me: "Shoot me Robbie, shoot me".

'I half crawled over to him, "Hold her boy," I said, "Let's have a look-see". "Shoot me Robbie; give me your gun . . . the pain's awful . . . and I know I won't get over it. Do the right thing . . . shoot me".'

Soldiers in all wars have faced this horrifying dilemma: mates with terrible injuries begging to be put out of their misery. Many know that help is either too far away or simply not available and are racked with guilt at their inability to save their mate. Some are haunted by the experience for the rest of their lives. Like Tom Roberts, most cling to the hope of saving their mates and draw on superhuman strength to get them help. Tom managed to get Bill Jury to the nearest aid post, where the doctor immediately gave him morphine and sent him back to an advanced dressing station, leaving Tom with his thoughts:

'I feel very, very tired. It's difficult not to get upset when you see a pal covered in burns and in agony – looking to you for

*assistance, absolute trust in you, doing everything you tell him –
and you can do nothing except keep his fighting spirit up. Strong,
vigorous ruthless Bill.'*

Bill Jury died just 24 hours later. His only brother had been
killed a month earlier.

The Diggers of the 9th Division at El Alamein won praise
from friend and foe. The enemy paid them a compliment by
massing most of the famous Rommel Panzer Corps along their
front because they considered them so dangerous. The British
commander of 30 Corps wrote to the Australian commander,
General Sir Leslie Morshead: '. . . this breakout was only made
possible by the Homeric fighting over your divisional sector'.

The British commander in chief, General Montgomery,
said: 'I want to congratulate you on the magnificent work your
division has done on the right of the line. Your men are
absolutely splendid and the part they have played in this battle
is beyond all praise.'

Montgomery would repeat this fulsome praise on the 25th
anniversary of the battle, when he said: 'When all did so well
it would hardly seem right to single out any for special praise.
But I must say this – we could not have won the battle in
12 days without that magnificent 9th Australian Division.'

The 9th paid a heavy price for its role in the El Alamein
triumph. During the full El Alamein campaign it lost 1225
men killed or died of wounds, 3638 wounded and 946
captured. Some individual units, in the thick of the fighting,
were devastated. From a complement of more than 650 men at
the start of the offensive on 23 October, it had been reduced to
just 41 men a week later.

The 9th Division's successes were underpinned by the
quality of leadership, at all levels, shown by its members. One
study of the Division, *Bravery Above Blunder*, by John Coates,
points to more than 50 occasions of privates commanding
platoons and another 20 where NCOs led companies in action.

This remarkable depth enabled many of the Division's individual units to recover from massive losses and to rebuild with a core of experienced veterans passing on their spirit to the new recruits. Most of the Division's battalions had enough reinforcements pass through them during the war to make up four separate battalions.

Perhaps surprisingly, given the typical Digger's penchant for letting off steam when out of the line, the men of the 9th Division actually won praise when they arrived in Palestine for leave following the victory at El Alamein. Even more surprisingly, it was the British commander of the Cairo Area who noted, as reported in Barton Maugham's official history for the Division, that: 'during recent leave, 9th Australian Division troops were the best behaved in Cairo'.

The 9th Division's superb performance was given a final accolade by Britain's General Alexander, the commander of the Middle East Command, at a special parade of the entire Division at Gaza Airport, where he concluded by saying:

Wherever you may be my thoughts will always go with you and I shall follow your fortunes with interest and your successes with admiration. There is one thought I shall cherish above all others – under my command fought the 9th Australian Division.'

After El Alamein, the Division returned home for leave and retraining for the climactic jungle campaigns ahead of it in New Guinea and Borneo.

TEN

The spirit of the POW

Some of the finest examples of the spirit of the Digger have come from men far away from the clamour of battle. They've come from those placed in the position most dreaded by all soldiers – that of prisoner of war. Falling into your enemy's hands is one of the many hazards of combat. Depending on the time, the place and the enemy it can be a deliverance from danger or a trip to hell on earth.

Some Diggers were unlucky enough to fall into enemy hands in the first battles we fought in World War II. During the delaying actions against the might of Rommel's Afrika Korps at Er Regina outside Benghazi, the late Corporal Vic Murray's section from the 2/13th Battalion was overrun by a large force of Germans. After a brief, furious firefight, Vic was badly wounded in the knee as he went to the aid of one of his men shot in the head. As he tried to drag his mate to safety, he turned to find a German officer's pistol against his temple and heard the classic words echoed in a score of war movies: 'For you, the war is over!'

But for men like Vic Murray it was just the beginning of a harrowing experience of years in captivity, which would push their courage, their mateship, their faith and their health to the extremities of endurance. Many ex-POWs suffered a lifetime of health problems; many had their lives shortened by the physical or psychological damage done to them during their captivity.

They could never be adequately compensated for their sacrifices: their lost years; their impaired health; the mental and physical cruelty they endured; the lack of recognition.

Much of our understanding of the German and Italian POW camps in which our Diggers were incarcerated comes from movies and, God forbid, US television series like *Hogan's Heroes*. These images were rarely countered by the facts, because most ex-POWs were reluctant to speak about their experiences except with those who had shared them. Few movies have successfully captured the constant stresses that played havoc with the minds and bodies of the POWs, caused by the cumulative effect of the deprivation of freedom, feelings of powerlessness and abandonment, boredom, poor nutrition, and random and orchestrated terror tactics. Certainly, some camps were relatively civilised, and their POWs were treated with various levels of respect and humanity. Some were allowed limited fraternisation with local communities and received food to sustain them. But the vast majority of camps and their regimes subjected the POWs to a grinding dehumanising process, ranging from isolation to overwork, even torture, and leading to permanent impairment of their health.

The one thing that showed superhuman resilience was the spirit of the POWs. As a body of men they upheld the highest traditions of the Digger – and in many instances set new standards of courage, initiative, endurance and resilience – while maintaining overall discipline and individual dignity and humanity in the face of the most trying conditions. In most camps the ingenuity of the POWs rose to new heights. Sergeant Angley Ogilvie of the 2/15th Battalion, a POW in Italy, was credited with making cricket balls and baseballs from a magical combination of rubber from worn-out gym shoes, tin foil from cigarette packets and lengths of wool unravelled from socks. These materials formed the core of the balls and twine from Red Cross packets was plaited to form the outer cups, which were then stitched together. This provided hours of vital entertainment and morale-boosting diversion. Others used their imagination and skills to create a wonderful range of essentials, from methods of enhancing food and transforming clothing, to building ovens and surprisingly sophisticated cooking utensils out of tin boxes and other scraps. Many POWs passed the long hours with games like cards, chess and all manner of outdoor sports through to the ever-present two-up. In fact, in one camp the Diggers made sure that, after their regular whitewashing of the chapel, they always had sufficient paint left to mark out the stones that formed the two-up ring.

And the Australians and New Zealanders generally managed to commemorate Anzac Day, whatever the circumstances. At Campo Concentramento No 57 in Italy, the guards were persuaded to allow the Anzacs to celebrate what they were told was a religious day on 25 April 1943. They were astonished when the normally crumpled Aussies and Kiwis appeared on parade, as the 2/15th Battalion history relates:

'. . . smartly dressed as possible, shaven and boots cleaned. The senior RSM fell in the parade, the orchestra converted to a band for the occasion and the parade marched past the NZ Padre (who held the rank of Major) with great precision. A full salute, completion of the march past and the parade was then dismissed. Next day the men appeared just as lackadaisical as ever in front of the puzzled Italian commander.'

As bad as the conditions were for our POWs in Italy and Germany – and some were treated appallingly – they paled in comparison with the inhuman privations and brutality meted out to those unfortunate enough to be captured by the Japanese. Much of this can be attributed to the attitude of the Japanese towards POWs, explained by the British colonel, Laurens van der Post, in his foreword to *The War Diaries of*

Weary Dunlop:

'For them, surrender was the final depravity which deprived the human being of the right to live with honour, and a life without honour with oneself and one's society, I knew from my own pre-war experience in Japan, was utterly impossible.

'So one started life as a Japanese prisoner-of-war with this complex poison of guilt, shame and dishonour already subtly at work in one's system and one's state of mind unusually vulnerable to the helplessness and apparent hopelessness of one's physical situation.'

When Singapore fell on 15 February 1942, the Japanese captured 130,000 British and allied troops, including about 15,000 survivors of the Australian 8th Division, which had fought a brave but ill-fated rearguard action against the invaders. Lance Corporal Frank Jackson of the 2/10th Australian Field Company was one of those who took part in the defence against the final Japanese assault on Singapore. He recorded his thoughts in a privately published memoir:

'At this time I witnessed the very great bravery of my section officer Lt Charlie Heathcote. He supervised the loading of our wounded on to several of our remaining trucks. In a defiant and most fearless manner he stood there, a fine target, with his revolver in his right hand and a parang in his other hand directing the loading and ordering the drivers to get the hell out of it.

'At the same time he cursed the Japanese with every adjective in the book. As soon as the last truck was loaded and rolling, Charlie was executed quite deliberately by some cold blooded yellow bastard who was obviously waiting for such an opportunity. This is how a brave soldier gave his life for his mates.'

Frank Jackson recalled vividly the feelings of the Diggers after the surrender:

'We were all completely exhausted, acutely depressed, very emotional and to some degree ashamed of our performance. Few spoke, some wept, but beneath it all we wondered what our relatives at home in Australia would think of us. We had let them down and in such a short campaign.

'Singapore was devastated. Wrecked buildings, vehicles and bloated bodies were strewn everywhere. The Japanese, from memory, did not molest us except to keep us moving. The civilian population, particularly the Chinese, were very kind to us. At great personal risk they gave us cool water and fresh fruit. In some instances, I was given words of hope and encouragement; why I never knew, particularly after our failure. Japanese flags were displayed at every vantage point and indeed on just about every house.'

Another Digger swept up in the Japanese net was the late Sergeant Stan Arneil, a member of the 2/30th Battalion. Stan stole a diary and some pens, pencils, ink and rubbers during his early days as a POW working on the Singapore docks. He recorded his harrowing experiences, under constant threat of death if he were discovered:

'We arrived at Selarang Barracks, Changi after dark. We were utterly exhausted and slept on the ground where we were halted within the perimeter. It had been for most of us the bitterest day of our lives; we had no idea of what lay ahead and gained strength from each other as we talked quietly together. There was no laughter, no singing, just a deadly question mark as to what the future held for us.'

Stan Arneil eventually published his diary in 1980 as *One Man's War*. It's a compelling chronicle of the terror and soul-destroying deprivation he and his mates suffered from February 1942 until the survivors were finally released and returned home in October 1945. Stan emerged from the ordeal a magnificent man, full of courage, kindness and compassion. His record paints a chilling picture of the slow disintegration of the POWs' health, but it also emerges as a testament to the protective and healing powers of mateship. Stan and his fellow Diggers put their faith in each other. They forged an unbreakable bond, and those who survived emerged as blood brothers – mateships that endured for the rest of their lives. Indeed, many, like Stan, believed their harrowing experiences made them better men. They learned selflessness and compassion and love and, while they never forgot the mindless cruelty of their captors, few wasted precious energy on grudges.

But after the surrender of Singapore, as they waited stunned and uncomprehending with their fellow Diggers in Changi, men like Frank Jackson and Stan Arneil could not have imagined in their worst nightmares the fate that awaited them. Their early months as prisoners in the Changi area were bad enough. Changi was a small village on the coast of Singapore Island, where the Diggers had camped when they first arrived in Singapore late in 1941. After the surrender it was where the main body of POWs was housed. There at least they had solid buildings, water, electricity, and they could barter and scrounge to get food from the local people. As Stan Arneil wrote:

'The portrayal of the "dreaded Changi" camp brings a smile to the faces of many former prisoners of war who longed for Changi as almost a heaven on earth compared to some of the dreadful places to which they were taken. It was possible to remain at Changi and rarely see a guard; the camp was administered by Brigadier "Black Jack" Galleghan almost as it would have been at any Australian Army camp.

'It was a good arrangement for the Japanese Army because they were relieved of the day to day problems of dealing with a large group of prisoners and it was a good deal for us because we had faith in the ability of Black Jack to obtain the best conditions for us at all times.'

Initially, the Japanese housed the Australians in Selarang Barracks, the British in Roberts Barracks alongside it, and the civilian women and children in Changi Gaol – until May 1944. By that stage the population of 50,000 that had been on the Changi peninsula had been reduced to about 5500. The Japanese then moved all the huts and reconstructed them around the gaol, but they occupied that area for only about 15 months. Lieutenant Colonel Frederick 'Black Jack' Galleghan was made the senior Australian commander after the Japanese removed all senior officers and moved them to their own camp in Formosa, believing they were having an undue influence on their troops.

In those early stages the situation in Changi was tolerable, as most units retained their identity and functioned through their chain of command. The only direct contact most POWs had with the Japanese was when they were needed for working parties, which began as daily events into Singapore and then expanded to detachments being moved there for longer periods of work. Immediately, the Digger's penchant for adaptation and resourcefulness emerged, as Stan Arneil recalled:

'We loaded tinned pineapple for Japan and each man ate pineapple until he could eat no more. Nothing was given to us but within almost no time at all the troops became accomplished thieves. In eating food the trick was to use our army Jack-knives to open tins, eat the food immediately and replace the tin in the box. There were countless thousands of empty tins which were sent to Japan from Singapore.'

Stan also noted some early differences in attitude between the Diggers and their British fellow prisoners:

'I remember watching with amazement as a small group of Englishmen washed from a tin bucket not much bigger than a tin hat. The English had been working on a resin cargo, a dirty job, and had simply taken off their singlets to wash from the bucket.

'Within a few feet of them Australians were standing stark naked under the showers enjoying every minute of the cold water. We found it hard to understand but we were apart from them and made no comments to them about this. They were a cheerful bunch and we had no wish to offend them.'

Early on, Frank Jackson recalled a warning from one of his senior officers, which proved prescient:

'I for one was amazed at his pessimism when he told us in no uncertain terms that we could forget any chance of relief from the allies and to dig hard and to grow vegetables to supplement our rations which in his opinion would shortly become inadequate. He also informed us at the same time that we would not see Australia again for some years at the very least. Needless to

say the remarks were a great shock to us all, but in due course we just realised how close to the mark he was.'

During the working-party period, relations between captors and captives were at their most reasonable. Frank Jackson recalled an experience, remarkable in light of the subsequent tribulations to which he was subjected, which occurred while his working party was on a mine-salvage patrol at the Mersing Mine:

'As this was our last evening in Endau, the meal was our final party in the area. We sat down to an excellent repast, each Australian being seated between two Japanese, with Lieutenant Karkawici taking the head of the table. Each of us, in his turn, was required to sing a national or a folk song, whilst several of our officers sang verses from their old school songs.

'Our host, who had been a student at Tokyo University and, incidentally, had played Rugby against a Sydney University team which visited Tokyo in 1934, sang his old house song in Latin. He also produced a bottle of "Black and White" Scotch whiskey, labelled with the Union Jack overprinted over the label with "Britain Delivers The Goods".

'After the meal, cigarettes and coffee were enjoyed by all, and an interesting demonstration of ju-jitsu was given by several of the guards. This was followed by a short bout by a couple of our budding pugilists. The evening was quite the most unusual of my P.O.W. existence. War was far from us. The usual atmosphere between captives and captors was replaced with that between hosts and guests.'

But this incident was unique, and the atmosphere quickly soured back in Changi as the Japanese stepped up their work demands of the prisoners while, at the same time, resorting to threats and bashings to achieve their aims.

Shortly afterwards, the Japanese announced that they planned to make a propaganda film on life in the camp. Frank Jackson was there:

'They made it known they wanted the boys to sing as they went through the gate. The boys refused and things began to get

electric. When it appeared obvious that something had to be done one bright spark suggested that they sing the unprintable version of "Bless 'em All!" The suggestion caught on like a bushfire. Shouldering their tools they marched through the gate bellowing this parody. If the Nip ever attempted to screen that – well! He never succeeded in humiliating or cowing them no matter what he did.'

In April, the Japanese ordered Black Jack Galleghan and his British counterpart to provide 7000 workers to be sent to an unnamed destination. Although they had no idea at the time, these unfortunates were the men of 'F Force', who were part of those sent to build the infamous Burma–Thailand Railway. Their treatment was unparalleled for its barbarity in modern warfare.

About 62,000 POWs worked on the Railway. Of these 30,000 were British, 18,000 were Dutch and 13,000 were Australian, plus a little-known group of about 700 Americans. More than 200,000 forced Asian workers, who were originally promised high salaries and lured there by Japanese propaganda, were also ultimately forced to join them. Stan's diary records their arrival in Thailand:

'1st May 1943. Arrived at Temple Camp after a wicked night. Half the chaps have dysentery and stomach pains to say nothing of blistered feet and must be carried with their gear. Doug vomited all night and the effort of carrying his gear left me too exhausted to even talk this morning. We are right on the river and the Thais are trading here so instead of sleeping (I defy anybody to sleep during the day-time in Thailand) we bought some sago and had a swim. My boots are in a bad condition and I have to tie a piece of rubber beneath the sole of the boot.

'4th May 1943. Horrible march last night arrived exhausted at a big base camp to which the railway has penetrated. We met D Force who told us that they were transported here in trucks. We are exhausted and our bodies are crying for sleep. We move on again tonight. It is an effort for us to keep our eyes open.

'17th May 1943. Today we arrived at the Mecca of our

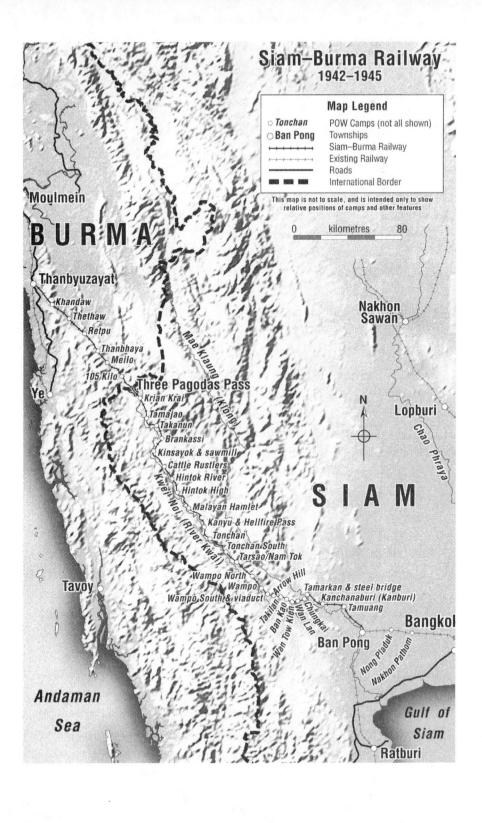

Siam–Burma Railway
1942–1945

Map Legend

○ Tonchan	POW Camps (not all shown)
○ Ban Pong	Townships
┿┿┿┿	Siam–Burma Railway
────	Existing Railway
────	Roads
▬ ▬ ▬	International Border

This map is not to scale, and is intended only to show
relative positions of camps and other features

0   kilometres   80

Moulmein

BURMA

Thanbyuzayat
  Khandaw
   Thethaw
    Retpu
  Thanbhaya
   Meilo
 105 Kilo
Ye
      Three Pagodas Pass
        Krian Krai
       Tamajao
        Takanun
       Brankassi
      Kinsayok & sawmill
      Cattle Rustlers
      Hintok River
       Hintok High
       Malayan Hamlet
       Kanyu & Hellfire Pass
        Tonchan
        Tonchan South
         Tarsao/Nam Tok
       Wampo North
        Wampo
      Wampo South & viaduct

Mae Klaung (Klong)

Kwei No. 1 (River Kwai)

Nakhon Sawan

Lopburi

Chao Phraya

SIAM

N

Tavoy

Andaman
Sea

Takilan
Ban Kao
Wan Tow Kien
Wan Lan
Chungkai
Arrow Hill
Tamarkan & steel bridge
Kanchanaburi (Kanburi)
Tamuang

Bangkok

Ban Pong

Nong Pladuk
Nakhon Pathom

Gulf of
Siam

Ratburi

dreams, Shimo Sonkurai the land of milk and honey, the end of the journey. We have travelled 190 miles and finished up in old bamboo, roofless huts and with a diminutive creek like a buffalo wallow in which 2000 men will eventually bathe, draw water for drinking and wash clothes.

'Soap is a thing of the past and food is fairly tight. The food consists of rice and a little onion and towgay gravy. No roofs on the huts and the heat is terrific.'

With F Force was another remarkable character from the 2/30th Battalion, the famous 'Changi photographer', Private George Aspinall, a 26-year-old motor mechanic from the Riverina. In one of the most remarkable feats of the many accomplished by our Changi POWs, George Aspinall managed to take an extraordinary series of photographs with a cheap Kodak folding camera, which he kept hidden in a belt around his waist with the camera in the small of his back. After his initial film supply ran out, he used cut-down X-ray film and developer from a disused X-ray machine at the camp hospital. His images provide the most vivid record of our Diggers' horrific experiences and span the period from the surrender to near the end of the Railway when, with no more film likely and ever-increasing searches, he broke up the camera and threw the pieces down a well. George Aspinall later wrote of Shimo Sonkurai (or No 1 Camp):

'The camp commander Lieutenant Fukuda lined us all up and left us in no doubt as to intentions and our future. The railway would be built, he said, and every available body would be used to build it. It didn't matter about anybody's life, Japanese or Australian. "If Australians have to die, if Japanese have to die, the line will be built".'

Under the Geneva Convention, officers could not be forced to do manual labour. This led to differences in the performances of some officers, as George Aspinall noted:

'Some of them took their badges of rank off and went out on work parties to take the place of sick men. But others stayed in camp all the time. One senior officer in particular was famous

for sitting under his mosquito net and doing nothing. He lay back there issuing orders and making life difficult for his own officers, and for the rest of us. He's dead now, but I won't name him.

'It is a known fact that very few officers died on the Railway compared with the one-in-three death rate of the men. But most behaved well – even taking bashings from the Japanese for insisting that conditions be improved. All the doctors were magnificent. You won't find any ex-prisoner-of-war who has anything but the highest praise for the way the medicos looked after us.'

The POWs' lives revolved around food, or the lack of it. They found that necessity dictated that any kind of sustenance was better than nothing. George Aspinall wrote:

'Occasionally we would get cases of prawns, sent unrefrigerated of course. They would just be putrefied shells, eaten out by maggots. Our medicos said that if this mess was thoroughly boiled it could be eaten and would give us some protein. So that was made into what we called prawn soup. At least it gave the rice a prawny flavour . . . or more likely the boiled-up maggots provided the flavour, because they had been living on the prawns. We ate anything we could get our hands on, it didn't matter how bad it tasted, as long as you could eat it.

'The Japanese had a peculiar attitude to our rations. We always had a number of men who were too sick to go out to work. So the Japanese would count the number of men not working and subtract that number from the issue of rice or vegetables or any foodstuff made available on that day. Their idea was that if a person was sick, he didn't require food. So if there were fifty men sick on a particular day, we were fifty men's rations down. That's where our internal organisation took over. The cooks would be told how many men had to be fed and some people we called rice quality experts would look at a dixie or bucket of rice very closely and say, "There's enough for three-quarters of a pint, or half a pint per man", depending on how many had to be fed.'

The Diggers banded together for survival. Malnutrition, overwork, the punishments of the guards and the climate combined to batter the constitution of even the most robust into submission. Under these conditions, all privacy and any pretence vanished and men saw deep into each other's hearts and lives, as Stan Arneil recalled:

'Thailand was a time when all artificiality disappeared and men saw themselves and others as they really were. It was a time of kindness to one another which would have to be seen to be believed but the circumstances engendered a mutual co-operation as a means of life preservation.

'Thailand was a bitter experience with almost no light patches. The dense bamboo jungle with its cruel thorns crowded us into the narrow strips on which we were working. The sun rarely ever shone during that wet season. I never heard a bird sing.'

It was in this grim, daily fight for existence that Stan saw the differences in approach between the Diggers and their British counterparts begin to emerge:

'The British, who comprised approximately half the force, were a happy go lucky lot who did not have the apparent determination either to live or to take preventative action to reduce disease. Whereas the Australians were fanatical in their efforts to prevent the blowflies contacting the rice and depositing the cholera germs, the British regarded such efforts as something of a joke. The Australians scrupulously collected each single grain of rice which may have dropped on the ground when the rice was issued and at meal times sterilized their dixies [food containers] *in cauldrons of boiling water before receiving their rice. The British rarely bothered to sterilize their personal food containers and allowed rice dropped at meal issues to ferment on the ground providing breeding grounds for the cholera carrying blowflies. The British died at the rate of almost two to one of the Australians.'*

::

The Railway cost more than 100,000 lives – about 245 men for every kilometre. Some 10,549 POWs died during construction, most of their graves being found when the Allies searched along the tracks afterwards. A further 2000 died in captivity during the two years following the completion of the Railway, predominantly from the illnesses and injuries from building it, even though life became much easier for them once the Railway was completed. Unbelievably, an estimated 90,000 Asians died building the Railway, and most were not Thais. (Some reports claim that Thais built the Railway, but Thailand had signed a pact with Japan granting them right of passage and the Japanese were anxious not to disturb the arrangement. Thais on the Railway worked as contract labour, and the Japanese rarely beat them because of their nebulous political alliance.)

One of the main causes of death was cholera, which struck with devastating effect at Shimo Sonkurai. Once cholera took hold among the wasted bodies, it cut a deadly swathe through F Force. Those who contracted it were isolated from the main body of the men, placed in a special area which soon became known as 'Cholera Hill'. For most, being moved there was a death sentence, and its inhabitants died with terrifying swiftness. George Aspinall saw it first-hand:

'Cholera is an awful business. A man can be dead within hours, as the body just hurls out all its fluid in violent explosions of vomiting and diarrhoea. A cholera patient can lose half his body weight in hours, and become totally unrecognisable, even to his friends.'

Stan Arneil recalls that the Last Post was being played so often at one stage that they decided to restrict it to once a week because of its impact on morale (during a period where half a dozen POWs were dying each day at Cholera Hill):

'26th May 1943. Do not consider me relishing the gloomy side of affairs, but since yesterday afternoon five chaps have died from cholera, three of them from our unit. The situation is going from bad to worse and fifteen chaps were admitted to the cholera tents

this morning. I just saw a cove carried from one of the huts, grey of face and limp of body. The ground is becoming covered in slime where these have bogged or vomited.'

'2nd June 1943. Six deaths in 24 hours, three admissions only. We may have the cholera beaten. Malaria now almost as the cholera was. Tip work party today of all the fit men. 240 men went to work, we marched in here 2000 strong.

'20th August 1943. Eight more dead. More rain, more mud. Rumours of the camp shifting on Sunday. Starting to get tinea and beri beri again. The former from the continuous wet feet and the latter from this awful diet.'

Later in that entry Stan again refers to the difference between the British soldiers and the Diggers:

'Nine out of ten people dying here are Englishmen, even though the Australians outnumber the Chums by three to one. They seem to give up the ghost without a fight at all. I cannot under-stand it at all because the spirit of the English at the start of the war was so brave.'

Even allowing for the natural 'team' bias that may have accompanied Stan's view, it's clear that there was a difference in the way the Diggers and the Tommies dealt with their time in captivity. Many dispassionate sources have mentioned the way the Australians banded together and the positive impact that mateship had on their chances of survival. Stan's proud boast was: 'No Digger died on the Railway without his mates holding his hand'. Years later, whenever he spoke in depth of his fellow POWs, manly tears welled in his eyes and he spoke of them with love and respect. He had no doubt that the mateship and love with which they cocooned each other was a major contributing factor to their subsequent survival. He saw this mutual protection as acting as a spiritual and psychologi-cal safety net, which allowed them to draw strength from each other so that those bending under the strain could be supported by others with greater resilience at that time. They would repay the debt at some later stage, when the tables might have turned:

'3rd September 1943. Four years today! [since Stan joined up] *In the last two days three of the finest chaps in our unit have died, Tucker, Hurry and Guy, all from A Coy. Malnutrition and cardiac beri beri is doing most of the killing now.*

'I worry about the Englishmen under my care. They practically walk to the cremation pyre. They stop eating, lay down and refuse to live. It is incredible, instead of hanging grimly on to life with both hands they start to criticise their meals and that is the finish. Meals here, particularly breakfast is almost revolting but most of us regard it as a legitimate ticket home and religiously poke it down. I must get home.'

The POWs battled a deadly range of diseases and sickness, which threatened their weakened constitutions, including beri-beri, malaria, dysentery, tinea and the constant scourge of tropical ulcers. George Aspinall worked as a medical orderly, helping in the medical huts on the Railway where doctors like Bruce Hunt heroically struggled to keep the ulcers under control:

'One of the methods used to treat them was to scoop out the bad flesh of the ulcer with a spoon sharpened on one side. It was desperation treatment really. The idea was to get back to the good flesh, in the hope that it would heal. I used to sharpen spoons for one of our surgeons, Major Bruce Hunt. I had a little honing stone, and would get hold of a solid tin spoon and sharpen the edge on one side, right around the handle. This sharp edge was used as a scalpel. Major Hunt became quite adept at using this spoon. He would cut by moving the spoon backwards and forwards, at the same time scooping out the bad flesh from the ulcer. It was an excruciatingly painful procedure, of course, and there were virtually no anaesthetics. I sometimes used to help to hold blokes down on the operating table while their ulcers were scraped, so I couldn't help but see what was happening.'

As a last resort, if the progress of the tropical ulcers could not be successfully arrested, the doctors were forced to amputate the affected limb, a terrible operation often witnessed by George Aspinall:

'I only know of one man who survived an amputation under these conditions. As far as I know he's alive today, but most died from the shock of the operation. Even so, many of the ulcer sufferers would be begging the doctors to amputate their legs. Some of the bad cases had the shin-bone exposed. You could see their tendons clearly. Sometimes the bone would go black and start to break down and rot. Then the flies would get in and lay their eggs, and the maggots would actually be in there, feeding on the bone marrow. They would start to work up, all the way up the leg. It used to drive blokes off their heads with the pain.'

The doctors who tended to the desperate needs of the POWs have emerged as the often unsung heroes of the period. The great Sir Edward 'Weary' Dunlop is perhaps the best known of them, but many POWs speak of the Western Australian Dr Bruce Hunt and Drs Albert Coates and Roy Mills in the same reverent tones they reserve for Weary Dunlop.

After he retired from his career as an engineer in the Australian Army, Colonel Terry Beaton became the curator of the Hellfire Pass Museum on the Railway. His work there inspired him to make a detailed study of the Railway and of its impact on those who were forced to build it:

'Dr Bruce Hunt saved countless lives at Shimo Sonkurai with F Force. When he arrived, 155 Australians had already died, mainly from cholera, and had been buried at the cemetery called "Cholera Hill". He did something incredible: he got the Japs to stop work for two days to clean up Shimo Sonkurai. Everyone pitched in and they cleaned up the camp, dug new latrines, fly-proofed them and they had no new outbreaks of cholera in F Force.'

Even digging a grave was an overwhelming task for the severely weakened POWs. Terry Beaton says:

'The graves were about five metres long, by about a metre wide, by about 75 centimetres deep and you put up to five into each grave. The normal thing was to try to burn and cremate the remains but if you didn't have timber for fires you had no other

choice but to bury. Some POWs told the guards they'd make a funeral pyre and put their mate on but they didn't have enough timber so when they knew the Japanese weren't looking they'd build the funeral pyre over a grave and when the timber burned through he would fall into the grave and they would bury him, partially cremated, rather than leave him for the animals.'

Terry Beaton has calculated that, on the Railway, the Australian fatality rate was 18 per cent, the British about 22 per cent and the Dutch 16 per cent.

'The reason the Dutch had the lesser rate was that they came from the tropical climate (it was the Dutch East Indies) and many of them knew tropical medicine and which plants to use. On every working party they would come back with some greenery.

'Weary Dunlop worked on the Thai side of the Railway, Albert Coates was on the Burma side. Both did an incredible job. Albert Coates amputated 120 legs using a borrowed butcher's meat saw because he had almost no instruments and the anaesthetic was often physically knocking the men out or putting some leather between their teeth to bite down on while their leg was sawn off.

'Even with tropical ulcers: four men would hold the victim down as the doctor scraped out the ulcer each day with a spoon to try to clean the wound, create blood flow and regenerate it. When that didn't work, the last resort was to take the limb off.'

Terry Beaton discovered that one of his relations, Frederick Michael Beaton, suffered that fate: 'Albert Coates took off his leg but toxic shock and toxaemia took him.'

All the while, under the brutal direction of Japanese engineers, the building of the Railway continued. In total, the POWs and the Asians who laboured with them built an astonishing 688 bridges (eight steel and concrete, 680 timber), a total of 14 kilometres of bridges alone, for a Railway that extended about 400 kilometres through the jungles of Burma and

Thailand. F Force started with about 7000 men. In nine months 3096, or 44 per cent, died during the construction. Many more died in the following months from disease or the impact of their privations.

Terry Beaton has created a magnificent tribute to those who gave their lives on the Railway. During his time as curator of the Hellfire Pass Museum, he painstakingly researched and drew a map of the Railway and all the camps and cemeteries along it. It shows the scale of the suffering and the sacrifice of those forced to build it:

> 'When you walk the railway in many places the dry-stone rockwork that these men made is incredible. I am an engineer and, looking through dispassionate eyes, I have to take my hat off to the Japanese for their surveying skills and their ability to build a railway. And whether the POWs like it or not, it was an achievement to build the railway in seventeen months – but at a huge cost.'

The speed with which the Railway was built was all the more remarkable because previous British surveys had concluded it would take five years to build. In addition to the POWs, the Japanese used Malays and others, originally as volunteer paid labour. But where people wouldn't volunteer the Japanese would go into a village saying they were going to put on a film night. The naive local Malays would turn up expecting a movie, and the Japanese would surround the gathering, drag out all able-bodied men, put them in trucks and send them to the Railway. They were originally told they'd be gone for three months. When they hadn't returned after five and no money was forthcoming, not surprisingly the volunteers dried up. That led to the press-ganging. More than 90,000 of these Asian peoples perished building the Railway because their Asian masters treated them far worse than even the POWs. They had to conform. In some areas they worked alongside the POWs, and many believe they brought in the cholera. When that was suspected the Japanese shot them, threw them into rice sacks and into the river, thus spreading the disease down to the lower camps.

Both POWs and Asian workers suffered from the physical cruelty of their captors, as George Aspinall attested:

'There was a lot of corporal punishment. A senior officer would slap or belt a junior officer. That officer would bash a sergeant who would bash a three-star private and on to the lowliest private. He would take it out on a Korean guard who would then bash the prisoners-of-war! We were the last cab off the rank in status although the poor Asians used as forced labour were even worse off than we were. They died in tens of thousands on the Railway. At least we had our military discipline. They had nothing.'

Terry Beaton analysed the causes of death on the Railway, and the vast majority seemed to have died from dysentery:

'But what was the main cause of death? Really it was malnutrition. The fact that they had a poor, small diet, meant they didn't have the natural ability to resist infection. So when these diseases came along and most prisoners would have multiple diseases – malaria combined with dysentery and beri-beri, etc. It was really a guess as to which killed them but really it's likely to be the dysentery.'

Outsiders have asked the POWs why they built the Railway so well. The POWs have always maintained they built it to the minimum standards the Japanese would accept: anything less and they would make them tear it down and start again and would punish them mercilessly. To save their lives, they simply built it to the minimum standards they could get away with and that depended largely on the standard of the guards and engineers at any time. 'They could only be concerned with their survivability and their five kilometre section of the railway', Terry Beaton says.

Most lost their lives on the Railway from May to September 1943, when the Japanese High Command cut three months off the completion date – from 18 to 15 months. This was the infamous 'speedo' period, and it occurred during the wet season. The men went from working a normal day, from 8 am to 5 pm, to working 16 hours a day for 100 days with sometimes a Sunday off. No wonder, as the rain and the constant damp combined with cholera, they dropped like flies.

As the Railway neared completion, the Japanese started moving men through from Burma – the sickest first, then the less sick – until all the POWs were brought into Thailand, where they went into one of three 'fattening camps'. There they were given improved food and the fitter men were put onto rust-bucket ships and sent to Japan to work in the coal mines, copper mines and factories. From 1942 to 1945 more than 30 ships were used by the Japanese to transport about 30,000 POWs to various locations. Ironically, 15 of those ships were sunk by Allied action – including two that were carrying 1500 prisoners who had survived the Railway and that were sunk by the USS *Pamponito*. The US ship went back, searching for what they thought would be Japanese survivors, and found Australian and British POWs. Just 177 were rescued out of the group. The others perished.

Sadly, of a total of about 15,000 POWs sent by sea, only 5000 made it safely. Some 10,000 were lost to friendly fire.

Back in Changi, life was more tolerable and the POWs had some degree of control over their lives. Here they drew on their spread of individual skills and their collective powers of ingenuity to do what they could to improve their situation. They established a 'limb factory', which made artificial limbs for their amputee mates. The factory also repaired their precious surgical instruments. A 'rubber factory' extracted latex from local rubber trees to make sandals, to repair clothes and even to make dental plates. Some POWs used lighting conductor wire to make nails to repair boots, and others repaired clothes by building machines to unravel old socks to create cotton thread. Grass extract was used as a remedy for vitamin deficiencies.

At Changi, the POWs fell back on discipline to avoid idle minds. They organised an extensive variety of study courses, concerts and sports. Laurens van der Post noticed that the Diggers' attitude to these courses also set them apart:

'And their intellectual curiosity, love of learning and discussion, which sometimes would continue long into the day and night as a private argument in the barracks, was endless and, for me, one of the most marked and endearing characteristics of the Australian soldier.'

But one of the most difficult hurdles faced by the POWs was the isolation, from the war, the outside world and particularly from their families. As this entry from Stan's diary shows, mail from home arrived sporadically, if at all:

'18th April 1944. Twenty bags of mail at the gaol, almost double the last quantity and all Australian. We have not obtained permission to sort it but that should come any time and then, if my luck holds, I may receive a letter from Ruby. The latest date of the mail is September '43 which would be now thirteen months older than I have received up to date.'

The POW experience brought out the best in most and the worst in some. Many used the experience positively, reasoning that if they could survive it, they could survive anything that life was going to throw at them. Terry Beaton interviewed many ex-POWs:

'It wasn't just the railway but also afterwards. Some went into conditions in Japan and were looked after very well by the Japanese people in their area. Others, one I know of, received more beatings in Japan. A lot of the beatings were issued by Korean guards, who were the most brutal. The POWs will say that while they were captured and held by regular troops, there was very little animosity and very few beatings. But when they were handed over to the POW branches, the Japanese became more brutal but the majority of the severe beatings they had came from the Korean guards when they arrived on the railway. Many accounts of the Japanese absolutely laying into the Korean guard who lost face and would then lay into the Australian who had caused the problem in the first place.'

While mateship was crucial in the survival of the Diggers, an equally important factor was luck. For a start, you had to be lucky in the group in which you were placed. For example, Weary Dunlop's group on F Force lost perhaps 10–20 per cent while another group lost 200 of 600. Again, one group was kicked off the train and force-marched to their camp – 20 kilometres a day for two weeks and three days until they made 295 kilometres – and then put straight to work. Another group was sent by truck. The British camp at Sonkerai had cholera and huge losses; another camp had almost no cholera.

But perhaps the POWs' greatest luck came when the Japanese finally surrendered. Originally, all internees were to be exterminated if the unthinkable happened and the Japanese were defeated. But because it was Hirohito, the God-Emperor himself, who announced unconditional surrender, the blind obedience of the guards saved the POWs. The Japanese people had never even heard the Emperor's voice before.

When General Blamey accepted the surrender at Morotai on 9 September 1945 from Lieutenant General Teshima, the commander of the Second Japanese Army, he said:

'In receiving your surrender I do not recognise you as an honourable and gallant foe, but you will be treated with due but severe courtesy in all matters.

'I recall the treacherous attack upon our ally, China in 1938. I recall the treacherous attack made upon the British Empire and upon the United States of America in December 1941, at a time when your authorities were making the pretence of ensuring peace.

'I recall the atrocities inflicted upon the persons of our nationals as prisoners of war and internees, designed to reduce them by punishment and starvation to slavery.

'In the light of these evils, I will enforce most rigorously all orders issued to you, so let there be no delay or hesitation in their fulfilment at your peril.'

::

So how did those shadows of Diggers who remained alive survive their unspeakable ordeals? Overall, it was a combination of mateship and willpower. Their determination never to give in was critical. An indomitable spirit sustained them individually and as a group. And, while they looked after each other, they had a low tolerance for those among them who failed to pull their weight or who thought only of themselves. Terry Beaton has explored the subject:

There was a term on the railway, "White Nips" – either someone who collaborated or those who were "Jap happy" meaning those who tried it on for their own survivability or conning their way out of work or taking advantage of their privileges which made it easier for them but harder for their mates. But today the survivors will never "dob" on their mates, even when they go through obvious turmoil in the decision.'

George Aspinall agreed:

'I think we survived because we were determined that we were going to get home and that we could put up with anything the Japs threw at us, no matter how hard or tough it was, in order to get home. Everyone helped each other as much as he could, and that was one of the things that got most of us through. There were one or two cases of men behaving selfishly, like trying to get more food than the others, but these incidents were rare. If something like that did happen, the individual concerned would be singled out and given a quiet talking-to by one of us – not necessarily an officer or NCO. He'd be told to pull himself into line or he'd get a belting from his own people. But that wasn't necessary very often. Most did the right thing, and that's how we kept together and survived.'

Stan Arneil turned his suffering into a positive force:

'Those terrible years though were good to me; they taught me of values which are not usual in civilian life. The co-operative principle of sharing good things and bad together, of respect and love for one another, despite differences in (pre-war) social scale, are attitudes which shaped my life.

'I do not personally regret having been a prisoner of war,

perhaps it was a privilege, but the years will not ever go away and a memory trigger, such as the death of a former comrade, recalls incidents so vividly.

'I can still feel the blazing heat on the "drome" or the sweat running from my body as we worked in the foetid heat of the tunnels of Johore.

'I can feel the biting cold of the rain in Thailand pelting ceaselessly on to our near naked bodies and I will never forget the sinking feeling of hearing the dreaded cry of "Currah! Currah! Speedo! Speedo!"

'I can recall those magnificent young men who never lost hope even as they faded from robust health to walking cadavers.'

Laurens van der Post looked back on the horrors from a higher plane and, in doing so, was able to find meaning:

'. . . we had discovered a way of living in prison as if it were not a prison and instead an immense opportunity for re-educating ourselves and freeing our minds and imaginations for life in a way they have never been free before. We had discovered, as I put it to the Japanese General who announced his surrender to me in September 1945 in urging him to emulate the example, how to lose in a way that losing became another kind of winning.'

ELEVEN

New Guinea and beyond

The 9th Division regrouped after its Middle East triumphs and began training for forthcoming campaigns in New Guinea and Borneo. There it would fight alongside the Diggers of the 7th Division, who had distinguished themselves on the Kokoda Track and at the beachheads of Buna, Gona and Sanananda. The two forces worked in tandem to cut off the Japanese withdrawal from Lae on the Salamaua Gulf, about 200 kilometres north of Port Moresby. The 9th Division stormed the swampy beaches at Finschhafen, on the Huon peninsula, on 4 September 1943, and the 7th Division was flown into Nadzab, inland from Lae, three days later. The 7th drove up the Markham Valley and the 9th moved up the coast.

The battle for the Lae-Nadzab area was crucial to establish Nadzab airstrip as a base for the Allies to bomb the Japanese stronghold at Rabaul, the capital of nearby New Britain Island, from which Admiral Yamamoto was conducting the entire Japanese southwest Pacific campaign. In this short but decisive battle, the Diggers of the 2/4th Field Regiment, an artillery unit armed with 25-pounders, impressed the Americans with their daring and inventiveness. They were so keen to join the action that they volunteered as a group to be parachuted in, with their guns, to support the American 503rd Paratroop Regiment – this despite the fact that they had never parachuted in their lives. US General George Kenney wrote in his memoirs:

'It's hard for me to believe that anything could have been so perfect. At the last minute the Australian gunners who were to man the 25-pounders decided to jump with their guns. None of them had ever worn a parachute before but they were so anxious to go that we showed them how to pull the ripcord and let them jump . . . General MacArthur swore that it was the most perfect example of discipline and training he had ever seen.'

Earlier, after the Owen Stanleys campaign, while the battered veterans of the 2/14th Battalion, the saviours of Isurava, were recuperating outside Port Moresby, a fresh-faced lieutenant from Wollongong, south of Sydney, Nolan Pallier, joined them as a reinforcement. He remembered being checked out by Phil Rhoden, then 2IC of the battalion:

'He would have been a captain then. I was about 23. They didn't want these young blokes from NSW, they wanted Victorians and their own sergeants promoted, which was only right. And Phil explained that. It was not blunt but right to the point. I was one of three new young officers. From the start, they treated us very well. We were taken into the family. It was like a big family and closer than any militia battalion.

'Then they sent us back to Cairns in Australia, to the Atherton Tablelands. They were reinforced and we trained there and we went back into the Ramu and Markham valley campaigns. I reformed 9 Platoon, a famous platoon from the Owen Stanleys. It was very knocked about. The whole battalion looked knocked about.'

Phil Rhoden recalled meeting 'Noel' Pallier for the first time:

'I couldn't believe he was old enough to shave. He looked so young – the blokes called him "the boy" – but he looked likely and he was keen and willing to learn. We needed new blood and he brought enthusiasm. I knew the old hands would knock him into shape.'

Back in Australia, Noel Pallier remembered the first time

he met one of the heroes of the battalion, a youthful-looking, self-effacing man with smiling eyes. Sergeant Lindsay 'Teddy' Bear had served in the Middle East and then won a Military Medal for bravery at Isurava, where he had been wounded in the action in which Bruce Kingsbury won his Victoria Cross:

'I didn't see Teddy until we were back in Australia and he'd recovered from his wounds and he came back to us at the camp at Ravenshoe on the Atherton Tableland. I can remember the very day I met him. Two or three chaps were there as the reinforcements marched in every three and four days and this bloke came up and gently said "G'day". We clicked right from that G'day.'

The experienced veteran Teddy Bear would serve as sergeant under the tyro officer Lieutenant Noel Pallier. This teaming of the practical, hard-headed and experienced NCO with the young graduate officer is one of the central planks of the subunit system that has served the Australian Army so well. It often results in a fascinating amalgam of gung-ho exuberance and battle-hardened caution, which provides the unit with a leadership team possessing a combined balance greater than its individual parts. Noel Pallier remembers his early feelings of apprehension:

'Nobody knows how they will behave till they're confronted. I had a reasonably protected life. I was a shy boy, still a shy nature. I probably thought that at some times but it didn't worry me but I didn't think I was any hero or anything special.

'I went away. I thought I was fairly well trained then as an infantry officer, not brilliant, just an ordinary chap. I went away with a feeling that the Japs had to be stopped. I'd really never known any Japanese people. I was to learn about the Japanese from their army which I didn't have a lot of respect for. They were tough good soldiers from their point of view but we were a cut above what they did. Their atrocities were beyond belief.

'I used to think what would happen if I lost a leg or an arm. I'm not saying I wasn't afraid of being killed – I knew that could happen – but I was more concerned if I lost a leg or lost an arm.

I might have been thinking of the future but I can remember that well. I never really thought I would be killed but don't let anybody tell you they weren't frightened. At some time or another, if they went into real action they were frightened or they weren't mortal. But being frightened and doing your job is a lot different to being frightened and not doing your job. That's the difference between heroes and others.'

Once they'd reached New Guinea, Noel's platoon was flown up the Markham Valley and they began chasing the Japanese up the valley until they hit Dumpu, a village down from the Finisterre Range, where the Japanese decided to make a stand.

Earlier, at nearby Wampum, the battalion had been involved in a firefight that ended the brilliant combat career of their commanding officer. Lieutenant Colonel Ralph Honner, former CO of the 39th Battalion at Isurava, had led the 2/14th with equal flair and distinction. Ralph had exposed himself to danger many times as he led from the front. As a company commander with the 2/11th Battalion in Syria and Crete and again as CO of the 39th Battalion at Isurava, he had often dismayed his men with his disregard for his personal safety as he moved among them, encouraging and directing them and moving into harm's way to better appreciate the situation. At Wampum his luck ran out, as Noel Pallier recalled:

'At Wampum we'd stopped for the night and deployed around the track. We heard a few shots and saw two fellows running flat out along a track in the valley. I remember saying what the hell's going on down there. They ran into a thicket of jungle and disappeared. We were sitting in the long grass and suddenly there were flop, flop, flop, bullets hitting near us.

'Colonel Honner had taken Gerry O'Dea to have a look at A Company up the track. But A Company had moved to the higher ground above the track. He and Gerry kept walking and the next thing they knew they were fired on by the Japs.'

The ball-and-socket joint in Ralph Honner's hip was shattered by a machine-gun burst. He was bleeding profusely and could barely move. His companions dragged him into the kunai grass and ran back past Noel Pallier's position for help:

'So Ralph was in the grass just in front of the Jap positions. He told me later while he was waiting for assistance, he could see the Japs searching for him and he was badly wounded. He drew a pin out of a grenade and lay doggo. If they'd have seen him eye to eye, he said he was going to take some of them with him.

'Alan Avery went up to get the Colonel out and as he got near he wondered how he was going to find him. He couldn't yell out Sir or Colonel or anything. So he yelled out "Honner!", "Honner!" so the Japs wouldn't know who we were after. Eventually Ralph responded and when Alan reached him, Ralph was covered in blood and there were millions of little black ants feeding on the blood. He'd been there for some time. He said to Alan: "We're going to attack this position" and Alan said "I'm sorry Sir my orders are to bring you out". He knew Ralph was in a bad way. Ralph said: "Who gave you those orders Mr Avery?" and Alan replied it was Captain O'Dea. Ralph said: "Oh I think my orders are still a little bit above Captain O'Dea so get your walkie talkie going". He called up an attack. It wasn't until the attack was evidently successful that Ralph would let them take him out. Through all of that Ralph's voice was calm as always.'

The young Noel Pallier remembered being overwhelmingly impressed by the demeanour and the professionalism of Ralph Honner, Alan Avery and the others during the drama:

'Anything these men did they would try to do well, no matter what it was. Whether it was playing up, they'd play up well. If they were fighting, they'd fight well.'

Just as he'd done at Isurava, Phil Rhoden took command of the battalion. He would lead it with wisdom and courage until the end of the war. Noel Pallier's greatest test was rapidly approaching. The young officer was about to grow up in a hurry.

On patrol near Dumpu, Noel's platoon had taken a brief meal break after a long morning's trek when they were caught in a hail of fire from the high ground above them:

'It was too steep to get up and there were big rocks in the flat part of the valley and you could hear the bullets ricocheting off them. The natural reaction was to grab your gear and run for the cover of the river banks about 100 or 150 yards away. That we did and when we got to the river bank it was a sheer drop where it had been carved away by the fast flowing river. But we soon got down there, climbing or jumping and we took cover.

'We could see the Japs' smoke firing at us from up in the hills. Georgie Pottinger was a Bren gunner and when he appeared next to me he didn't have his gun with him. I said in army language "You didn't leave your gun out there did you?" and he said nothing, just slumped against me. When I grabbed him, the blood just came through his shirt and I knew what was wrong.

'You couldn't see where the bullet went in but it blew a big hole out the back. We made a stretcher and gave him a morphine needle and wrote the time in indelible pencil on his forehead, so they'd know later.

'We then had a firefight with the Japs and they had the knocker on us – they had the surprise on us and the high ground. But, for some reason, I wasn't going back without that Bren gun. The bullets were flying everywhere, off the stones and through the trees. I decided I'd go out and get the Bren gun. I didn't know how I'd find it but I crawled until I could stand up and run to the area we run from. I told them what I was going to do and ordered them to cover me and I crawled out and I expected to be hit any time – this is for a Bren gun mind you, not a man!

'I stood up and ran and when I got there I couldn't see the Bren gun. I ran about and then I caught sight of it, just where George had dropped it because he was too badly hit to carry it. I was running across to the gun and had almost reached it when My God somebody spoke behind me: it was Teddy Bear.

'He'd followed me out. He was the 2IC of the platoon and I'd told him not to but I reckon he thought Noel will get hit and I'll be there to pick him up. I got the gun, Teddy picked up a couple of magazines and we ran back and scrambled down the bank *to safety. That was Teddy Bear. That was the feeling in that platoon.'*

Noel Pallier and his men carried George Pottinger through the rugged 10 kilometres back to their base camp to the Casualty Clearing Station. He rallied there but died some days later when they tried to put him on a plane to evacuate him.

Noel Pallier's greatest challenge had now arrived. His platoon was ordered to take a razorback ridge high in the hills around the famous Shaggy Ridge. Alan Avery's mob was on the next hill and the 2/22nd Battalion was deployed up in the mountains near Shaggy Ridge. This is some of the steepest country in New Guinea: all single-track ridges plunging to deep ravines and valleys. By this stage Noel's platoon had been reduced to 28 men. Noel recalled:

'My orders were very brief: "Capture the hill before dark". Couldn't be briefer.

'If you'd have seen that hill and how steep it was. We were hanging with our heels dug in so we wouldn't slide back down the mountain. The Japs had moved in and they dug in. It was part of their system of trying to cut you off. That's why I was ordered in to take the hill. I could see it through field glasses. We didn't know how many were up there. They'd dug in the day before along the razorback track. Alan Avery saw it from his standing patrol below.

'An assault along the razorback track would have been the last resort and we wouldn't have got there. The only way was around the sides, up the razorback, digging in our heels and climbing up yard by yard.'

Noel Pallier's artillery support had only 19 rounds for their 25-pounder gun. The plan was to fire one shot every minute:

'I reckon now it was perfect. After a shell goes off you get your head down and then you wait awhile then stick your head up and that's when the next round came over.

'The 25 pounders, fired over open sights, from back in the valley at battalion headquarters, were very effective. We could nearly hear the shells go past as they went up the hill. You'd hear

the bang, back in the valley, and fair dinkum it seemed to be just right there on you as it whistled past. It was music to us!

'When we got along there a little bit, moving in single file and staying low, and because the Japs didn't clean us up getting into that position, we got the feeling, hey, we're going to make it. Before that you had a feeling: this is nearly hopeless, you know, but we've got to go. The others have told me since that they felt exactly the same.'

After hours of clambering, sliding and crawling up the sheer sides of the hillside, dodging grenades rolled down from the heights past them and avoiding the sniping from above, Noel's platoon eventually made it to within striking distance of the razorback:

'We got into position, jammed up together and that's where I gave the order: "Fix bayonets!" then, for some reason, I added: ". . . if you like!" It's not natural to push bayonets through someone. And for a split second I remember thinking I wonder how many of us will come through this. I really did. Teddy Bear was right next to me. I seemed to think clearer after a few shots have been fired and you think of things you'd never think you'd think about.

'I was looking back and forth, making sure everybody was ready, and Teddy was saying, almost under his breath, "Let's get stuck into them! Let's get stuck into them!" I looked again and yelled out "Charge". The blokes looked at each other, and then at me, and we all burst out laughing! Fancy yelling out charge, you could see how steep it was but you had to give some kind of command and off we went. Our Vickers gunners were very good and they supported us beautifully. The bullets were tearing up the ground just in front of us. The Japs were dug in, with just their heads above the edge and, with the curve of the hill, their field of fire wasn't that far. They knew we were there but not exactly where. They scattered grenades across their front, like throwing out a bag full of them down the hill.'

Noel's men had made it closer to the Japanese defenders than they thought when they charged. Immediately it broke into vicious hand-to-hand fighting, all in! Even the reserve section charged up on the left. The Aussies yelled at the top of their voices as they charged – a tactic used to instil fear into the enemy – and it worked! Noel:

'We pushed on and the grenades came down at us. I got hit by shrapnel from a grenade but I struggled to the top. Then Teddy got a bit further ahead and I remember he'd always give the impression that he could take on the whole Japanese army. I heard "Hi Ho" [Corporal Edward "Hi Ho" Silver] *talking to his Owen gunners saying: "Johnny Crane, you stop on my left side with that gun" and to the other, Billy Howarth: "Billy you stop on my right hand. And don't youse bloody well move from there". He was a born leader of men and a very brave man old Hi Ho.*

'In any attack there's the organised part, then there's the hand-to-hand fighting as I see it when nobody's really in command because everybody's dealing with the enemy just in front of them. And, in all of that confusion, the Japs had enough discipline to duck down in the foxholes, wait until some of our blokes went past, and then open up behind them. We were a wake-up to that most of the time.

'It went down to bayonets and you couldn't describe what went on with your close family of friends in that sort of fight. We gradually overcame them and when the Japs were dealt with they were pushed aside until we'd taken the position.'

The official history reveals that, as did so many Diggers, Noel Pallier was underplaying the intensity of the fighting at Pallier's Hill: on the night of 10 October 1943 a Japanese company of about 60 troops was set in strongly dug-in positions on a dominating feature overlooking Kumbarum and connected to Kings Hill by a razor-edge ridge about 1 kilometre long. The position completely cut the supply line to the 2/27th Battalion. The enemy firing from it panicked the native carrier trains attempting to get through to the 2/27th.

Because of the narrow and steep approach, the Australians could use only one platoon in the attack. It crept to within

35 metres of the position before making its final assault. Teddy Bear led the initial wave with two sections, one on either side of the ridge line up almost sheer cliff faces through heavy fire and a barrage of grenades rolled down from above. Teddy was the first to the top. Hit three times, he still managed to pick off enemy troops until his rifle was empty, then he began an amazing bayonet charge, where he killed three or four and sent at least ten more to their deaths by driving them or, by some accounts, literally pitchforking them over the sheer precipice. The position was taken at a cost of more than 30 Japanese killed.

For his part in the attack, Noel Pallier was Mentioned in Despatches:

'Lieutenant Pallier led 9 Platoon in the attack. Although wounded in both legs in the last stages of the attack he continued to direct and encourage his men displaying a high standard of personal courage and gallantry. The operation was completely successful and resulted in over 30 of the enemy being killed and the line of communication being cleared.'

In honour of his magnificent effort in leading his men to capture that remote hill, Noel's superiors named the feature 'Pallier's Hill'. The official citations give weight to the enormity of the achievements of 'the boy' and his men: Noel and Lance Corporal 'Lofty' Back were Mentioned in Despatches; Corporals E.P. 'Hi Ho' Silver and J.H. 'Bluey' Whitechurch won the Military Medal; and Sergeant L.A. 'Teddy' Bear won the Distinguished Conduct Medal. His recommendation read:

'The success of this most difficult attack was largely due to the magnificent part played by Sergeant Bear. He showed complete disregard for his own safety and displayed outstanding personal gallantry throughout the attack. The example he set was an inspiration to his men.'

Noel Pallier has never forgotten the feelings he experienced when the battle died down:

'[Corporal J.H.] *"Bluey" Whitechurch later wrote that we all seemed to be hysterical after we'd done it and he was sort of right. It was a feeling that it was unbelievable that we'd made it to beat them on that hilltop. Then things cooled down and machine gun from the Japs' reserves further back started to pick us up. We thought a counter attack was coming but it never amounted to anything.*

'Somewhere on the hill, in the fighting, I got hit again. At first you don't even pinpoint when you got hit. The pain hits you later. You can feel the bullets hit the ground but you don't realise you've been hit immediately because your blood's up.

'We weren't cold blooded men but we had to use the bayonet then. We had no choice. You're fighting for your life. When you see a man getting out of a foxhole, clipping his bayonet on, you know it's either him or you and you do what you were trained to do. Correct action becomes instinctive. You were trained to make the correct move but you don't think about it. You couldn't imagine Teddy Bear to be ruthless but that's what happens in war. Had we not fought like that, we would never have survived.'

Now in his early eighties but, as always, appearing many years younger, Noel Pallier is looking with bemusement at an old photo of Pallier's Hill and the surrounding countryside. They show a ridge line like a giant Stone Age axe protruding, cutting-edge up, out of the jungle:

'Looking at the photos now, I find it hard to believe that we could have taken that hill. We were so isolated. We were so on our own. It was like a mediaeval castle. Every man that day did his job. I didn't see everything. I didn't see Billy Parfray who got his arm almost blown off. He did an excellent job. Every man who went in with me should have been decorated but the Australian army don't do things like that.

'It was about 9 o'clock at night when they got us wounded blokes back down and the doctor had a go at us. The blokes helped us down with one on each arm and they skidded down the hillside. That bloody hurt, I can tell you.

'Teddy got one which skidded through the back of the

shoulder, one across the knee, two or three bullets or bits of shrapnel. He could still sort of half walk but he was using a rifle as a crutch, leaning on the barrel. When he cooled down he looked at it and saw there was one up the spout and the safety catch off. He was so annoyed at himself that he hurled the rifle off into the valley. One day somebody will find that rifle.'

Noel Pallier and Teddy Bear remained mates for the rest of their lives. After he recovered from his wounds, Teddy was chosen for officer training. He topped the course, won the Baton of Honour and served as a platoon commander in Borneo. After the war he named his son, Nolan, after his mate. Typically, he made no special mention of the name to Noel. It wasn't until young Nolan's wedding, many years later, that Noel received the confirmation he always suspected:

'It wasn't until the wedding breakfast that he told everyone how his son Nolan was named. He said he was lying on a hill in New Guinea, wounded with another bloke not far away, also wounded and he said: "If ever I have a son I'll call him after this fellow". He never said anything to me but he never forgot it. Typical Teddy.'

Teddy Bear was, in many ways, the embodiment of the Digger. He was a ready wit with an ever-present smile, a loyal mate. He worked his way through the ranks, serving his military apprenticeship as a private, then a corporal, in the Middle East, where he showed superb courage and leadership skills. At Isurava he rose to the occasion again, taking command of the platoon after his CO and sergeant had been killed and charging into the advancing enemy with a Bren gun.

He showed remarkable endurance and courage again after Isurava when, crippled by his wounds, he and a mate, Russ Fairbairn, took a fortnight to inch their way back down the Kokoda Track to Moresby. Because of his wounds, Teddy could only shuffle sideways. Russ had a bullet near his spine. Together they linked in a bizarre, excruciating marathon dance through the mud, across the streams and up and down the steep hills and gullies, pulling and pushing each other to safety. Both recovered.

Then Teddy came back for more in New Guinea and rose to new heights, passing on his skills to Noel Pallier as sergeant of his old platoon, a platoon which by war's end had won one Victoria Cross, one Distinguished Conduct Medal and seven Military Medals. Finally he rose to become an officer. It's hard to imagine a man better suited to lead in battle.

After the war Teddy reverted to the other, more dominant side of his personality and took a Diploma in Bible Studies. He and his wife Martha worked as youth counsellors in schools. Alzheimer's disease claimed Teddy in 1999.

The Japanese resistance in New Guinea was fatally undermined by the Battle of the Bismark Sea, which prevented their forces from being reinforced. The Australian 3rd Division took Lae and Salamaua and the 7th Division fought through the Markham Valley to win Dumpu. After bitter fighting around Shaggy Ridge, the 9th Division took Finschhafen. The Australian forces were then withdrawn home and readied for the last, island-hopping campaigns of 1944–45, which saw the Japanese threat finally extinguished.

In the final campaigns, public opinion had tired of the war. Many people, including Diggers, were questioning the necessity of risking lives in what became known as 'backyard' campaigns (mopping up Japanese forces that had been bypassed by the main Allied advance and left to wither on the vine). But, as the distinguished military historian Gavin Long wrote:

> *'Always a realist and therefore the more keenly aware of the probably doubtful value of the tasks to which he had been relegated, nevertheless the battle wise Australian soldier fought on to the end with the same devotion and skill that he had shown in the decisive battle of earlier years.'*

Ironically, the campaign to capture Balikpapan on Borneo in

July 1945, the last large-scale campaign of the Pacific war, was the biggest Australian joint-forces operation of World War II.

According to his biographer, William Manchester, MacArthur was aware of the doubts creeping into the troops as the war ground to an end. He exposed himself to danger by attending the landings at both Brunei and Balikpapan to assure the troops that he was not asking them to do something for which he himself had no stomach. Whether the Diggers who saw him regarded his actions the same way is open to debate. Nevertheless, the Australians fought with their customary flair and courage, and soon cracked the defences of the desperate, dug-in defenders.

By this stage the Americans had decided that they had suffered enough casualties (particularly after the bloody fighting at Iwo Jima and Okinawa) in trying to bring the Japanese to their knees. US military planners estimated it could cost another million casualties if they continued their current conventional operations to conquer Japan itself. They decided to use the atom bomb. The impact of that decision, first at Hiroshima and then at Nagasaki, brought the Japanese Emperor out of centuries of seclusion to surrender personally, telling his stunned people that they must 'endure the unendurable and suffer the insufferable'.

MacArthur accepted the surrender on board the US battleship *Missouri*, on 1 September 1945. General Sir Thomas Blamey signed the document on Australia's behalf. (Among the witnesses was Sergeant 'Bluey' Whitechurch, who won a Military Medal at Pallier's Hill.) General MacArthur captured the feeling of the moment:

'Today the guns are silent. A great tragedy had ended. A great victory has been won. The skies no longer rain death — the seas only bear commerce — men everywhere walk upright in the sunlight . . . and in reporting this to you, the people, I speak for the thousands of silent lips, forever stilled among the jungles and the beaches and in the deep waters of the Pacific which marked the way . . .'

By war's end, the Australian Army had suffered 18,000 deaths, 22,000 wounded and 20,000 prisoners of war out of the 400,000 who had served outside Australia. The Diggers of World War II had matched, and in many cases surpassed, the deeds of their fathers. They had enhanced the reputation of the Digger.

TWELVE

War in Korea

Sadly, the peace which the world so desperately hoped for after the end of World War II did not eventuate. While Australia struggled with the demobilisation of the half-million servicemen and women still in uniform at war's end, Europe and the Super Powers were embroiled in the tensions that became the Cold War.

With the Soviet Union's Joseph Stalin ruthlessly wielding power both at home and against his neighbours, the communist expansion began to gather pace. By 1948, Poland disappeared behind what Winston Churchill called the 'Iron Curtain'. Czechoslovakia followed soon after. Germany was split in half, with the communists controlling East Germany. A Soviet push to swallow Berlin was thwarted only when the Allies broke the blockade with a remarkable airlift of supplies. The communists also made rapid gains in Asia, taking control of the great prize of China when Mao Tse-tung defeated the Nationalists under Chiang Kai-shek. The French were struggling against the Viet Minh in Indo-China while Malaya, Burma and Indonesia were all trying to contain communist insurrectionists.

Many dreaded World War III. Indeed, the Americans prepared for that eventuality. They tried to counter the communist expansion: first, with the Marshall Plan, which provided aid to threatened nations; second, by joining with its

Western European allies to form a military alliance called the North Atlantic Treaty Organisation, or NATO.

But a test of strength between the two forces was inevitable. The showdown was eventually played out on what was effectively neutral ground – the remote Korean peninsula. Here, in the predawn of Sunday, 25 June 1950, the tension exploded into violence when the North Koreans, trained and backed by the Soviets, invaded South Korea, armed and trained by the USA. The North Koreans launched a massive artillery bombardment against the South Korean defences along the 38th parallel, the artificial boundary since 1945. Since 1910, Korea had been a Japanese Protectorate. After Japan's WWII capitulation there was a rush to fill the void. The Russians occupied the northern half, which contained most of the country's industries, while the Americans hurriedly countered with a blocking move into the southern half, which served as Korea's agricultural base. The Soviets provided the North Koreans with all the modern weapons of war. On the other hand, the Americans withheld many essential elements – tanks, heavy artillery and fighter planes – because they were concerned the South might try to conquer the North. Consequently, the South was no match for the might of the North, and within three days the communists overran them and captured many key southern cities, including the capital, Seoul.

The United Nations dismissed the absurd North Korean claim that it was not invading the South but merely defending itself against a South Korean invasion. The UN Security Council passed a motion calling for an immediate end to the conflict and demanding that North Korea withdraw its forces back above the 38th parallel. That same day, US President Harry Truman ordered General Douglas MacArthur, then in supreme command of the Occupation Forces in Japan, to use his forces to assist South Korea.

Then, for the first time in history, the UN Security Council called for member states to come to the aid of South Korea and

CHINA

Baishan

Tonghua

Hyesan

Kimch'aek

Sea of
Japan

Kanggye

NORTH
KOREA

Hungnam

Sinanju

Wonsan

PYONGYANG

Demarcation line 1953

Maryang San

38th Parallel

Kangnang

Sariwon

Chunchon

Kaesong

Kapyong

UN line
24th Jan 1951

SEOUL

Inchon

Wonju

Suwon

Ch'onan

Andong

Pohang

SOUTH
KOREA

Taejon

Kunsan

Taegu

Kyongju

Masan

Pusan

Kwangju

Sunchon

Mokpo

Yellow

Sea

N

Cheju

Cheju-do

0   kilometres   200

to help it repel the attack. Truman proposed MacArthur as commander of the UN forces in Korea, and the participating nations agreed. Australia was one of the first countries to answer the call, first with the RAN's frigate HMAS *Shoalhaven* and then with the destroyer HMAS *Bataan*. Operating in his usual style, using carefully controlled press releases, MacArthur requested the use of the RAAF Mustang Squadron, stationed in Japan, then promptly released his request to the world media. An embarrassed Robert Menzies agreed to the request.

Realising the North Koreans were relying on their surprise attack to conquer the South before the rest of the world could react, MacArthur called for, and received, US Infantry troops to bolster the collapsing South Korean Army. The RAN and the RAAF Mustangs were in action early as the UN forces tried to slow down the North Korean advance sufficiently to deploy their ground troops.

Australia's first casualty was Squadron Leader Graham Strout, killed in action during an air strike against the railway at Samchok. The RAAF played a prominent role in the crucial air defence, which harassed the North Korean advance and allowed the UN land forces to make a difference. MacArthur, in what turned out to be a master stroke, split his forces: landing the US 10th Corps at Inchon, on the eastern coast, level with Seoul and well behind the then front line; and the US 8th Army in the South. He trapped the North Koreans in the pincer and cut their supply route. They faltered and then collapsed under the weight of MacArthur's forces. By 29 September the UN forces had driven the North Koreans out of the South and MacArthur was able to hand back Seoul to its South Korean president, Dr Syngman Rhee.

The Australian contingent, the 3rd Royal Australian Regiment, was below full strength when the war came. It was brought up to its full complement by a special recruiting campaign which drew an enthusiastic response, including a substantial number of experienced WWII combat troops.

3 RAR arrived two days before MacArthur reclaimed Seoul and missed most of the fighting. But they were soon called into action. The UN forces, led by the USA, decided to take advantage of the defeat of the North Korean forces by continuing their advance past the 38th parallel and driving the communists before them. The ultimate aim was to unite Korea under the control of Syngman Rhee.

The Australians' first major battle was near the North Korean capital of Pyongyang. Here the 3rd Battalion was part of the general advance across the 38th parallel. It passed through Pyongyang to reach Yongju, where it was ordered to help relieve US paratroopers who were in difficulty. The Australians performed superbly. They claimed 270 North Korean dead at a cost of just four wounded. The British commander of the Commonwealth Brigade to which they were attached later wrote:

'I saw a marvellous sight. An Australian platoon lined up in a paddy field and walked through it as though they were driving snipe. The soldiers when they saw a pile of straw, kicked it and out would bolt a North Korean. Up with a rifle, down with a North Korean and the Australians thoroughly enjoyed it.'

Towards the end of October the North Korean forces seemed to be at the end of their tether, and it looked as if the UN forces would push right to the border between North Korea and China. But MacArthur had ignored a series of warnings from China that if he continued to advance they would intervene. On 27 October 1950, as the winter set in, 27 divisions of Chinese troops, 300,000 in all, attacked without further warning.

MacArthur completely misjudged the situation and, while he was sending out a press release advising what he called his final 'decisive effort in Korea', the Chinese split the UN forces with a massive thrust, decimating the South Korean Corps and savaging the US 8th Army. The US 2nd Division lost one-third of its troops during the disastrous withdrawal.

The Chinese assault pushed the UN forces out of Pyongyang and then drove them south. By 4 January 1951, Seoul was again in North Korean hands. The UN successfully counterattacked and, for the fourth time in under a year, the South Korean capital changed hands.

MacArthur renewed his call for an all-out attack against China. But, by this stage Truman had had enough: 'We are trying to prevent a world war, not to start one.' On 11 April, he shocked both America and the world when he announced he was replacing the great man with General Matthew Ridgeway. The move signalled a renewed drive by the Chinese. Once again they broke through the UN defensive line, and 3 RAR, which had been relieved and was resting at Charidai, was ordered on an hour's notice to shore up the Kapyong Valley where the Chinese threatened to break through.

The South Korean division defending the area had broken, and was retreating down the Kapyong River Valley with the Chinese hard on its heels. The Australians established a defensive position where the river and another stream joined. The Chinese took advantage of the South Korean retreat and joined in the chaotic flow of Korean troops. In the confusion, some Chinese troops slipped behind the Australians. Captain Reg Saunders, the first Aborigine to win a commission in the Australian Army (and brother of Harry Saunders, a gallant and much-loved member of the 2/14th Battalion in World War II who died at Gona), recognised the danger, as quoted in Norman Bartlett's *With the Australians in Korea*:

> *'The clamour on our front became easily recognisable as that of a defeated army in retreat. I had heard it before in Greece and Crete and earlier in Korea. I must admit I felt a little dejected until I realised I was an Australian company commander and if my morale got low then I couldn't expect much from my troops. This served to buck me and I lay down in a shallow trench and had a little sleep.*

'The sound of small-arms fire awoke me and soon after the crash of tank cannon in B Company area. I could also see flashes of fire coming from the direction of battalion headquarters and I realised that the enemy were now in a good position to cut off the companies.'

The Chinese launched a series of human-wave assaults against the Diggers. But, in another example of the endurance and courage of the Digger, the men of 3 RAR overcame the odds, as the official historian of the Korean War, Robert O'Neill, wrote:

'The Chinese seemed to have enormous numerical superiority and their attacks increased in frequency to become one continuous onrush of troops. All three Bren gunners of the 1 Platoon were killed or wounded and the fighting strength of the platoon was reduced from thirty to thirteen.'

Yet another Anzac combination played a crucial role: the New Zealand artillery helped the Diggers hold their ground under these relentless assaults by bringing their fire to within 50 metres of the Australian positions. The Diggers, the US 72nd Tank Battalion and the Canadian Princess Patricia's Light Infantry Battalion, fighting alongside each other and supported by the 16th NZ Field Regiment, eventually weathered this firestorm. They inflicted massive casualties on the Chinese, who eventually broke off the attack.

It transpired that the three UN units had withstood an attack by a full Chinese division. The Australians had lost 32 dead and 59 wounded, but the Chinese death toll was between 500 and 600. Ironically, some of the heaviest fighting had taken place on Anzac Day 1951. All three units received a Presidential Unit Citation for heroism. The citation read in part:

'. . . the seriousness of the breakthrough on the central front had been changed from defeat to victory by the gallant stand of these heroic soldiers [who] displayed such gallantry, determination and esprit de corps in accomplishing their mission under extremely difficult and hazardous conditions as to set them apart and above other units participating in the

campaign and by their achievements they brought distin-
guished credit on themselves, their homelands and all
freedom-loving nations.'

The Chinese offensive petered out by the end of April. The
Chinese had suffered 70,000 casualties, compared to the UN's
7000. By 15 June, when the UN forces had recaptured the
ground as far as what became known as the Kansas Line,
north of the 38th parallel and south of the Imjin River, both
sides entered into a series of cease-fire talks. The talks initially
attracted great optimism, as both sides appeared to accept that
their original aims of a total victory over their opposition were
unrealistic. No-one could have predicted that the talks would
drag on for another two years and one month before an
armistice was finally concluded.

In the meantime, on 28 July, the Australians became part of
the 1st Commonwealth Division under British Major General
Jim Cassels. This division, in turn, formed part of the US 1
Corps under US Lieutenant General John 'Iron Mike'
O'Daniel, a renowned gung-ho leader in the Patton mould.

In October 1951, the Commonwealth Division joined three
other UN divisions in 'Operation Commando', an advance
designed to adjust the front line and eliminate the Chinese
advantage over some of the high ground. General O'Daniel
placed the Commonwealth Division in the vanguard of the
attack and ordered the Diggers of 3 RAR to capture a steep
hill, called Maryang San by the locals and known as Hill 317
by the UN forces.

The Diggers were now commanded by Lieutenant Colonel
Frank Hassett, a 33-year-old Duntroon graduate who had
proven himself with a fine record in the Middle East and the
Pacific in World War II. He wrote of his first impressions of
his men, as quoted in *The Battle of Maryang San*, by the
Australian Army HQ Training Command:

'I found the battalion in good heart, though some thought they
were being forgotten by Australia. All looked fit, lean and con-
fident, as they were entitled to do after performing so well in

*their first arduous winter campaign, culminating in their epic
defence at Kapyong. There were more older soldiers in 3 RAR
then than I was to see in later years in our regular battalions.*

'*Many were K Force volunteers, patriotic and adventurous
young men fired up by experiences and stories of the Second
World War. The battalion reminded me very much of Second
World War battalions after a hard campaign. These were
warriors, in the sense that their job was to close with the enemy
with butt and bayonet and they had done this well.*'

Before the battle, Hassett assigned specific tasks to his
various company commanders. One of them was Major 'Basil'
Hardiman, commander of D Company:

'*About a week before the big operation the CO called an officers'
conference. I don't recall the details but afterwards Colonel
Frank [Hassett] asked me to come down to his caravan. After
the pleasantries, such as enjoying a can of beer, he told me of the
projected operation and that my company had been selected to
lead an assault on the final objective – Hill 317 (Maryang San).
I thought of that steep, totally bare, conically shaped hill rising
sheer out of the valley. It seemed an impossible task. I must have
gone pale and looked awful, bad enough for Colonel Frank to
say – "Are you alright Bas?" I am positive that for a second my
heart actually stopped – skipped a beat – it was as if I had just
received a death sentence. However I hastily gulped down the
rest of my beer, managed a smile and said I was fine.*'

Frank Hassett was well aware of the task facing his battalion, as he recalled:

'*The battalion was given an enormous task – a long approach
march with open flanks and an attack to a depth of over 3000
metres against a well-equipped, well-sited enemy, determined to
stay. Further, two companies had been designated as Brigade
reserve and there was no telling what they would have to do in
this role or what shape they would be in when they returned to
the battalion.*'

Frank Hassett also succinctly summed up both the lone-
liness of the commanding officer in these circumstances and

the emotional differences between him and the men he is about to place in harm's way:

'Only the CO has the time, the background detail perhaps the experience to appreciate fully the problems and inherent dangers in an operation of this nature. At the company level and below a spirit of excitement, adventure and confidence prevailed. It was only sensible to leave it like that.'

The battle began in the early hours of 3 October 1951, with two companies of 3 RAR starting their advance on Maryang San at 3 am. By 8 am they had taken their first objective, Hill 199, and were joined by British Centurion tanks. The Diggers had surprised even themselves, as 7 Platoon Commander Lieutenant Maurie Pears, recalled:

'We were down to two sections but this was unknown to us. Somehow we reached the top of the feature and sheltered behind some rocks. The enemy was firmly entrenched and opposing further movement with small arms fire. We sent one section to flank from the left whilst we held the ridge line. They made no progress.

'We sheltered behind granite boulders which seemed the size of peanuts, trying to contact the reserve for some help but contact was lost. At this stage Jack Gerke got fed up with waiting and so did the Bren gunner Jim Burnett. Jack screamed up with his trusty McFadzean and urged us forward. Burnett blasted onwards with his Bren at the hip, Mark Young with the Owen, and the remaining elements of 7 Platoon (about eight of us) surged on to the position.

'The sight of these desperate, wild-eyed Australians must have been too much for the Chinese. They withdrew. But they left 19 dead and 3 prisoners were taken. The guts and determination of Gerke, Burnett and Young and his leading section had won the day. It was a substantial victory against overwhelming odds. My overall memories are of total confusion and amazement that we were not all killed.'

Two days later, under cover of thick mist, B and D Companies 3 RAR, with Centurions in support, attacked the eastern ridge of Maryang San itself. Despite the earlier successes, the final assault was a prodigious task. The Diggers had to cover a kilometre to the first Chinese defences and then another 1500 metres through a mutually supporting Chinese bunker system. Although they didn't know it at the time, the 320 Australians faced around 1200 fresh Chinese infantry troops.

The Diggers performed with great dash and spirit, and their swift advance made quick inroads on the lower Chinese defences, as Private Jim McFadzean later wrote:

'. . . D Company made a magnificent contribution, literally tearing the heart out of the Chinese positions on the lower features leading to 317 [Maryang San]. In these actions D Company killed 68 Chinese, wounded a large number and took 30 prisoners. Their cost was three killed and 14 wounded. Surprise, speed and aggression had won the day.'

Frank Hassett then called on Captain Jack Gerke's C Company to make the final attack on the summit of Maryang San. Climbing on hands and knees because of the steepness of the terrain, Gerke's men launched an outstanding assault on the summit, taking the defenders by surprise and winning the ground before nightfall. Frank Hassett:

'I judged C Company's immediate follow-up to be a faultless performance; the company did everything right, from ready acceptance of a most difficult task, to the sweeping over Pt 317 [Maryang San] with great dash, to providing depth to its position at first light the following day. I mentally gave full marks to Jack Gerke. Not many officers could take on that sort of task and execute it so well.

'Too few realise how often battles turn on the efforts of a handful of gallant infantry. There were thousands of men in the Commonwealth Division and Maryang San was a principal objective. Yet in the final assault on the last major feature in front of Point 317 the attacking platoon led by Clark was less than half strength, down to some 17 men, its losses including the platoon sergeant and two of the three section commanders.

'The platoon was in no way deterred by its casualties, of the *fact that every advantage was with the Chinese – numbers, volume of small arms fire, deep cover and pre-planned mortar and artillery fire. Nor was it a blind rush by 11 Platoon. Its tactics were good and the supporting fire, including that from the other two platoons, carefully laid on.*

'I have used 11 Platoon as an example, the other platoons were equally good. It is small wonder that, over the years, experienced commanders have stressed the need for good infantry and have often waxed lyrical in its praise.'

The Diggers of 3 RAR earned their place alongside the finest feats of arms achieved by their predecessors. Jack Gerke and Frank Hassett both won Distinguished Service Orders for their roles at Maryang San. Maurie Pears won one of ten Military Crosses awarded for gallantry there:

'I have a lot of fragmentary and disconnected memories of this attack and the aftermath. A visit to the Norwegian MASH; my first sight of a Swedish female; finding a piece of meat in the ham and beans; smoking three packets of Camels a day; dreaming of Dawn Lake in the concert party; the humour of men under woeful conditions; Mark Young pulling me into line when my inexperience showed; the always cheerful Reg Whalley reduced to tears having to sew up the dead – he grieved for all of us; the misery of the misplaced Koreans; sleeping in the snow or in a hole in the ground; putting Barbosal on the frostbite; ripping the skin on frozen gun barrels; spraying DDT on the hair and crotch to get rid of the lice; McFadzean groaning under the weight of the WS [wireless set]; *the courage of the stretcher bearer, Bill Massey; 'Horse' Goggin firing a 3-inch mortar without bipod or baseplate; Morrison passing the bottle around for collective urine to cool the Vickers; arguing with Karl Schmidt about who would cover who and his saying "Do as you are bloody well told, Sir, or we'll both be bloody killed". We were battle weary but stood up to it well.*

'But the deep and enduring memories are those of the men who saved my life and shaped my future. I am in their debt. I have seen little of them since that time and wonder how those

men who deserved so much have fared. I fear they are yesterday's heroes left with yesterday's promises.'

In addition, 3 RAR won two Distinguished Conduct Medals and ten Military Medals, and another 13 Diggers were Mentioned in Dispatches. Frank Hassett would become general and be rewarded with a knighthood for his contribution to Australia's military, but Maryang San always held a special meaning for him:

'The fighting of 3rd battalion at Maryang San was a sequence of stories of ordinary soldiers rescuing their mates, plugging gaps, pushing on hard, ignoring wounds to stay in the fight. They were not fearless in the sense of impetuous or hot-headed. They were prepared to accept great risks, they knew what had to be done and they were determined to do it.

'There are plenty of brave soldiers the world over, and some of them are very skilful also. But it is the added qualities of commonsense, initiative and concern for his fellows, so amply demonstrated by 3 RAR at Maryang San, that put the Australian soldier in a class apart. Unquestionably, the soldiers won the Maryang San battle, not just because they were brave, but because they were smart also. They recognised that, if we were to get 317 [Maryang San] at all, let alone without massive casualties, then they would have to move quickly. This they did.

'There was no heroes' welcome home for these warriors. They left from Australia as individuals or in small groups and returned the same way, unheralded and unsung. Somehow, it did not seem to matter. There was much quiet satisfaction just in knowing one had fought at Maryang San.'

The Korean War dragged on until an armistice ended hostilities on 27 July 1953. The Australian contribution was modest in numbers but substantial in quality. In all, just over 18,000 Australians served in our armed forces in Korea, around 11,000 of them from the Army. During the war 293 Diggers gave their lives, of the total of 339 killed in action and 1216 wounded from all three services.

::

Our involvement in Korea under the United Nations banner won widespread support at home and gained us considerable respect internationally. It would be a different story in our next major conflict in Vietnam.

THIRTEEN

The Vietnam War

'There's the smell of sweat, there's the smell of blokes who've pissed themselves. There's the smell of the gunfire and the projectile propellant, cordite or gunpowder. There's the smell of the rice and the smell of the explosives. I can smell it right now.'

Dennis 'Arab' Ayoub, retired Australian Army major and Vietnam veteran, relives his first firefight as a young sapper in Vietnam:

'When an action starts there's the smell of leaves being broken and branches being torn off and earth being kicked up and there's the dry earth and there's the wet earth and there's the smell of that. As people are scrambling through the leaves and the decaying layer of flora on the floor of the jungle, there's the smell of that stuff. I can tell you exactly what they are. I don't care how you train a soldier, you can't prepare him for that. To do that you'd almost have to kill a bloke and that's not the idea.

'It's not the firefight. It's these smells which stay with you for the rest of your life. And the noise. The noise levels are immense. All these dimensions of noise . . . wack wack, wack, boom, wack, wack, wack, brrrt, wack wack. And yelling, "Get here", "Get that fucking gun here!" And all these are compacted. A cacophony of sound.

'But to me the jungle is a comforting smell. I like sleeping in the jungle. If I went back to the Daintree, I'd fall in love with it again.'

Southeast Asia, 1965

Dennis Ayoub was one of the 47,000 Diggers who served in Vietnam during what was Australia's longest war. It started when our first training team landed at Tan Son Nhut Airport in Saigon on 3 August 1962 and lasted until our troops were finally withdrawn in December 1972. At the height of our involvement, our Vietnam contingent reached a maximum of about 8000 Diggers. Our total casualties were 520 killed and 2400 wounded.

But these bald figures in no way reflect the impact of the war on the Australian psyche. It was the first war in which we'd fought without Britain. It was the first war the United States ever lost. It was the first war played out in living rooms, via television, particularly in the USA, where the graphic images had a substantial impact on public opinion. And while the Australian troops involved were never defeated there in any battle, their presence in Vietnam cleft our nation in two. For the first time in our history, while our Diggers were away fighting, large crowds of Australians at home were protesting at their involvement; some were even marching under the enemy's flag and collecting funds to support that enemy against them. It was a division that would have a deep and lasting impact on many of the Diggers. For the first time, when they returned home, Diggers would be treated as pariahs and not as honoured veterans by a significant propor-tion of the Australian people. Their treatment has long rankled with many Vietnam vets, as the former commander of 3 Field Troop there, Colonel Alec 'Sandy' McGregor, recalled:

'When our Vietnam vets came back, they were put on the plane and while they were on it they were told to get into their civvy clothes. They arrived at midnight and were given a briefing: "Don't talk about the war. It's a year out of your life. Forget about it. The public don't like it. The press don't like it. Don't talk about it".'

Australia's involvement in the Vietnam War was a gradual process. At the start few Australians had any idea where Vietnam was, let alone what was happening in this far-away country where our Diggers were required to fight. Dennis Ayoub's introduction was probably typical:

> *'Our Staff Sergeant Major stood out on the parade ground one day and said: "I need some volunteers for a place called Vientiane". (Along with most of us, he'd never heard of this place called Vietnam.)*
>
> *'I was 18. I didn't even know where Melbourne was. I didn't even know where the ACT was. Almost all of our troop volunteered to go, with some exceptions, some who were married, some too young or inexperienced, etc.'*

Following the recently completed Korean War, the balance of the region was upset irreparably when the French were comprehensively defeated at their base at Dien Bien Phu, in central North Vietnam, in May 1954. The communist-controlled Viet Minh (who were supplied by China and Russia) bombarded, then laid siege to Dien Bien Phu. In a clear sign of things to come in the Vietnam War, the French hopelessly underestimated the tenacity and fighting capacity of their foes. In a superhuman feat, the Viet Minh dismantled and dragged artillery pieces up through the dense highlands surrounding Dien Bien Phu, then battered the 16,000-strong French garrison into submission by smashing their airstrip and surrounding them with 50,000 Viet Minh troops.

While a stunned world watched and sat on its hands, after a 55-day siege the garrison was forced to surrender. Under the subsequent Geneva Accords, signed on 21 July 1954, France lost her South-East Asian colonies and Vietnam was spilt in half, east–west, along the 17th parallel, with an 8-kilometre-wide Demilitarised Zone (or DMZ) along the border. North Vietnam fell under communist control while South Vietnam was briefly governed by the Emperor Bao Dai and then, in late 1955, became the Republic of Vietnam under President Dinh Diem. Diem and his brother Nhu were assassinated on 2 November 1963. More or less continual political instability followed.

Fearing further communist expansion in the region, the US-led Western nations formed the South-East Asia Treaty Organisation (or SEATO). Under it, the United States, the United Kingdom, France, Australia, New Zealand, Thailand, the Philippines and Pakistan agreed they would act in concert to defend military aggression against any of the signatories. They also designated 'protocol' states, whose security was guaranteed by the treaty. One of these was South Vietnam.

The gradual escalation of the communist forces in South Vietnam, from a few thousand in 1959 to more than 100,000 by 1964, saw a reciprocal growth in US military 'advisers' until they'd reached 16,000 in 1963. President Diem made a plea for assistance to the world's anti-communist heads of state, including Prime Minister Sir Robert Menzies, in early 1962. Then the United States put pressure on the Australian government for advisers, citing our proven expertise in jungle fighting, and Menzies agreed to commit our first training team of 30 instructors in May 1962.

Retired Colonel Mike McDermott served as a young lieutenant on what was officially known as the Australian Army Training Team Vietnam but became known as 'the Team':

'I went to Da Nang. I was flown out by Air America, the air arm of the CIA and I flew past this area the crew called "Death Valley". "You don't want to go up there sir", said the pilot.

'I had a job there for about three weeks when I was supposed to be acclimatised and then I was located further south, about 30k, and then, sure enough, where did they send me back to, Death Valley, and that's where I spent most of my time. I found out later the Americans had lost 2000 killed and 14,000 wounded there. The Vietnamese lost more. And it wasn't a very big valley.'

Many members of the Team worked, like Mike McDermott, with the indigenous tribes of the central highlands mountains in Vietnam, known by the French collective name of Montagnard. These tribes – 30 or more distinct groups – were formed into paramilitary units, which then harassed the communist lines of supply into South Vietnam. One of the most remarkable operators among the Team members there was a 28-year-old Queenslander, Captain Arthur Barry Petersen. Barry Petersen's war experiences with the Montagnard tribes in the Darlac Province in South Vietnam's central highlands read like a chapter out of a Robert Ludlum thriller. In fact, many believe he was the inspiration for the central character in Francis Ford Coppola's acclaimed movie *Apocalypse Now*. For two years Barry Petersen ran an independent field operation based out of the Darlac Province capital, Ban-Me-Thout. His work was supplied and funded by the US Central Intelligence Agency but he had unfettered operational control.

First, he learned the languages and won the confidence of the local tribes. Then, training them in groups of 100, he amassed a Montagnard army of more than 1000 tribesmen. He was so successful he was made a tribal chieftain and given the name 'Dam San', after a legendary Rhade tribal warrior who was never defeated in battle. Barry Petersen effectively became a Montagnard warlord. He adopted the native dress and led his men in battle against the Viet Cong (the Vietnamese communists) in an endless cycle of raids, ambushes and patrols aimed at disrupting their infiltration and destroying their supplies and crops. He designed a tiger badge for his troops, and they became known as the 'Tiger Men' of Truong Son Force.

However, the Montagnards' ultimate aim was independence, and they harboured a deep distrust of the South Vietnamese that regularly threatened to undermine their relationship. In late 1964, Petersen's intervention averted a major Montagnard revolt against the South Vietnamese government. It brought him praise from the US Commander in Chief but was to prove his undoing. Mike McDermott explained:

They flew in General Westmoreland and Peterson briefed him and Westmoreland said to the CIA: "Why can't the Americans

*do this? Why does it have to be an Australian to be so success-
ful?" Peterson knew that was the death of his whole tour
because the CIA would withdraw their support because they'd
been publicly embarrassed in front of their chief. He was then
kicked out of Vietnam by the South Vietnamese because they
saw he had too much power.*

*'He used to wear a skirt and a little vest and he got a Cross of
Gallantry with the Silver Star from the Vietnamese Army. The
Australian Army sent him back as a company commander. He
wasn't allowed to go back to the north because he might lead
them in a revolt. I would say the CIA would still have him under
surveillance.'*

Barry Petersen also won the Military Cross for his gallantry
in Vietnam. Another of that remarkable Team was Warrant
Officer Kevin 'Dasher' Wheatley, who was training and
serving with a Vietnamese/Montagnard unit in Quang Ngai
Province when they came under attack in November 1965.
For his heroic and selfless act in staying with his wounded
comrade, Warrant Officer R.J. Swanton, when his South
Vietnamese troops broke and left them after they were
overrun by a large Viet Cong force, Dasher Wheatley posthumously won the Victoria Cross – the first awarded to a
Digger since World War II and the first of four won by
members of the Team.

Somehow, Wheatley dragged his mate more than 200
metres under heavy fire through the open paddy field, where
they had been ambushed, to the edge of the jungle. He held off
the attackers until he ran out of ammunition. Then he was
seen to pull the pins from two hand grenades and to coolly
await the oncoming enemy. Some time later observers heard
two grenade explosions, then several bursts of machine-gun
fire. At first light they found the two bodies side by side. In the
highest traditions of the Digger, Dasher Wheatley had refused
to leave his mate.

The other members of the Team to win VCs were Major
Peter Badcoe, a bespectacled, scholarly character, renowned

for his fearlessness in combat, who won his VC posthumously for gallantry in a series of actions on 23 February, 7 March and 7 April 1967; Warrant Officer Ray Simpson, for actions on 6 May and 11 May 1969, when, while commanding a South Vietnamese company, he made a lone stand covering his troops as they recovered their wounded during a fighting with-drawal; and Warrant Officer Keith Payne, for a similar series of incidents in Kontum Province at the end of May that year. Ray Simpson was another remarkable Digger, having served in World War II, Japan, Korea and Malaya, prior to his three tours with the Team.

Keith Payne's citation for the VC pointed out his 'repeated acts of exceptional personal bravery and unselfish conduct in this operation . . . an inspiration to all Vietnamese, United States and Australian soldiers who served with him.' Both Keith Payne and Ray Simpson survived the conflict.

Lieutenant General Sir Thomas Daly, the Australian Army chief for most of the Vietnam War, summed up his views of the Team in a letter to the Team's CO on 30 July 1969:

'It is always rewarding talking to these chaps [Team members]. *They are the salt of the earth and all those who know them cannot but be inspired by the tremendous job they are doing for Vietnam and Australia.'*

In April 1965 the Australian government agreed to an American request and sent a battalion, the 1st Battalion Royal Australian Regiment, to Vietnam to work alongside the US 173rd Airborne Brigade in the Bien Hoa-Vung Tau region. It marked a new phase in the war. The Americans were rapidly building up their forces in Vietnam – from around 80,000 to more than 200,000 during 1965. The Australians settled into operations similar to those conducted by their forebears in Kokoda and New Guinea in World War II and in the 'Malaya Emergency'. One of the platoon commanders was the young Lieutenant Peter Cosgrove. He'd been in Vietnam for less than a month when he led his platoon in a sustained action in which he won the Military Cross.

Today he declines to talk about that action, but others recall the young Lieutenant Cosgrove as a platoon commander brimming with energy and exuding a natural leadership. A burly rugby second-rower, he was tough, forthright and decisive, and clearly relished a physical challenge. But he also showed another deeply rooted characteristic, which has flourished as he has gained experience and perspective: compassion. This was perhaps his most widely respected character trait when he later came to prominence as the commander of the Interfet force in East Timor and subsequently as the Commander in Chief of our defence forces.

In Vietnam, Peter Cosgrove's platoon was out on patrol when it found itself confronted by Viet Cong forces on three sides. Cosgrove instinctively summed up his options and immediately ordered his men to do the one thing the enemy did not expect: attack.

Peter Cosgrove's training kicked in. Realising he was outnumbered and outgunned, he reasoned his men's best chance rested on a surprise breakout before the enemy's superior numbers could be brought to bear and ultimately overpower his Diggers. Lieutenant Cosgrove's determination and leadership under fire enabled his platoon to wrest the initiative from the Viet Cong and eventually to prevail. He credits the calibre of the Diggers he led:

You learn all kinds of things. You learn a lot about yourself because the Diggers mirror in their own reactions how you're performing and perhaps the strengths and flaws of your own character.

'I was on the steepest learning curve imaginable. Leaving Duntroon as one of its less promising graduates, about half way up the class, I think I probably had some strengths which suited me for infantry, I was a pretty determined player of sport – a knockabout sort of a figure, not afraid of hard work or the sort of privations of infantry life, so I would have carried that with me but into a totally unknown environment.

'I was very lucky, I had a bit of an apprenticeship as a young commander with a quite experienced and polyglot lot of soldiers in 1 RAR in Malaysia where I was a team commander for four or five months effectively before going off to Vietnam. So I was technically not too bad and I'd also had this experience with good NCOs helping me and sort of training me before I took over this bunch of hard cases in Vietnam.

'All of these guys had been there a while and there was a trickle flow of reinforcements coming in and old hands moving on but the nucleus of this mob had been together since before the battalion went on operations.'

Peter Cosgrove went in as a 'Reo' (a reinforcement officer), taking command of an existing platoon. He was the new boy. Luckily, he inherited a well-trained team with good NCOs:

'The team had its own discipline and jungle skills. These were all good. So they were quite confident in each other, they just had to find me out.

'And I was pretty shy. But shy's not quite the right term because you actually had to make decisions and give orders and go around and talk to people. But I suppose I held back a little simply so that I wouldn't offend by coming on too strong, not in terms of the decisions but in terms of establishing rapport. That was probably reasonable.'

Peter Cosgrove joined his platoon while it was on an operation, one which had by then become somewhat routine to his men. They knew they could handle the heat. They weren't so sure about the new bloke. For his part, Cosgrove faced a timeless question which most men, and all Diggers, ask themselves at some time: how will I react when my turn comes to face combat? Cosgrove:

'I can remember on one of the first battles – I think it might have been the first one – that the medic in the platoon was giving me a sort of idiot grin as we were moving through on what was called "the sweep" – you've fired at the enemy, they've fired at you and then you start to advance on them. It's actually an attack. And this guy glanced across at me and afterwards

I said to him "What were you grinning about?" and I realised it was pure relief on his part because I was doing my job.

'I was very lucky the training kicked in, all the drills you do, all the fellows were rearing to go so I didn't have to argue the toss with anybody or make an intricate one hour plan. It was quite plain that we'd been shooting in this particular area at people who'd been shooting back. This is in deep jungle, so we just did a left hook with one of the sections and I went with the section and we killed some enemy in that battle. So, from that point of view, we'd resolved the danger to ourselves very emphatically and I'd answered some questions from myself, I'd answered some questions on their behalf I guess, and off we went.

'About the only thing they were concerned about was that every platoon gets a little battle weary, especially if they've seen soldiers who were comrades being carted off wounded progressively during the year, or dead, so a new boy comes in full of enthusiasm.'

The 'new boy' remembers clearly his baptism of fire. His platoon had stopped advancing up a track because they'd received a radio message ordering them to pause while HQ made inquiries to ensure there were no friendly forces in their path:

'It was a track that looked like it had had a lot of use, so we stopped with a section across the track, the other two sections from the edge of it all the way round to the back. We put a machine gun facing up the track and I put a sentry at the front of the machine gun and we settled back quietly to wait for them while we sorted out further permission to continue up the track.'

Although they'd seen signs of a Viet Cong bunker system nearby, the Aussies weren't aware that it was, in fact, within striking distance of them and that the occupants had already detected their arrival in the area:

'Maybe they smelt us. Maybe they heard some movement in the bush. Anyway they came sneaking out of the camp along the same track to see what it was that had occurred and our sentry *saw them coming and fired at them and then came zooming back into our position.*

'We engaged the area and then we attacked the area where we'd seen them and we killed them – killed two and one went away about a zillion miles an hour and we knew he was wounded.

'I remember when the first shots rang out and I rushed forward to the machine-gun about the same time that our man was zooming back in. As soon as he was safe with us, we fired into the area. The only inertia was that I was firing into the area and the officer really ought to be thinking "OK good you're all fine, that's good".

'Then one of my corporals said "I've closed up on the left" and I said "Good. We'll do the sweep from the left". I supposed there was five seconds or so when I was shooting like a soldier would be shooting instead of thinking like an officer should be thinking. There are times when you think and times when you shoot.'

Like a footballer after he makes the first tackle in the game, Peter Cosgrove was then able to relax sufficiently to allow his training to kick in as a reflex action:

'I went from not having a clue what combat's like to saying well, that's what it's like, and the transition was instantaneous. I suppose I'd been carrying around a certain sense of anxious expectation from when I was warned to go to Vietnam. Back in Malaya I got told you're going to go to be a reinforcement and then you'll go on to be an infantry platoon commander in Vietnam.

'Probably from that time somewhere back then must have been this sense of anxious anticipation or expectation and it probably reflected itself in checking things all the time and being almost paranoid about the accuracy of navigation and that sort of thing. All the things – where, when – and if the moment arrives you want to make sure that you've done all you can in preparation.

'I felt sorry that my men had to break in a new officer, where their anxieties were heightened by the fact that I had in my

hands and in my brain, so to speak, the authority and oppor-
tunity to put them in much more danger than was reasonable.
I could do so by getting it wrong, that's obvious. I could even do
so by being very right but being very aggressive.'

One of Peter Cosgrove's main concerns was the responsibility he had as a platoon commander for the safety of his men.
He developed a compelling devotion to maintaining his
vigilance:

'I didn't want to entertain the remotest whiff of slackness
because the moment you take your eye off the ball that's when
you get hurt. I remember late in my tour when I was command-
ing a different platoon my soldiers suffered the only casualties
that my various platoons suffered while I was the boss.

'I sent out a half platoon patrol to check on a particular area
and to get from where we had spent the night to where I wanted
them to do the job involved passing down what you might call a
geographic jug point – a tall hill with a spur line leading off it,
a brief flat part and then a swamp. And the swamp was just the
edge of a little canal where sampans and fishing boats ply their
trade.

'It seemed to me that this little jug point – the little flat
part – was a good spot to get ambushed. So I said to the fellow I
put in charge of this half platoon: "Mate, remember, don't use
that. Go up the hill a bit." And we settled down. I was staying
round this little jungle base I'd set up on this day and they'd been
gone for about twenty minutes when, boom! They got hit by a
claymore mine – knocked over the first three guys.

'They'd used the flat part and the enemy had thought "Oh
we've seen those guys use the flat part a bit". So they set up a
mine, blew up the first three blokes. The mob I had back at the
base and I ran forward and I thought my heart was going to
burst. We ran about a kilometre and a half through ankle deep
soft sand in our webbing and rifles.

'When we got there we found that they were in a bit of
disarray. They'd sort of recovered to the point of being ready to
defend themselves. But the blokes who'd hit them with the mine

had shot through very smartly. We made an error and it was because we took the soft option.'

Vietnam once again brought out the ingenuity in the Digger. One of the most outstanding examples was the way our engineers reacted to the discovery of what turned out to be an extensive labyrinth of tunnels from which the Viet Cong were waging war. From the start of their tour, the engineer unit of 1 RAR, under Major Sandy McGregor, found themselves delousing all manner of booby traps and unexploded bombs. In early 1966, during 'Operation Crimp', the Australian battalion was with the Americans in the Ho Bo Woods, about 20 kilometres north of Cu Chi in the Binh Duong Province, when it stumbled on an underground bunker system. Sandy McGregor's mob was called in. He recalled that before he left Australia he'd been primed to expect anything:

'I'll always remember when we were about to leave, I asked my commander: "Precisely what do we do over there? What's our main task?" He said: "McGregor. Go and do what engineers do!" You know I only realised later how wonderful that was: do whatever you need to do.'

Up to that stage, when the Americans discovered a tunnel, they had dropped a smoke grenade down it, blown air through it to locate the other entrances by observing where the smoke emerged, then blown the tunnel up. They, and their commanders, had regarded it as beneath them to actually chase the Viet Cong down the tunnels. Sandy McGregor's mob saw things differently:

'We decided the best thing to do was to go into them. I had assumed that the Americans were also going into them. My theory was that if the enemy was living and working down there, that there had to be one hell of a lot of intelligence down there, number one: weapons, ammunition and that sort of thing; but the second thing is that darkness is a great leveller.

'Out in the bush Australians became second to none. They're bloody good bush soldiers and, in the darkness, they took them on. In tunnels, it was the same thing. It's a great leveller. They're scared that we're coming in. We're scared of them. That's OK. What we found, generally speaking, was that as we came in, they went back. And we found a lot of intelligence.'

Dennis 'Arab' Ayoub was a sapper (a private in the engineers), and part of McGregor's team. Although he would later win a commission and retire a major, he has never forgotten the terrifying experience of being a 'tunnel rat':

'Have you ever snorkelled? You know the rasping sound when you breathe and you can hear nothing else? Well that's all you can hear when you're in the tunnel. You can hear the air going down your airways and you can hear this thump, thump, thump as your heart beats. And you're trying to make your heart quieter because you fear that someone can hear that. Your senses are absolutely acute.

'It's very hard to control your fear. I think if I'd gone down on my own – well, I'd probably have done it then, but I wouldn't do it now. I knew that it had to be done. What really concerned me was that if anything happened they'd never get my body. That was the only thing that really worried me. It wasn't the fact that I might get killed – because I knew I wouldn't – that's the invincibility of the Australian soldier.

'A firefight's a bit like you're driving across the Harbour Bridge and someone cuts you off and you skid and then regain control and think: "Shit I could have been killed!" But you could reasonably expect it to occur because you're driving. The actions I was in you could reasonably expect to occur because you were in that place. But the tunnels were a different thing altogether. You had to summon up enough guts to go down there again and again.'

Dennis was one of many Diggers struck by the experience of the Australian contingent just before he arrived in Vietnam. The Diggers lost two soldiers on a patrol. Their bodies were never recovered. It struck at one of the basic tenets of the

Digger in combat – that they always bring back their wounded and dead:

> 'They think they were shot from tunnels and the bodies disappeared. It's silly to say I wouldn't have minded being killed but I would rather have had the normal courtesies accorded to me. And I think the Vietcong were the same. They had to get the bodies back for the proper burial.
>
> 'You didn't do stupid things but you just knew it wasn't going to happen to you. I just was always worried: how will they be able to explain it? Where's Dennis? Oh he's in a hole somewhere.'

Working down the tunnels was a process of trial and error. There had been no training that prepared the Diggers for the work. Sandy McGregor took the lead:

> 'It was scary going down the tunnels but the very first tunnel we discovered I went down it. I got my staff sergeant to hold a rope around my legs. I could trust him. I was lowered down with a torch in one hand and a bayonet and a pistol. You've only got two hands, so it was push the torch, fiddle on the ground with the bayonet, then push the torch, a metre at a time.'

Dennis Ayoub helped to refine the technique:

> 'You'd sneak the gun around first, then put your head around, then flash the torch on trying to get your eyes accustomed to the light. Then you'd immediately turn the torch off and see if you could remember the picture. If there was nothing there, then you'd move on.
>
> 'But you knew if the light was shining and there was another angled tunnel, up or down, you would have been seen. So they were backing off as you were moving forward.
>
> 'Most of us had a bit of whinge, or had a bit of fear or your guts were churning. There were certain areas in the tunnels where when you got there you just knew you were in deep shit.
>
> 'The shafts were usually circular and you had two options: you could go down head first or you could go down feet first. Now we used to figure if you went down feet first you'd have a tendency to drop and your arms would be locked and you wouldn't know what to do.

'*The best thing to do was to get someone to tie a rope around your legs and we used to get a pistol and a torch and slide down, perhaps two metres. You'd put your weapon around, your torch around and then you wriggle to let the bloke holding your rope know, then you'd flick on the torch and if it was okay you'd let him drop you down.*

'*If they were going to have a mine, that's where they'd have the mine. If they had Panji stakes and you went down feet first, the stakes would go through your foot and you'd be stuck and you wouldn't be able to get out. But if you went down and put your hand down and you felt around and there were no Panjis, no collapsible board with the nails on the inside of it which snapped on to your hand, or there were no trip wires or anti-personnel mines, then you were okay. But you would have to be careful you weren't touching around the inside and they might have had something there as well.*

'*To go down that hole it would take a good five minutes. I don't know how long it would take down the tunnel, I never checked, but you might be down there for forty, forty five minutes. One bloke once went down there in daylight and came back out it was dark and everybody had gone home because they'd forgotten he was down there. He was so fucking angry, so pissed off! He had to make his own way back, in the dark.*'

Corporal Bill Gallagher was working down a tunnel system during 'Operation Crimp' when he collapsed. The others had to rush down, and luckily were able to get him out alive. Sandy McGregor realised what had happened:

'*Basically the air was rotten and we'd done it when we'd pumped in the smoke. I felt very much responsible for that. I should have twigged that the smoke was going to burn up oxygen and our blokes were not going to be able to breathe. But, of course, it was standard operating procedure from the 173rd Airborne Brigade to blow smoke and find other entrances and that's what we did.*

'*General Westmoreland didn't want guys to go down the*

tunnels. He didn't tell me. He thought it was almost below their dignity to go down the tunnels but after we took out so much gear, equipment, lists of intelligence, hit lists of Americans in Saigon, even photos of Chinese advisers, all sorts of stuff, he decided to develop a team of people who could go down tunnels and get all the right equipment and it became the order to search out tunnels. But we were the first.'

Dennis Ayoub was among the Diggers who rushed to extricate Bill Gallagher. They knew he was in an area where the tunnel dropped to a lower level. The tunnel was about the size of the coffin it almost became for Bill Gallagher, just big enough for Dennis and the others:

'I was then eleven stone and I was on my hands and knees and my bum used to scrape against the tunnel and my head used to hit the top of the tunnel as I crawled along with a torch and a pistol.

'Somehow we had to get down and behind Bill to push him back up. He was unconscious and he was gagging. Probably the best thing he did was to be overcome by the fumes because he was using less oxygen.

'I didn't realise I was claustrophobic until I did that. I was petrified about going down again – I did – but I was petrified because of the space there. If I have to get under the house even today, I'm scared. I had to get under my mother's house recently after she died, and it brought it all back to me.'

During 'Crimp', Sandy McGregor's team stumbled onto a tunnel system so massive that its exploitation could have changed the course of the entire Vietnam War. Sandy sums up the situation in his book, *No Need for Heroes*:

'We had gone to find and destroy the Saigon-Cholon/Gia Dinh political and military headquarters of the Viet Cong. By the time we left we knew we'd found it and we were pretty sure we'd destroyed it. History shows that the former assumption was correct while the latter was well off the mark.'

Working in four teams of six men, each attached to an infantry company, the engineers worked underground from daylight until dark. They discovered and extracted an extensive array of intelligence. Sandy wrote:

'We had investigated tunnels for 700 metres in one direction and 500 metres across that line. We still had no idea how far the tunnels extended. We had taken out truckloads of equipment and documents, including photographs of the Viet Cong's foreign advisers and a hit list of political and military figures in Saigon whom the VC wanted to assassinate.

'I'd be very surprised if some of the VC papers returned to the Vietnamese by the USA in July 1993, as part of the two countries' reconciliation over US troops Missing In Action, weren't from the half ton extracted from the tunnels under Ho Bo Woods.'

Sandy and his team had discovered underground hospitals and classrooms with so much gear that their American superiors assumed they must have found the Viet Cong HQ they'd been seeking. Two of Sandy's team, Les Colmer and Barry Harford, reached a trapdoor which they discovered, after a painstaking search for booby traps, led to a new third level. But, alarmed at the ticking sound they heard on opening it, they withdrew and sought further instructions. They were told to leave the area and blow all the entrances and to make them unusable to the enemy.

Two decades later, Sandy discovered that on the other side of that trapdoor lay the military HQ of the southern command of the Viet Cong. The enemy had withdrawn down their tunnels and held off attacking the tunnel rats, hoping to bluff the searchers into believing they were of little strategic importance:

'The Viet Cong had pulled back as far as they could without abandoning important installations. The next step would have meant bloody warfare which we would probably have won, but at a terrible cost.

'Would it have changed the course of history? The Viet Cong planned the Tet Offensive of 1968 from those tunnels. Ten years later they launched the final assault on Saigon from there, by which time the network had grown from 200 to 400 miles.'

Sandy discovered that the Viet Cong had started digging the tunnel complex as far back as 1945, during their war of independence with the French. As many as 5000 troops lived and worked in the complex, many without seeing daylight for up to six months at a stretch:

'If we had continued for another couple of days, we would have discovered and ultimately destroyed their underground city. It is not stretching the imagination to see how that could easily have led to the capitulation of Hanoi. As it turned out, the Americans' decision to pull out led only to the fall of Saigon.'

But that was to come. In the meantime, the Diggers acclimatised themselves to a strange form of warfare, where the enemy was often a phantom and most of what they saw was a deadly illusion: rice caches that were massive booby traps; innocent villagers who were Viet Cong; grenades wired in trees; mines everywhere; panji pits; enemies without uniforms who became expert insurgents and night fighters. It is to the great credit of the Diggers who served in Vietnam that they proved yet again they were capable of maintaining their focus in this twilight zone. Dennis Ayoub:

'First you looked for booby traps. When you found one, you knew something big was around: a rice cache, ammunition cache, a tunnel. The traps could be vines across the track, panjii pits, twigs or leaves turned the wrong way, things too neat. In one, there were 14 booby traps, grenades, set in the trees around the entrance. Not all of them were set because they had to get down there too quickly.'

Later on, the Viet Cong changed their style of booby traps. They took mines out of the minefields and they even used US M16 'Jumping Jack' mines against the Diggers by putting them in and around tracks. The Diggers were constantly alert. Dennis Ayoub recalls:

'When I slept in the jungle I used to sleep straight on the ground. I had an insert of a blow-up Li-Lo which I inflated about a third full and I slept with that under the back of my neck and down the centre of my back. I'd sleep with my heels on the

ground, my bum cheeks on the ground and my shoulders on the ground. I'd sleep with my rifle straight down my stomach.

'You'd only hear the sentries changing every hour. When the next bloke moved, just the rustle of his clothing was enough to wake you. You wouldn't startle but your eyes would just open. But in the meantime you'd been sleeping so that you knew you were asleep and resting but you were aware of any sound. You could rest because soldiers can teach themselves to go, not into a deep sleep where you snore, but like a coma where you meditate. You can hear the outside noise but you could rest.

'You could wake up by the clock. If you knew you were on sentry duty at ten o'clock you'd wake up right on time, a few minutes before and when the previous sentry came to get you, you'd be immediately ready.'

Mike McDermott recalled a similar constant state of tension:

'I'd lie down at night up against a tree with my weapon there and I'd watch. I'd listen for the change of sentries. I always slept on my right side, north-south. I'd do it by compass so if something happened during the night I'd know immediately, that was north-east or west, or whatever.'

One of the major differences from previous wars in the Diggers' service was the presence of National Servicemen, or 'Nashos' – young men selected for a two-year term in the Army by a national conscription ballot. On 10 November 1964, Sir Robert Menzies had announced his government was introducing conscription, referring to the increased 'risks in this corner of the world'. All 20 year olds were required to register for the ballot (except for Aborigines, non-naturalised migrants, employees of a foreign government and those already members of the military forces). The government needed only a modest number of conscripts to serve. It was limited to 4200 in 1965 and then 8400 a year thereafter, from a pool of 750,000 young men eligible from 1965 through to 1972.

The ballot was conducted by choosing marbles representing birth dates. Then the selected men faced a series of tests to determine whether they met the Army's medical, psychological, educational and security standards. The result was that almost 64,000 conscripts served in the Army between 1965 and 1972. Of these, 19,450 went to Vietnam (where they made up less than half of each unit in which they served). In Vietnam, 200 National Servicemen were killed and another 1279 were casualties. Retired Army Sergeant Major Wally Thompson worked with many of them:

'In Vietnam we had National Servicemen and in many ways they were more mature than the regulars because they'd been out in the workforce, they knocked around a bit more, they'd had a career and because they were slightly older, from 19 through to 21.

'There is a bit of a myth about National Servicemen being forced to go to Vietnam. They were all volunteers. But, even so, if you've trained with a whole lot of blokes, you're not going to be the dingo who didn't put your hand up, so there was a lot of peer pressure.'

The Australian Army's insistence on training its soldiers to a satisfactory level before committing them to combat was adhered to with the National Servicemen who served in Vietnam. The training generally took up to a year out of the two-year National Service period and included basic recruit training, jungle training at the Jungle Training School at Canungra and, where appropriate, specialist training. This was in contrast to many US conscripts sent there. Much of this can be attributed to the greatly reduced numbers of our soldiers who served in Vietnam. Whereas the Americans were forced to train their troops on a massive scale, the Australians received the same level of individual training and testing that had been available to their forebears. Wally Thompson:

'Every soldier must be proficient in the use of his weapon and then to fit into the lowest element, which is a section. That's

THE SPIRIT OF THE DIGGER

*company collective training. Then you progress to unit training
and that then is testing through a unit: a CO putting plans out
and testing individual companies as to whether they're up to
speed.*

*'Everyone who went to Vietnam had to be rubber stamped
that they went through Canungra. They're sorting out: are we
up to speed but they're also looking at leaders at all levels. Even
up to Canungra stage, there were people sacked from private to
Major who weren't considered up to speed. The culling process
continued right until they embarked.*

*'When the average soldier went away, he would have been
three months recruit training, then they would go to the infantry
centre for their initial deployment training aimed at making
them a soldier working in a section in a platoon environment.
Once they completed that, usually another three months.
Soldiers who went to Vietnam were, in the main, well prepared
and trained.*

*'If soldiers aren't trained properly, they will take a lot of casu-
alties. They don't know how to use their weapons correctly.
They don't know how to work tactics properly within their area.*

*'People, individually, doing brave acts, is not how it should
have to happen. Someone shouldn't have to sacrifice his life for
the rest. It does happen on occasions but we train everything
for a team to avoid that.'*

Many of the lessons learned by our World War II Diggers
against the Japanese on the Kokoda Track and subsequently in
New Guinea, Borneo and Malaya were applied by the Diggers
who fought the Viet Cong. They had some benefits that the
Diggers on the Kokoda Track would have welcomed with
open arms, as Wally Thompson pointed out:

*'Blokes in Vietnam knew if they were wounded, we could get
them back on a helicopter and they'd have the best medical treatment they could get within half an hour. When they arrived back
at Vung Tau, they'd be stripped off and straight into a surgical
team. You couldn't get that back in Australia. So that's why the
death rate was so low there.*

'If that had been on the Kokoda Track the death rate wouldn't have been so horrendous. Most soldiers aren't killed instantly; they die of shock or haemorrhage. I can't understand how the Fuzzy Wuzzy Angels got them back along that Track.'

Retired Colonel Ted Love believes the continuation training the Vietnam veterans received during their service played a major role in maintaining their high morale:

'Combat power has two elements: one is human and one is physical. I can teach you all the physical stuff, like how to fire your mortar or drive your truck or fire your gun but, on the personal side, I want your morale to be high. I want you to know what you're going to do and why you're doing it. I want commitment and peer-group loyalty and then medical, dental and spiritual support, communication and mail. And medical services in the field.

'In Vietnam the standard was if somebody was injured or hit, 20 minutes to a surgery team. And you must have logistic backup for all these things. Unless you're a contented person who's highly trained with the gear, you've got a problem.'

While the Americans tended to rely on the use of overwhelming force and firepower, regularly 'telegraphing their punches' by heavily bombarding an area before inserting their troops, the Australians tended to rely on stealthy patrolling. The Diggers avoided operating alongside the Americans, preferring to work with small patrols which operated quietly in the jungle. They often challenged the Viet Cong at their own game. Contact with the enemy led to rapid-response drills, which rarely saw the Diggers caught in a static situation and inflicted heavy casualties on the enemy.

Brigadier Ted Serong, CO of the Team, summed up the difference between the two forces:

'Conventional soldiers think of the jungle as being full of lurking enemies. Under our system, we do the lurking.'

US Commander General Westmoreland also recognised the difference, noting the Australians were 'thoroughly professional . . . small in numbers and well trained, particularly in anti-guerrilla warfare . . . the Australian Army was much like the post-Versailles German Army in which even men in the ranks might have been leaders in some less capable force'.

The courage and skill of the Vietnam Diggers, including the Nashos, came to the fore on the afternoon of 18 August 1966 in a rubber plantation at a place called Long Tan.

The Australian 1st Task Force had only recently established a defensive base at Nui Dat, in the heart of the Phuoc Tuy Province. The Viet Cong effectively controlled the area and regarded the Australians' presence there as a direct challenge. They decided to teach the new arrivals a lesson and to establish an early superiority over them. It later transpired that the Viet Cong had also hoped a bloody defeat of the Diggers would encourage the growing anti-war movement in Australia. The Viet Cong plan was simple. They would stage a surprise mortar attack on the Australian base, knowing this would draw out a reaction force that would seek out the mortar positions. They prepared an extensive ambush aimed at wiping out this reaction force.

The mortar attack began at night on 16 August. It caught the base unawares and wounded 24 soldiers. The base artillery responded with a barrage. All night the Diggers at the base waited for the anticipated attack. It did not come. At dawn on 17 August, B Company 6 RAR moved out to search the area. They found five mortar sites but no enemy troops. The following day, D Company swapped places with B Company and headed toward the Long Tan rubber plantation. They had no real expectation of encountering the enemy, which traditionally melted into the jungle after a strike to fight again another day. Each member of D Company carried three days' rations and 60 rounds of ammunition.

They entered the rubber plantation around 3.15 pm on 18 August 1966. After a small initial exchange of fire, which lured the Australians' 11 Platoon further into the killing zone, the Viet Cong sprang their trap. As the heavens opened with a torrential tropical downpour, the Diggers were caught in a firestorm, pounded by mortars, grenades, machine-gun and rifle fire from the front and both flanks. The young Diggers dug in as best they could and returned fire, but in less than 20 minutes they'd lost a third of their number killed or wounded. Nearby, 10 Platoon tried to move up to support their beleaguered mates but were immediately pinned down by massive fire from three sides, still more than 100 metres short. The company commander, Major Harry Smith, recalled 10 Platoon to the main company position as the Diggers formed a defensive perimeter. The situation was now critical. The 108 men of D Company were surrounded by 2500 Viet Cong troops, the bulk of whom were Main Force Viet Cong soldiers rather than the provincial troops the Australians generally faced.

Harry Smith called for an air support strike to enable his trapped forward platoon to pull back to the main group. But the driving rain prevented the American Phantom bombers from locating the target, and they headed off to a secondary target.

Around this time, 11 Platoon's CO, Lieutenant Gordon Sharp, a Nasho from Sydney who had recently been commissioned, was killed. His place was taken by Sergeant Bob Buick, who coolly kept his surviving men at their posts. At least half the platoon were now casualties. Bob Buick then regained radio contact, as he recalls in Lex McAulay's *The Battle of Long Tan*:

'The rain was very heavy, and visibility about 100 to 150 metres, when I decided to call artillery onto my own position, knowing that with ten of us left out of 28, and no ammunition, we could not survive more than another ten or fifteen minutes.

'Captain Maury Stanley [the attached NZ artillery officer] reminded me of the rules of artillery fire when I requested the fire mission, but I told him of our situation. The fire came and landed about 50 to 100 metres to our front, and right in amongst the heaviest concentration [of the enemy].'

Lex McAulay also recounts a classic piece of black Digger humour that occurred in the midst of this cauldron:

'The constant blaring of bugles was heard from the trees as the VC units manoeuvred for their assaults. In the waterfall of sound enveloping the scene, shouted orders would easily be lost, whereas the sharper tones of the bugles pierced the noise of explosions and firing. There seemed to be no tune or melody, just blasts to signal "wait!", "ready!" and "go!"

'Brian Reilly heard someone say with dry Aussie wit, "All we've gotta do is hit the fuckin' bugler!"'

Now 12 Platoon tried to break through to relieve Bob Buick and his men. Creeping through the blinding rain, they made it to about 75 metres away from their mates when they too were pinned down by the enemy's firepower, which was still pouring in on three sides. The Platoon's commander, Lieutenant David Sabben (a rare volunteer for National Service), decided the only way the men of 11 Platoon could find their way to his position was if he set off a coloured smoke bomb. Bob Buick's survivors saw the signal and were able to sprint back through the fire to join Sabben's men, losing another man killed in the process.

The rain was protecting the Viet Cong from the American air strikes but miraculously two RAAF choppers, flying at treetop level, dropped desperately needed ammunition into the Aussies' position just when the defenders were down to their last 100 rounds.

George Odgers, in his *100 Years of Australians at War*, quotes a D Company Digger describing the continuous Viet Cong assaults:

'A solid line of them – it looked like hundreds – would suddenly rush us. The artillery would burst right in the middle of them and there would be bodies all over the place. The survivors would dive for cover beside these bodies, wait for the next attacking line, get up and leap over the dead to resume the rush. They were inching forward all the time over their piles of dead.'

Back at Nui Dat, Task Force Commander Colonel Colin

Townsend had mobilised his force. He accompanied A Company and a group from B Company out in armoured personnel carriers to relieve the trapped troops at Long Tan. All the while, the Nui Dat artillery (an Anzac combination of two Australian and one New Zealand field batteries) bombarded the Viet Cong positions with deadly accuracy, thanks to the inspired work of the Kiwi forward observer attached to D Company, Captain Maury Stanley of the NZ 161 Battery.

The carriers charged past the D Company position and into the enemy positions beyond. They then returned to the central D Company position and readied themselves for the massed attack they were certain would follow. But shortly afterwards the rain stopped and, through the mist and fast-fading light, the Diggers saw the Viet Cong troops rising and drifting away through the rubber trees.

At first light the next day, the reason was clearer. The enemy had sustained enormous casualties. Australians moving through the battlefield counted 245 Viet Cong bodies and saw that many more had been dragged away. Private 'Pom' Rencher, an Englishman who had joined the Australian Army, helped to bury the VC dead, as he recalls in *The Battle of Long Tan*:

'It took three days to bury them, with the constant hum of flies around. Burial was for humane reasons, and for hygiene. Captured VC documents later showed respect for the Australians because they buried the dead at Long Tan. The document said: "They buried our dead, they are a true enemy". That is, we didn't abuse them. Some Americans cut off hands or ears, or buried them with an ace of spades sticking up, that sort of stuff.'

The Diggers had lost 18 dead and 24 wounded. 'Pom' Rencher recalled the eerie scene that confronted him when he returned to 11 Platoon's position:

'My mates lying in an arc, facing outwards, with rifles still at the shoulder as if they were frozen in a drill and it only needed a touch to bring them back to life again . . . They looked very

peaceful and dignified, dying in place, doing their duty. And that's when the tears started. I don't suppose anyone was dry-eyed. I know I wasn't.'

Lex McAuley reported that General Westmoreland came to lend his moral support:

'"Wild Bill" Doolan created newspaper headlines when he addressed General Westmoreland in classic Digger language. The General walked up to a group of Australians digging the graves, and said: "You've done a good job fellows, but this is the dirty part". Doolan replied: "She'll be right mate. We can handle it".'

For its remarkable performance at Long Tan, D Company was awarded the Presidential Unit Citation. It read:

'D Company Sixth Battalion, Royal Australian Regiment, distinguished itself by extraordinary heroism while engaged in military operations against an opposing armed force in Vietnam on 18 August 1966. While searching for Viet Cong in a rubber plantation north-east of Ba Ria, Phuoc Tuy Province, Republic of Vietnam, D Company met and immediately became engaged in heavy contact. As the battle developed, it became apparent that the men of D Company were facing a numerically superior force. The platoon of D Company were surrounded and attacked on all sides by an estimated reinforced enemy battalion, using automatic weapons, small arms and mortars. Fighting courageously against a well armed and determined foe, the men of D Company maintained their formations in a common perimeter defence and inflicted heavy casualties upon the Viet Cong. The enemy maintained a continuous, intense volume of fire and attacked repeatedly from all directions. Each successive assault was repulsed by the courageous Australians. Heavy rainfall and a low ceiling prevented any friendly close air support during the battle. After three hours of savage attacks, having failed to penetrate the Australian lines, the enemy withdrew from the battlefield carrying many dead and wounded, and leaving 245 Viet Cong dead forward of the defence position of D Company. The conspicuous gallantry, intrepidity and indomitable courage of D Company were in the highest tradition of military valor and

reflect great credit upon D Company, Sixth Battalion, The Royal Australian Regiment and the Australian Army.'

For their vital parts in the battle, Captain Maury Stanley was awarded the MBE, Major Harry Smith won a Military Cross, WO2 Kirby and Corporal Carter the Distinguished Service Medal, and Sergeant Bob Buick the Military Medal.

Perhaps the section commander of A Company, Ross Smith, best summed it up when, speaking to Lex McAulay, he recalled his image of Long Tan:

'. . . the comradeship, the valour and the amount of artillery; the legend of Anzac upheld.'

Australia's involvement in Vietnam would continue for another six years. The Diggers there survived the infamous Tet offensive in early 1968, when the Viet Cong, having made a solemn ceasefire pact for the traditional Buddhist sacred celebratory period, launched a massive attack on Saigon itself. Although the attacks were a military disaster for the Viet Cong, they hardened the already strong anti-war opinion in the United States and Australia. Later that year the Diggers triumphed in what the Diggers called 'Coral', an attack on their Fire Support Bases 'Coral' and 'Balmoral', which had been established to block enemy infiltration of Saigon. The Australians lost five killed and 19 wounded but repulsed the enemy while inflicting hundreds of casualties. Subsequent successes in major engagements at Binh Ba and Long Khanh saw the Australians maintain their reputation and respect.

But the political will behind the war began to falter, and the United States ultimately decided on a 'Vietnamisation' policy under which they would withdraw their troops and replace them progressively with South Vietnamese units.

In December 1969, Australian Prime Minister John Gorton foreshadowed a reduction in our military commitment in Vietnam. On 22 April 1970 he announced he was withdrawing 8 RAR from duty without replacing it. By this time the Americans were also cutting their losses and handing the problem back to the South Vietnamese.

Only a small group from the Australian Army Assistance Group remained when the newly elected Whitlam government ordered them home in December 1972. A ceasefire agreement was signed in Paris on 23 January 1973, and on 29 March the last planeload of US troops left Tan Son Nhut Airport. Despite the pact, hostilities continued in Vietnam, with the North Vietnamese steadily throttling the South Vietnamese. On 30 April 1975, the Republic of Vietnam unconditionally surrendered.

For many Diggers the Vietnam War was an extremely painful experience, and many have been treated for post-traumatic stress disorder. Many have developed other illnesses and mental conditions they believe were related to their service. The prevalence of chemical weapons in the war zone opened up possibilities of more physical and psychological harm. The Americans used defoliants like 'Agent Orange' to destroy forests, aiming to expose the Viet Cong they believed were using them as cover. The extent of their use in Vietnam was extraordinary and nearly 20 per cent of the forests in South Vietnam – more than three million hectares – were destroyed between 1965 and 1971. After years of lobbying and pressuring by the Vietnam Veterans' Association, the Australian government finally established the Evatt Royal Commission to inquire into the effects of Agent Orange and other chemicals on the Diggers. The Royal Commission delivered its report in 1985 and concluded (in unusually colourful language):

'So Agent Orange is Not Guilty and the chemical agents used to defoliate battle zones in Vietnam and to protect Australians from malaria are not to blame. No one lost.

'This is not a matter for regret but rejoicing. Veterans and their wives are no more at risk of having abnormal offspring than anyone else. Veterans have not been poisoned. The number with general health problems is small, probably much smaller than amongst their peers in the community.'

Opinions vary on whether the Vietnam experience was harder, easier than or simply different from that of the World War I or World War II Diggers. Unlike their forebears, the Vietnam Diggers were committed to the combat zone for a limited period – usually a one-year tour of duty. The combat itself was, by turn, routine and intense, and was often conducted against an enemy difficult to distinguish from the general population. And much of the action was played out under the glare of media scrutiny.

Where earlier Diggers had been part of a one-in-all-in kind of war, the Vietnam Diggers had been sent off to war while the vast majority of their contemporaries simply got on with their lives. (In World War I 13.4 per cent of all men enlisted. In World War II the figure was 10.28 per cent. In Vietnam only 0.4 per cent of the eligible male population served.) Aside from their immediate families and friends, the community did not suffer hardship with them as it had in the earlier wars. And when the Diggers returned home, they often did so within days of being in combat, without the period of natural debriefing and cathartic comradeship experienced by veterans of the World Wars with their mates during the protracted journey home. Perhaps these were contributing factors in the angst that some Vietnam Diggers have experienced.

Like most Diggers down the years, the Vietnam vets rarely talk of the horrors they experienced, as Dennis Ayoub confirms:

'Blokes don't talk about things like that. The things we talk about are the funny things. It's some sort of block-out mechanism, some sort of denial mechanism. And we all know or can imagine what each has been through and we don't really talk about it.

'A lot of people were against us being in Vietnam but I thought well I joined the army and I was prepared to go there.

'I don't blame it for my daughter's epilepsy. I don't blame it for anything, scabies, my bad temper – I'm a bad tempered bastard anyway! Something to do with booze and cigarettes and

abuse of my life probably created all those circumstances and people not slapping me hard enough when they were trying to bring me back in line.

'I know that I became a very confident bloke after that. One of the reasons I didn't suffer from PTSD was because I was able to capture the fact that I was one of the toughies. But the war trauma manifested itself in other ways like the alcohol abuse, the cigarette abuse, letting my marriage fail, not maintaining your obligations, living on a reputation and other things.'

Our Vietnam vets laid many of their ghosts when they finally received a proper welcome home, 15 years late, on 3 October 1987, when the Welcome Home March in Sydney gave them their due as Diggers who did their duty when called on.

FOURTEEN

Keeping the peace

The Digger's proud record as a warrior has been matched by his performance as a peacekeeper. Although we had some involvement in the Occupation Forces in Japan after World War II, our first real peacekeeping role came under the aegis of the United Nations when we provided a handful of military observers to the UN Security Commission for Indonesia from 1947 to 1951, which tried to mediate during the conflict between Sukarno's revolutionaries and the Netherlands.

From 1953 through to 1978 we contributed small numbers of troops and support personnel to peacekeeping contingents in the Middle East, the Congo, Yemen, West New Guinea, India and Pakistan, Syria, Sinai and Lebanon. In 1979 we stepped up the level of our commitment and played significant roles in UN peacekeeping duties in Rhodesia-Zimbabwe, Sinai, Iran, Namibia, Afghanistan, the Gulf of Oman, Iraq and Kuwait, Western Sahara, Cambodia, the former Yugoslavian states, Somalia and Rwanda.

Peacekeeping is now a global growth industry. The United Nations has about 50,000 peacekeepers deployed throughout the world, and at any given time we have some 2000 personnel involved in various UN-sponsored forces.

Some military experts believe that using Diggers in a peacekeeping role diminishes their effectiveness as soldiers in times of war. Major-General Duncan Lewis, Commanding Officer of our Special Air Forces (SAS), a 32-year Army veteran with service commanding battalions in East Timor, disagrees:

'I think peacekeeping, peacemaking, peace enforcement – all of the range of peace-related operations – are nothing more than an extension of military operations. I mean it's just one end of a spectrum and I see it as a continuous spectrum.

'Soldiers are optimised for fighting wars. That's their base objective and that's where this criticism comes from. But while you may be optimised for war fighting, and I think that's entirely correct, it's always easier to train down. What is far more difficult is going the other way: that if you were to optimise peacekeeping, you would find that it would take months, if not years, potentially years to get your force up to being able to do more robust military operations. It's like a footy team: train hard, play easy.'

When the Iraqi forces, under their dictator Saddam Hussein, invaded neighbouring Kuwait on 2 August 1990, the United Nations acted quickly. Saddam had banked on a swift strike giving him control of Kuwait before the world could react effectively. But the day after the invasion the United States and Britain announced they would send naval support to the Kuwaitis, and the Soviet Union joined with them in calling for a ban on arms sales to the Iraqis.

The UN Security Council then passed a resolution calling on the Iraqis to withdraw from Kuwait and threatening force and sanctions if they didn't comply. The Australian Hawke Labor government supported the UN resolution and quickly committed three of our RAN ships to the Coalition forces. The Army sent an anti-aircraft detachment to provide protection on board HMAS *Success*. The RAAF provided transport support.

When Saddam Hussein called the United Nation's bluff and failed to comply with its ultimatum to pull his forces out of Kuwait by 15 January 1991, the UN Coalition forces, under

US General Norman Schwarzkopf, launched 'Operation Desert Storm', starting with massed air strikes on Iraq. The Coalition soon had control of the Iraqi skies and followed up with a land offensive, which began at 4 am on 24 February.

It was the first of the live-to-air, computer-style wars, and it played via CNN in living rooms around the world. Members of our RAN contingent reported they could see missiles being launched from nearby US battleships and then watch them explode in Baghdad live on CNN. Hussein's bravado, in which he promised 'The Mother of All Battles', proved hollow and, just 100 hours after the UN offensive began, US President George Bush Senior was on television, saying: 'Kuwait is liberated. Iraq's army is defeated. Our military objectives are met . . . this is a victory for all mankind and the rule of law.'

Estimates of Iraqi losses ran as high as 100,000 killed (but more realistically perhaps 50,000) for the loss of 131 Coalition troops killed in action and another 100 killed in the now seemingly inevitable accidents that accompany modern American troop deployment and action.

The RAN's involvement won high praise. The US Navy commander, Vice Admiral Stanley Arthur, called it magnificent: 'The US Navy will be proud to sail in harm's way with the RAN, anytime, anywhere.'

While our SAS was on call to deal with anticipated terrorist responses during the Gulf War, it was not needed. The only involvement of our Diggers was a 75-strong medical and engineering team sent to assist in the protection of the Kurds in Iraq, who staged a revolt to break Saddam's stranglehold over them. The United Nations stayed clear and Hussein's forces brutally repressed the uprising, killing thousands and causing an estimated two million Kurds to rush to the borders trying to escape. Our team assisted for a little over a month before handing its duties over to UN-sanctioned civilians.

::

Until our commitment to East Timor in 1999 (considered in detail in Chapter Three), our most significant peacekeeping tasks were in Somalia and Cambodia in the early 1990s.

In Cambodia, Lieutenant General John Sanderson commanded the UN Force which oversaw the disarming of 250,000 Cambodians. The Australian Army also contributed 500 personnel in the form of the Force's Communications Unit. Both the commander and the Australian support unit received widespread praise for their performances.

Our role in Somalia was dangerous and required considerable diplomacy. 1 RAR, together with some supporting units, provided protection to those trying to deliver humanitarian aid to that strife-ridden country.

During the American-led anti-terrorist action in Afghanistan in 2002 our Diggers shone once again. Duncan Lewis saw it first hand:

'Afghanistan stands as a unique situation because it was very heavily Special Forces influenced. And it was a combination of [Australian] Special Forces on the ground and [American] air forces synergising their effect that created victory.'

Individual Diggers distinguished themselves in Afghanistan but, because of the need for continued security in the light of world-wide terrorist threats, their identities are kept secret from the public. Sergeant Y, serving with the Australians in Afghanistan, typified the standard of the team there. On Operation SLIPPER in March 2002, Sergeant Y was leading patrol Bravo Three of 1 Special Air Service Squadron, Task Force 64. His remarkable leadership skills and bravery under fire saw him win the Distinguished Service Medal. Continuing secrecy requirements mean that details of his actions have been withheld, but his citation reads:

'He displayed the highest level of commitment and dedication in commanding his patrol. He has made tactically sound assessments and decisions and displayed excellent leadership qualities under arduous conditions. His distinguished command and leadership from 2 March to 13 March 2002 are in the finest

traditions of the Special Air Service Regiment. The success and high morale of his patrol can be attributed directly to his performance of duty.'

By far our most controversial involvement in a 'peacekeeping role' was our involvement – via a 100-strong SAS contingent, some supporting ships and mine-clearing teams – in the US-led Coalition that toppled Saddam Hussein's regime in Iraq in 2003. As Duncan Lewis points out, there was little 'peacekeeping' at the sharp end in either Afghanistan or Iraq for our Diggers:

'I guess Iraq and Afghanistan are quite different from East Timor in that East Timor was a peace enforcement operation, while Afghanistan and Iraq were fully-fledged military operations. There was no peace enforcement or anything of that nature.'

Following the first Gulf War, Saddam continued his repressive rule. But the reaction to world terrorism, prompted by the 11 September attacks on New York and Washington in 2001, saw pressure mount in America for some proactive approach to pre-empt further attacks, and ultimately brought the Iraqi dictator back into focus. Many Australians shared these concerns after the shocking attack in Bali in October 2002.

The Australian government, under John Howard, supported the stance adopted by US President George W. Bush and Britain's Labor government under Tony Blair: that Saddam Hussein's regime continued to pose a grave international threat because of the repressive nature of his rule; because of his links to terrorist groups; and because they claimed he possessed, and was likely to use, 'weapons of mass destruction'. These were vaguely defined as chemical warfare agents and missiles exceeding the UN specifications. Internal differences within the UN Security Council, principally led by France and Germany, meant there was no prospect of a resolution to stamp the UN imprimatur on what Bush called 'the

Coalition of the Willing' to use force on Saddam to comply with their demands to surrender all weapons of mass destruction. Amid considerable dissension in Australia because the actions were not under the United Nations, the Howard government threw its full support behind the United States and Britain when they finally decided to go it alone in taking action against Saddam.

After another TV war, in which the Iraqi forces again were crushed under the massive weight of the Coalition's overwhelming force, the Australians played an unpublicised but by all accounts significant role behind the lines. The SAS Diggers carried out their dangerous activities without incurring any casualties, a source of great pride to their commander, Duncan Lewis:

'That was a fully-fledged war with thousands and thousands of ground troops, thousands of aircraft sorties by fast jets, sorties being flown each day, the use of significant armoured forces and so on. Special Forces in Iraq had a more niche role.'

The Australian SAS troops established their credentials in the Afghanistan conflict, and their performance there led to the Americans entrusting them with one of the most critical roles in the Iraqi conflict:

'. . . in our case, in the suppression of Iraqi weapons of mass destruction. There was a significant threat, and there will be debate as to how real or otherwise it was, but nevertheless, there was a significant threat of Iraqi Scud launchers from the west of the country. The horrific consequence of that, of course, is that they would be launched against the state of Israel and that would change the dimension and the balance of the operation.

'So there was an imperative to ensure that the Iraqis did not have the opportunity to launch Scud missiles at Israel. And I must say that the Special Forces operation in which we were involved contributed directly towards ensuring that that was the case.'

Our SAS virtually moved straight from Afghanistan to Iraq and, in doing so, maintained many of their direct connections with their American counterparts. This was reflected in the number of occasions our Diggers seamlessly called in air support directly from their American allies in the field. Duncan Lewis:

'Our task group in Afghanistan covered itself in distinction, achieving quite disproportionate results for the number of persons deployed, and I think we carried that reputation forward then directly into the planning for Iraq. We were an integral part, and I think a successful part, of a wider Coalition effort.'

Any doubts that the modern Digger has earned his right to stand alongside his forebears should be allayed by the outstanding performances of men like Trooper X during Operation Falconer in Iraq. Trooper X's patrol was ordered to clear an Iraqi installation to prevent it being used for the command and control of Iraqi ballistic missiles. Trooper X was the machine gunner in the exposed .50 calibre mounting ring in his armoured patrol vehicle. As it neared its objective, the Aussie patrol was confronted by an Iraqi special operations force of two vehicles and up to twenty heavily-armed troops.

The Diggers were outnumbered and the operation was in the balance until Trooper X swung into action. Exposed and under fire, he immediately destroyed the first Iraqi vehicle with a Javelin missile. This restricted the Iraqis' ability to manoeuvre. The Aussies then charged at the remaining Iraqis and Trooper X swept another supporting Iraqi position to the south with his machine gun. Showing remarkable coolness, he switched back to his Javelin system and destroyed the second enemy vehicle, dispersing nearby enemy soldiers who were setting up a mortar position. As the Diggers closed on the enemy position, Trooper X picked up his sniper rifle and, with his first round, hit and exploded the mortar tube the Iraqis were hastily setting up.

At this stage, individual enemy troops began to surrender but were intermingled with other Iraqis who were still fighting against the Aussies. Trooper X then showed superb marksmanship, firing selected shots at the Iraqis who were still fighting from cover and forcing them to surrender. Trooper X was awarded the Medal for Gallantry. His citation read in part:

> 'Throughout this engagement, Trooper X demonstrated skills and composure of the highest standard. He acted with very little direction and his decisions and subsequent actions had significant impacts on the outcome of the engagement. His actions in destroying the enemy vehicles gave the Australian forces freedom of movement and put the Iraqi forces under immediate pressure. For the entire engagement, Trooper X was subject to enemy fire passing close overhead. He readily accepted the personal danger and disregarded his own safety while acquiring the enemy vehicles with the Javelin. His conduct whilst in a hazardous situation in contact with numerically superior enemy forces was most gallant and led to the success of the action.'

Trooper X remains anonymous. His only recognition comes from his fellow SAS Diggers. This has always been the way for our Special Forces: from the Z Specials responsible for one of the greatest feats of war when they twice penetrated Singapore Harbour and destroyed thousands of tons of Japanese shipping, and the Independent Companies and forces operating in the islands to Australia's north in World War II, through to the SAS in Vietnam and afterwards. Duncan Lewis:

> 'Our operations are often conducted shrouded in secrecy and that's necessary of course in order to preserve the safety of the individuals who are deployed. These fellows are seriously in harm's way and we want to do everything to ensure that they remain as safe as we can possibly make them. The wider public doesn't get to hear the detail of what was done. But I think the couple of glimpses that come out of both Afghanistan and Iraq, through the commendations for Sergeant Y and Trooper X, give you an idea of the great spirit, the humanity, the courage, the generosity of the individuals that go to make up, not just Special Forces, but the wider Australian Digger, the wider membership of Australian military forces.'

The Army invests much time and energy in modern Diggers: in language training; in cultural awareness; and in ensuring they understand that the power of the local community, in many cases, outstrips military capacity.

'A local community is an enormously powerful instrument and if you can harness that instrument and have it work with you rather than against you, then you're quids in front.

'At the end of the day, you are trying to make this world a better place, a better community, and you don't do that by running around abusing – and I don't mean that in a verbal sense, but in a physical sense – the community. It's done by working with the community. And so quite often you'll find in the most amazing circumstances in the height of conflict a young soldier will defuse a situation by his ability to interact with the local community and, certainly, in the Special Forces world we regard that particular interaction as hugely important.'

Despite their extraordinary actions and their rigorous training, Duncan Lewis believes our SAS troops don't view themselves, as many of the public do, as 'super Diggers':

'They see themselves as being quite ordinary. They're only perceived by the wider media in this colourful and exciting light. What I think is that they are ordinary people in extraordinary circumstances. Ordinary, though, is playing them down too much, of course, because there is a very rigorous selection process.

'We are looking for soldiers who have the necessary endurance, both physical and mental; that have the necessary intellect and capacity to absorb high volumes of training. Their cognitive capacity and situational awareness must be high – knowing what's going on around them, not just constrained or confined to their lane but able to look at the wider issues or implications of their actions.

'We're looking for soldiers who can endure hardship and privation and, of course, we're looking for a soldier who has a sense of humour, who, at the end of the day, can see the funny side of all of this. We regard this as a balanced individual. We're

not looking for a superman, we're looking for a very balanced, capable individual.'

The Diggers have learned from the Americans' ability to conduct operations on a massive scale:

'They are able to do things militarily that other countries could only dream about, or in some cases, not even contemplate. We admire that but we also recognise that with scale, of course, comes some difficulty in understanding the particulars of a circumstance. And I think that's where Australian soldiers in particular have a strength. They work in quite small groups at the coalface level; they've got great character and an ability to engage both friend, foe and neutral in a humane and positive way. But, having said all that, of course, when push comes to shove we are just as gung-ho as the next American because you are there to achieve a mission and if that means having to prose-cute military operations vigorously, then we have to be able to do that, and we do it. But it is a very fine call when to press vigor-ously and when not.'

Diggers throughout history have shown an almost chameleon-like ability to switch from the role of the fierce warrior during wartime to that of a humane citizen after-wards. Duncan Lewis attributes this to the Australian leader-ship system, which allows the Digger room to make decisions within the overall command framework:

'Within my organisation there is a terrific respect for comp-etence. And people will sink or swim depending on their competence. And that is applied almost irrespective of rank: no matter what rank, whether you're a general or a private, you must be competent. So there's this respect for competence throughout the force, which I think is part of our make-up.

'We have a doctrine within the Australian Defence Force of 'directive control'. Essentially it says that you give a person the job, but you don't tell them how to do it. And that's a gross summary of the more intricate business of directive control, but it's nevertheless what it means. You give somebody a job, you give them some guidelines beyond which they may not go, but

within those guidelines they're free to move so long as they achieve the ultimate objective that you've set. And, of course, what this does is engender initiative and it means the guy on the ground, who can actually make the best call, will decide whether he should do this or that. But he also knows that his call must end up with [a specific] *result. The idea is to give subordinate commanders the necessary leeway to achieve the aim as they see it best done.'*

Perhaps the most pleasing thing to emerge from the war in Iraq in 2003 was that, despite considerable opposition to Australia's involvement, the respect that the overwhelming majority of Australians have for their Diggers ensured they were able to direct their criticism and displeasure at the government while still supporting our soldiers. This pleased Duncan Lewis greatly:

'I think the thing that sets the Australian soldier apart is humanity. That's the most important thing. They're human beings and they treat other people that they come across, whether they be friend, foe or neutral, as human beings. They've shown amazing degrees of compassion to those in need.

'I've always said: it's more difficult not to shoot someone than to shoot them. I think that's an axiom of modern military operations. It's more difficult and more challenging not to engage somebody by fire than not to engage them and my Special Forces blokes in both Afghanistan and Iraq have displayed time and time again that they're able to discriminate between those that they should engage and those that they shouldn't. And, of course, by not engaging it doubles the success because it's a win-win situation. I think that is very important.'

EPILOGUE

The spirit lives

Christ Church, South Yarra, Melbourne, March 18 2003

The old men's eyes were full of sad wisdom. They listened and they remembered, holding themselves with the proud carriage of those who have done their duty. They came, some from their sick beds, to farewell one of their beloved mates. They struggled to let him go, each knowing his own time could not be too far away. They sat in rows in the stark church, not in the front pews but, as always, a respectful distance towards the back. Their white hair stood out in relief against the heavy dark wood of the pews, their medals hung heavily across frail chests holding hearts that have withstood great sorrows and joys. Reverend Charles Sligo:

'Today, we farewell a great citizen of this nation. A distinguished soldier, a humble man of remarkable character, insight and integrity, Phil has set benchmarks of judgement, behaviour and ideals which will continue to radiate from him to those who know and loved him and listened to him. His influence will go on for a long time after his death.'

They came to farewell Phil Rhoden – a remarkable man. As with many of his age, his life was ruled by duty: to his much-loved wife of 60 years, Pat; to his daughter Judy and son Philip and their kids; to his country, which he served with bravery and distinction in its darkest hour; to the comrades who shared the risks with him, especially to those who never returned or who suffered then and later; to his community as a much-respected lawyer and as a leader in the administration of secondary schooling and youth development.

Phil led a richly diverse life, loved and enjoyed his friends, many of whom he cherished over his long life, and he retained an acutely analytical mind right to the end. One constant in Phil's life was his love and respect for the brothers with whom he fought.

So it is with most of our Diggers. Their bonds of mateship remain while there is breath left in them. Many of Phil's mates had gone before him: some never returned from the Middle East, and many fell in the jungles of New Guinea and now rest in the sacred earth at Bomana in Port Moresby. But others, like his lifelong friends and comrades Stan Bisset and Chas Butler, were there by his side for his final journey, just as they had always been.

Now 90, Stan Bisset had been Phil's mate for 75 years. They first met as schoolboys, then served together throughout World War II and had remained the closest of mates ever since. What memories must have flooded through Stan's mind as he looked at the coffin with the Australian flag draped over it. Stan trained as a choral singer and always led his battalion in song. The echoes of his powerful voice sound as he sings 'O God Our Help in Ages Past':

Time like an ever-rolling stream
Bears all its sons away;
They fly forgotten, as a dream
Dies at the opening day.

And Chas Butler is here, looking dashing as always, wearing his eye patch like the badge of honour it is. Phil helped get

Chas out when he lost his eye at swampy Gona after he was caught by a burst of machine-gun fire. 'You'll be right Chas, hold on', Phil said. 'I'm all right Phil but it looks like I'll be a one-eyed Melbourne supporter from now on.'

And he was. And Phil used to tell of the time at a game after the war when he and Chas were barracking for Melbourne and a Collingwood supporter yelled at them: 'I'm sick of you effing one-eyed Demons' supporters . . . oh, sorry mate!' They all had a beer afterwards, because the Collingwood bloke had fought at Gona too.

Phil was there in August 1942 at Isurava when Stan's beloved older brother Butch died in his arms at the side of the Kokoda Track. And he was there again 56 years later as Stan knelt at Butch's grave at Bomana War Cemetery when he returned to New Guinea for the first time.

In 1998, Phil led his men back to Papua New Guinea for the 2/14th Battalion's Last Parade, a chance to say a final farewell to the mates they had last seen 56 years earlier, when they were young and full of life with unlimited future. For Phil and his men it was a sacred pilgrimage, fulfilling promises made in the heat of battle in a jungle none were sure they would ever leave.

Just as he always did, Phil took the lead and found the right words:

'The Last Parade rekindled something that was already there and has been there for these past 56 years. It cemented it, if it needed cementing. It joined us together with those fellows that we left behind and did so much to win the day. We were the lucky ones. We could've been them and they could've been us. It was interchangeable. It was a matter of luck.

'We think of them in sorrow and with pride, but there should be a third feeling stronger than grief, greater than pride: a sense of fullness and of achievement.

'To us, their lives may seem to have been severely shortened. Yet in truth they were full lives. It is not how many years a man lives that matters but what he does with the years — many or few

*— that are granted to him. And those who sleep here did much
with theirs.'*

Phil Rhoden did much with his life. The spirit of the Digger
lived on in him. It will live on while ever we remember him
and the men like him who wore the slouch hat with pride.

Interviews by the author

Dennis Ayoub, Vietnam veteran, 25 October 2002, Sydney

Peter Cosgrove, Chief of ADF, 12 November 2002, Canberra

Ali Efe, Turkish historian, 4–5 December 2002, Gallipoli

Peter Hughes, Bali survivor, 7 January 2003, Perth

Duncan Lewis, Commanding Officer, SAS, 3 June 2003, Sydney

Ted Love, retired Colonel, 4 November 2002, Sydney

Mike McDermott, Vietnam veteran, 6 November 2002, Sydney

Sandy McGregor, Vietnam veteran, 15 October 2002, Sydney

Don Murray, retired Colonel, 28 February 2003, Sydney

Noel Pallier, WWII veteran, 1 November 2002, Wollongong

Wally Thompson, Vietnam veteran, 15 October 2002, Sydney

Brett Woodward, Army Corporal, 5 February 2003, East Timor

Endnotes

Prologue

1   'At first I thought why did she do that? . . .' (and following quotes): Peter Hughes, Bali bombing survivor, interview with the author, Perth, 7 January 2003.

4   'They are our real people . . .': General Peter Cosgrove, interview, Canberra, 12 November 2002.

1   The essence of the spirit
Page

7   'The fond dream of the return home . . .': Charles Bean, *Anzac to Amiens*, p. 537

7   'In the First World War when Bluey . . .': Wally Thompson, Vietnam veteran, interview, Sydney, 15 October 2002.

8   'I can remember . . .': General Peter Cosgrove, interview, Canberra, 12 November 2002.

9   'People say Australian soldiers . . .': Wally Thompson, as above.

9   'If the fellow says I won't let you down . . .': Peter Cosgrove, as above.

10   'An engineer commander once told me . . .': Dennis Ayoub, Vietnam veteran, interview, Sydney, 25 October 2002.

10   'Our infantry soldiers . . .': Peter Cosgrove, as above.

11   'They were appalled to find . . .': John Laffin, *Digger*, p. 35.

12   'Wars may be fought . . .': Wally Thompson, as above.

12   'He said "I wasn't concerned . . ."': Dennis Ayoub, as above.

12   'We have a thing in our army . . .': Wally Thompson, as above.

13   'The officers are the head . . .': ibid.

13   'There is a master-apprentice relationship . . .': Mike McDermott, Vietnam veteran, interview, Sydney, 6 November 2002.

14   'The Digger is normally . . .': Dennis Ayoub, as above.

14   'Keep orders to a minimum . . .': Wally Thompson, as above.

15   'Our Diggers have got this sort of restless ingenuity . . .': Peter Cosgrove, as above.

15   'They are two different things . . .': Wally Thompson, as above.

16   'Diggers idolise their section commander . . .': ibid.

16   'When I first met him . . .': Dennis Ayoub, as above.

17   'We had three majors . . .': Sandy McGregor, Vietnam veteran, interview, Sydney, 15 October 2002.

17   'Planning is done with the help of other people . . .': Ted Love, retired Australian Army Colonel, interview, Sydney, 4 November 2002.

20   'Soldiers know about the past . . .': Wally Thompson, as above.

2   Today's Diggers
Page

29   'The section commander's job . . .': Brett Woodward, Australian Army Corporal, interview, Maliana, East Timor, 5 February 2003.

29   'The strongest link in the section . . .': ibid.

29   'If I wasn't trying to enhance . . .': ibid.

30   'One of the first things . . .': ibid.

30   'You know "Jackman" . . .': General Peter Cosgrove, interview, Canberra, 12 November 2002.

31   'Some of the vernacular has changed . . .': ibid.

32   'The mantle is partly professional training . . .': ibid.

32   'When I get an opportunity to talk . . .': ibid.

35   'I've never seen such an outpouring . . .': ibid.

35   'My Dad was . . .': ibid.

35   'I grew up . . .': ibid.

36   'I know I squeaked into Duntroon . . .': ibid.

37   'I think that people want to be reassured . . .': ibid.

37   'At one stage in Timor . . .': ibid.

38   'When we were in Vietnam . . .': ibid.

38   'I've got to be capable . . .': ibid.

40   'I think we carry our national characteristics . . .': ibid.

3 The origins

Page

43 '. . . at the heart of white settlement in Australia . . .': Jeffrey Grey, *A Military History of Australia*, p. 2.

44 'One might imagine that Sydney was a purely . . .': Tim Flannery, *The Birth of Sydney*, p. 6.

44 'Its carefully cultivated concepts of personal courage . . .': Lawrence James, *Warrior Race*, p. xiv.

45 'It was a sentiment shared by warrior elites . . .': ibid., p. 71.

46 'It was not just that the Renaissance gentleman . . .': ibid., pp. 136-7.

47 'Many officers were frequently absent from their regiments . . .': Grey, p. 8.

47 'I do not know what the enemy will make of them . . .': ibid., p. 9.

49 'No man, be he Cromwell or Napoleon . . .': quoted in George Odgers, *100 Years of Australians at War*, p. 13.

51 'We tried to crawl from rock to rock . . .': Alfred ('Smiler') Hayes, journalist and novelist, quoted in Odgers, pp. 21–2.

52 'I cannot surrender . . .': quoted in Laffin, p. iii.

52 'This stand at Brakfontein . . .': quoted in Odgers, p. 28.

54 'fat-arsed, pot-bellied, lazy lot of wasters . . .': ibid., p. 29.

55 'The best assets of the Australian land forces . . .': quoted in Grey, p. 78.

4 Gallipoli

Page

58 'The Anzac soldiers on the battlegrounds . . .': Captain Ali Efe, Turkish historian, interview, Gallipoli, 4 December 2002.

62 'You can imagine the Turkish defenders' surprise . . .': ibid.

63 'The Australian was half a soldier . . .': Bean, *Anzac to Amiens*, p. 18.

64 'Australian and New Zealand Army Corps': Bean, p. 121; Laffin, p. 47.

64 'But my knowledge of the Dardanelles was nil . . .': quoted in Les Carlyon, *Gallipoli*, p. 25.

68 'We have two old sayings . . .': Ali Efe, as above.

68 'We are generally a secular country . . .': ibid.

68 'The Turkish soldiers' wives stayed at home . . .': ibid.

69 'On 25th April, 1915, at 0430hrs . . .': quoted in Hasan Basri Danisman, *Bloody Ridge Diary*, p. 8.

69 'This was it. We were scared stiff . . .': quoted in Odgers, pp. 49–50.

70 'A tug took us within 100 yards of the beach . . .': *Simply Hell Let Loose*, Department of Veterans' Affairs, p. 18.

70   'By this time we were all mixed up . . .': ibid., p. 18.

71   'Then I got up to the firing line . . .': ibid., pp. 18-19.

71   'Ross went out with four men along the beach . . .': Charles Bean, *Official History of the War of 1914–18*, Vol 1, p. 331.

72   'Their fire was getting absolutely murderous . . .': quoted in *Wartime*, Australian War Memorial, Issue 21, p. 59.

72   'Our lads all the time were behaving splendidly . . .': ibid., p. 59.

72   'Here is a tragic happening . . .': ibid., p. 59.

74   'Lalor stood up to see and resolved . . .': Bean, *Official History of the War of 1914–18*, Vol 1, p. 291.

74   'On Tuesday morning the 27th (Harry's birthday) . . .': Neville Kidd, *An Impression Which Will Never Fade*, p. 72.

74   'I got under cover as well as I could . . .': ibid., p. 73.

75   'The first day we landed . . .': ibid., p. 75.

77   'I do not expect you to attack . . .': quoted in Edward J. Erickson, *Ordered to Die*, p. 83.

79   'Of all the bastards of places . . .': quoted in Richard Reid, *Gallipoli 1915*, front cover.

79   'differed from experience . . .': Bean, *Anzac to Amiens*, p. 134.

79   'The condition of the men . . .': Reid, p. 65.

79   'Anzac Beach was a sight . . .': Bean, *Official History of the War of 1914–18*, Vol II, p. 61.

80   'The heat is great . . .': Kidd, p. 121.

82   'By 5 o'clock the 1st Brigade was in position . . .': Bean, *Anzac to Amiens*, p. 145.

83   'We charged over to the Turks' trench . . .': Kidd, p. 133.

83   'The signal for the assault . . .': Kidd, p. 137.

84   'One Turkish sergeant who was captured . . .': Kidd, p. 138.

85   'The night before the landings . . .': Kidd, p. 139.

85   'The Turks and the Australians lie . . .': Ali Efe, as above.

87   'The first line stood . . .': Bean, *Anzac to Amiens*, p. 155.

87   'The fusillade, which had slightly abated . . .': ibid., p. 155.

88   'The tempest broke out again . . .': ibid., p. 156.

88   'At first here and there a man . . .': ibid., p. 157.

90   'I was quite taken . . .': Don Murray, retired Australian Army Colonel, interview, Sydney, 28 February 2003.

91　'There is the same tradition . . .': Ali Efe, as above.

91　'The Turkish elderly local people . . .': ibid.

92　'The Turks could see them bathing . . .': ibid.

92　'In 1990, the 75th Anniversary . . .': ibid.

93　'From the Turkish point of view . . .': ibid.

95　'Those heroes that shed their blood . . .': inscription on Turkish monument at Anzac Cove.

95　'But the standard set . . .': Bean, *Anzac to Amiens*, p. 181.

5　Shelled to hell

Page

98　'They were a military force . . .': Bean, *Anzac to Amiens*, p. 183.

102　'Well, we hugged the trenches for a few hours . . .': *A Valley in France* by Elizabeth Whiteside quoted in *Simply Hell Let Loose*, p. 59.

102　'A machine-gun was rat ta tat tat tapping . . .': ibid., p. 67.

103　'Many wounded lay in front . . .': Laffin, p. 78.

104　'The value of the result . . .': Bean, *Anzac to Amiens*, p. 237.

104　'Technology now dominated the battlefield . . .' James , p. 418.

105　'. . . we lay down terror-stricken on a bank . . .': quoted in Odgers, p. 66-7.

107　'They were good strong soldiers . . .': Ben Shephard, *A War of Nerves*, p. 43.

108　'. . . did not merely probe character and nerve . . .': ibid., p. 44.

108　'I have had much luck and kept my nerve . . .': ibid., p. 44.

108　'. . . more densely sown with Australian sacrifice . . .': Bean, *Anzac to Amiens*, p. 264.

109　'The bombardment became so heavy . . .': ibid., p. 261.

110　'After fierce fighting above ground . . .': ibid., pp. 262–3.

110　'As a preparatory measure . . .': ibid., p. 318.

110　'For most conspicuous bravery . . .': official citation for Captain Harry Murray's Victoria Cross.

111　'. . . those whom they themselves would most desire . . .': Bean, *Anzac to Amiens*, p. 536.

112　'It was a point of honour . . .': ibid., p. 537.

112　'"Your troops are like dogs . . ."': James, p. 459.

113　'If he was to lead effectively . . .': ibid., p. 473.

113   'Special Orders of No 1 Section . . .': quoted in Odgers, p. 87–8.

114   'Australian and New Zealand troops were prominent . . .': James, p. 468.

116   'There went up from the unleashed line a shout . . .': Bean, *Official History of the War of 1914–18*, Vol V, p. 571.

120   'You bloody Australians . . .': ibid., Vol VI, p. 376

120   'The role of the infantry . . .': ibid., Vol VI, p. 277.

121   'The attack was a brilliant success . . .': Bean, *Anzac to Amiens*, pp. 461–2.

123   'Our fighting machine was no longer of real value . . .': ibid., p. 473.

123   'The cheering platoon at once . . .': ibid., p. 481.

123   'This brilliant action . . .': ibid., p. 483.

124   'Their records show . . .': ibid., p. 494.

124   'Such was the reputation . . .': ibid., p. 494.

125   'For the troops there the change went too deep . . .': ibid., p. 515.

6   Between the wars

Page

128   'Actually it was discipline . . .': Bean, *Anzac to Amiens*, p. 536.

129   ' . . . what actually happened . . .': ibid., p. x.

129   'There is little fear that a short history . . .': ibid., p. vi.

130   'The collection consists of the documentary records . . .': *The Australian War Memorial Canberra*, Foreword.

132   'Albany was the last sight of land . . .': quoted in press release by Regimental Sergeant Major of the Australian Army.

134   'In the event of war . . .': quoted in Odgers, *Army Australia*, p. 111.

134   'It is now generally agreed . . .': David Horner, *Crisis of Command*, p. 17.

7   World War II

Page

136   'In March 1940 . . .': David Horner, *Crisis of Command*, p. 18.

137   ' . . . we can no longer concentrate . . .': ibid., p. 18.

137   'There was no co-ordinated plan . . .': ibid., p. 20.

139   'My 100 men took 25,000 prisoners . . .': Ralph Honner, WWI veteran, interview, Sydney, 1991.

142   'To the eternal regret of everybody . . .': G.H. Fearnside, *Bayonets Abroad*, p. 91.

142   'There'll be no Dunkirk here . . .': quoted in Odgers, p. 121.

142   'The Germans were quite unprepared . . .': Fearnside, pp. 93–4.

143   'Far from proving a deterrent . . .': ibid., p. 94.

143   'The pattern that life was to follow . . .': ibid., pp. 95–6.

143   'The dust caused them the most discomfort . . .' ibid., p, 96.

145   'We've been into 'em . . .': Chester Wilmot, *Tobruk 1941*, p. 99.

145   'The German makes a very good soldier . . .': ibid., p. 168.

145   'The longer the odds Lord Haw Haw . . .': ibid.,p. 168.

146   'Our freedom from embarrassment . . .': Odgers, *Army Australia*, p. 138.

147   'The belief that Germany's power . . .': Wilmot, p. 313.

147   'They were in an exposed position . . .': Ralph Honner, as above.

8   The bloody track

Page

153   'Without any inhibitions of any kind . . .': quoted in Odgers, *Army Australia*, p. 151.

155   'War is largely a matter of confidence . . .': Ralph Honner, WWI veteran, interview, Sydney, 1991.

155   'The problems of our companies at Abuari . . .': Blue Steward, *Recollections of a Regimental Medical Officer*, p. 86.

156   'With the 53rd they had good blokes. . .': Ralph Honner, as above.

156   'We rehearsed what we could do . . .': ibid.

157   'We got a message from Port Moresby . . .': Kevin 'Spud' Whelan, interview, Sydney, 1991.

157   'Indeed, the strangest feature . . .': Ralph Honner, *The 39th At Isurava*, Australian Army Journal, July 1967, pp. 20–21.

158   'Should I leave the key . . .': ibid., p. 25.

158   'Mortar bombs and mountain gun shells . . .' ibid., pp. 30–31.

159   'A platoon or company attack was heralded . . .': ibid., p. 32.

159   ' . . . I do not remember anything more heartening . . .': ibid., p. 33.

161   'During the battle we had advanced . . .': Shigenori Doi, Japanese veteran, interview, Kochi, Japan, August 1991.

161   'Everyone should have got a gong . . .': Alan Avery, Kokoda veteran, interview, Brisbane, 1991.

162   'He came forward with this Bren . . .': ibid.

162   'Nobody knew its importance until later . . .': Phil Rhoden, Kokoda veteran, interview, Melbourne, 1998.

164   'If you got an abdominal wound . . .': quoted in Peter Brune, *Those Ragged Bloody Heroes*, pp. 128–9.

165 'His condition was pretty bad . . .': Don Duffy, Kokoda veteran, unpublished diary.

165 'At all times in action, McCallum . . .': official citation for Corporal Charlie McCallum's Distinguished Service medal.

166 'As a whole they [the 53rd] . . .': quoted in Raymond Paull, *Retreat from Kokoda*, p. 89.

169 'By the time we got back to Ioribaiwa . . .': Phil Rhoden, as above.

170 'Gona was hell . . .': Col Blume, Kokoda veteran, interview, Melbourne, 30 January 2002.

171 'As we were never in great numbers . . .': Ralph Honner, interview, 1991.

171 'The Australians have proven themselves unable . . .': quoted in Jack Gallaway, *The Odd Couple*, p. 118.

172 'Operational reports show that progress . . .': Horner, p. 209.

173 MacArthur's dispatches quoted in *Pacific War Encyclopedia*, p. 384.

173 'It's a very sorry story . . .': Odgers, p. 166.

173 'I think it is fair to say . . .': Horner, p. 232.

174 'Bob, I want you . . .': William Manchester, *American Caesar*, p. 325.

174 'The great hero went home . . .': ibid., p. 327.

175 'Charlie White, whom I taught at school . . .': Ralph Honner, as above.

175 'He told the men that they had been defeated . . .': quoted in David Horner, *Blamey*, p. 353.

176 'In Urbana Force . . .': Horner, *Crisis of Command*, pp. 247–8.

177 'One cannot compare the Australians . . .': ibid., p. 264.

177 'On one of his flanks . . .': Gryff Spragg, Kokoda veteran, interview, Sydney, February 2002.

177 'Although, therefore, undoubtedly much of the dash . . .': Dudley McCarthy, *South-West Pacific Area – First Year*, p. 394.

178 'Although instances of heroism . . .': quoted in Brune, *We Band of Brothers*, p. 237.

180 'We were fighting for Australia . . .': Phil Rhoden, as above.

181 'We do give high praise . . .': Ralph Honner, interview, 1991.

9   Alamein and after

Page
183 'In it there is none of the wild, heart-thrilling drama . . .': Dudley McCarthy, *South-West Pacific Area – First Year*, p. 3.

184 'In the Middle East, of course . . .': Phil Rhoden, Kokoda veteran, interview, Melbourne, 1998.

185   'She's on . . .': Tom Roberts, *Will We be Disappointed—After?*, p. 224.

186   'I don't think I'll ever forget . . .': ibid., p. 191.

187   'They turned to get clear . . .': ibid., p. 226.

187   'He insisted they come back . . .': ibid., p. 227.

187   'Capt Bill Ligertwood has died . . .': ibid., p. 230.

187   'It's no use worrying about your future . . .': ibid., p. 259.

188   'Some fellows say they lie there . . .': ibid., p. 226.

189   'Bill's face is black . . .': ibid., p. 214.

189   'I feel very, very tired . . .' ibid., p. 215.

190   ' . . . this breakout was only made . . .': Mark Johnston, *That Magnificent 9th*, p. 131.

190   'I want to congratulate you . . .': ibid., p. 131.

190   'When all did so well . . .': ibid., p. 131.

191   ' . . . during recent leave . . .': ibid., p. 135.

191   'Wherever you may be . . .': ibid., p. 136.

10   The spirit of the POW

Page

194   ' . . . smartly dressed as possible . . .': Barton Maugham, manuscript, p. 21.

195   'For them, surrender was the final depravity . . .': E.E. Dunlop, *The War Diaries of Weary Dunlop*, pp. vii–viii.

195   'At this time I witnessed . . .': Frank Jackson, unpublished diary.

195   'We were all completely exhausted . . .': ibid.

196   'We arrived in Selarang Barracks . . .': Stan Arneil, *One Man's War*, p. 11.

197   'The portrayal of the "dreaded Changi" camp . . .': ibid., p. 21.

198   'We loaded tinned pineapple . . .': ibid., p. 26.

198   'I remember watching with amazement . . .': ibid., p. 29.

198   'I for one was amazed . . .': Frank Jackson, unpublished diary.

199   'As this was our last evening in Endau . . .': ibid.

199   'They made it known . . .': ibid.

200   '1st May 1943 . . .': Arneil, p. 77.

202   'The camp commander . . .': quoted in Tim Bowden, *Changi Photographer*, p. 23.

202   'Some of them took their badges . . .': ibid., p. 67.

203   'Occasionally we would get cases of prawns . . .': ibid., p. 77.

204 'Thailand was a time . . .': Arneil, p. 93.

204 'The British, who comprised . . .': ibid., p. 91.

205 'Cholera is an awful business . . .': Bowden, p. 84.

205 '26th May 1943 . . .': Arneil, p. 96.

206 'Nine out of ten people dying here are Englishmen . . .': ibid., p. 122.

207 '3rd September 1943 . . .': ibid., p. 124.

207 'One of the methods . . .': Bowden, p. 85.

208 'I only know of one man who survived . . .': ibid., p. 86.

208 'Dr Bruce Hunt saved countless . . .': Terry Beaton, retired Australian Army Colonel, interview, Melbourne, 13 December 2001.

208 'The graves were about five metres long . . .': ibid.

209 'The reason the Dutch had the lesser rate . . .': ibid.

210 'When you walk the railway . . .': ibid.

211 'There was a lot of corporal punishment . . .': Bowden, p. 93.

211 'But what was the main cause of death? . . .': Terry Beaton, as above.

213 'And their intellectual curiosity . . .' Dunlop, p. xii.

213 '18th April 1944 . . .': Arneil, p. 173.

213 'It wasn't just the railway but afterwards . . .': Terry Beaton, as above.

214 'In receiving your surrender . . .': quoted in Horner, *Blamey*, p. 555.

215 'There was a term on the railway . . .': Terry Beaton, as above.

215 'I think we survived . . .': Bowden, p. 81.

215 'Those terrible years . . .': Arneil, p. 4.

216 '. . . we had discovered a way of living . . .': Dunlop, p. xiv.

11 New Guinea and beyond

Page
218 'It's hard for me to believe . . .': George Kenney memoirs, quoted in Odgers, *Army Australia*, p. 174.

218 'He would have been a captain . . .': Noel Pallier, WWII veteran, interview, Wollongong, 1 November 2002.

218 'I couldn't believe he was old enough . . .': Phil Rhoden, Kokoda veteran, interview, Melbourne, 1998.

219 'I didn't see Teddy . . .': Noel Pallier, as above.

219 'Nobody knows how . . .': ibid.

220 'At Wampum we'd stopped for the . . .': ibid.

221   'So Ralph was in the grass . . .':ibid.

221   'Anything these men did . . .': ibid.

222   'It was too steep . . .': Noel Pallier, as above.

223   'My orders were very brief . . .': ibid.

224   'We got into position . . .': ibid.

225   'We pushed on and the grenades . . .': ibid.

226   'Lieutenant Pallier led 9 Platoon . . .': official citation.

226   'The success of this most difficult . . .': official citation.

226   '[Corporal J.H.] "Bluey" Whitechurch . . .': Noel Pallier, as above.

227   'Looking at the photos now . . .': ibid.

228   'It wasn't until the wedding breakfast . . .': ibid.

229   'Always a realist . . .': J. C. McAllester, Official History, *Men of the 2/14th Battalion*.

230   'Today the guns are silent . . .': quoted in Odgers, *Army Australia*, p. 226.

12   War in Korea
Page

236   'I saw a marvellous sight . . .': quoted in Odgers, *Army Australia*, p. 197.

237   'We are trying to prevent . . .': ibid., p. 199.

234   'The clamour on our front . . .': Norman Bartlett, *With the Australians in Korea*, p. 201.

238   'The Chinese seemed to have . . .': quoted in Odgers, p. 263.

238   '. . . the seriousness of the breakthrough . . .': Presidential Unit Citation.

239   'I found the battalion in good heart . . .': Australian Army HQ Training Command, *The Battle of Maryang San*, p. 7.

240   'About a week before . . .': ibid., p. 11.

240   'The battalion was given an enormous task . . .': ibid., p. 14.

241   'Only the CO has the time . . .': ibid., p. 14.

241   'We were down to two sections . . .': ibid., p. 37.

242   '. . . D Company made a magnificent contribution . . .': ibid., p. 58.

242   'I judged C Company's immediate . . .': ibid., p. 72.

243   'I have a lot of fragmentary . . .': ibid., p. 120.

244   'The fighting of 3rd battalion . . .': ibid., p. 124.

13 The Vietnam War

Page

246 'There's the smell of sweat . . .': Dennis Ayoub, Vietnam veteran, interview, 25 October 2002.

248 'When our Vietnam vets . . .': Sandy McGregor, Vietnam veteran, interview, 15 October 2002.

249 'Our Staff Sergeant Major . . .': Dennis Ayoub, as above.

250 'I went to Da Nang . . .': Mike McDermott, Vietnam veteran, interview, 6 November 2002.

251 'They flew in General Westmoreland . . .': ibid.

253 'It is always rewarding . . .': Odgers, *Army Australia*, p. 220.

254–9 'You learn all kinds of things . . .': Peter Cosgrove, interview, 12 November 2002.

259 'I'll always remember when . . .': Sandy McGregor, as above.

260 'Have you ever snorkelled? . . .': Dennis Ayoub, as above.

261 'It was scary going down . . .': Sandy McGregor, as above.

261 'You'd sneak the gun . . .': Dennis Ayoub, as above.

262 'Basically the air was rotten . . .': Sandy McGregor, as above.

263 'I was then eleven stone . . .': Dennis Ayoub, as above.

263 'We had gone to find and destroy . . .': Sandy McGregor, *No Need for Heroes*, p. 115.

264 'We had investigated tunnels . . .': ibid., p. 123–4.

264 'The Viet Cong had pulled back . . .': ibid., p. 125–6.

265 'If we had continued . . .': ibid., p. 126.

265 'First you looked for . . .': Dennis Ayoub, as above.

266 'I'd lie down at night . . .': Mike McDermott, as above.

267–9 'In Vietnam we had National Servicemen . . .': Wally Thompson, Vietnam veteran, interview, 15 October 2002.

269 'Combat power has two elements . . .': Ted Love, retired Colonel, interview, 4 November 2002.

269 'Conventional soldiers think of the jungle . . .': Ted Serong, *Vietnam Remembered*, p. 41.

269 '. . . thoroughly professional . . .': Odgers, *Army Australia*, p. 224.

271 'The rain was very heavy . . .': Lex McAulay, *The Battle of Long Tan*, p. 67.

272 'The constant blaring of bugles . . .': ibid., p. 88.

272 'A solid line of them . . .': Odgers, *100 Years of Australians at War*, p. 323.

273 'It took three days to bury them . . .': McAulay, p. 145.

273 'My mates were lying in an arc . . .': ibid., p. 132.

274 '"Wild Bill" Doolan created newspaper headlines . . .': McAulay., p. 134.

274 'D Company Sixth Battalion . . .': Presidential Citation.

275 '. . . the comradeship, the valour . . .': McAulay., p. 161.

276 'So Agent Orange is Not Guilty . . .': quoted in Gary Pemberton, *Vietnam Remembered*, p. 203.

277 'Blokes don't talk . . .': Dennis Ayoub, as above.

14 Keeping the peace
Page
280 'I think peacekeeping, peacemaking . . .': Duncan Lewis, Commanding Officer of SAS, interview, 3 June 2003.

282 'Afghanistan stands as a . . .': ibid.

282 'He displayed the highest level . . .': official citation for Sergeant Y.

283 'I guess Iraq and Afghanistan . . .': Duncan Lewis, as above.

284 'That was a fully-fledged . . .': ibid.

284 '. . . in our case, the suppressor . . .': ibid.

285 'Our task group . . .': ibid.

286 'Throughout his engagement, Trooper X . . .': official citation.

286 'Our operators are often . . .': Duncan Lewis, as above.

287 'A local community is an enormously . . .': ibid.

287 'They see themselves as being quite ordinary . . .': ibid.

288 'They are able to . . .': ibid.

288 'Within my organisation . . .': ibid.

289 'I think the thing that sets . . .': ibid.

Epilogue
Page
290 'Today, we farewell a great citizen . . .': Reverend Charles Sligo, eulogy at Phil Rhoden's funeral, Melbourne, 18 March 2003.

292 'The Last Parade rekindled something . . .': Phil Rhoden at Bomana Cemetery, Port Moresby, August 1998.

Bibliography

Anderson, Paul, *When the Scorpion Stings*, Allen & Unwin, Sydney, 2002

Arneil, Stan, *Black Jack*, Macmillan, Melbourne, 1983

—— *One Man's War*, Sun Books, Melbourne, 1980

Askin, Mustafa, *Gallipoli: A Turning Point*, Keskin, Çanak-kale, 2001

Austin, Victor, *To Kokoda and Beyond*, Melbourne University Press, Melbourne, 1988

Bean, Charles, *Anzac to Amiens*, Australian War Memorial, Canberra, 1948

—— *Official History of the War of 1914–18*, Angus & Robertson, Sydney, 1942

Bergerud, Eric, *Touched With Fire*, Viking, New York, 1996

Bourne, John, *The Great World War 1914–45*, Harper Collins, London, 2000

Bowden, Tim, *Changi Photographer*, ABC Books, Sydney, 1997

Breen, Bob (ed), *The Battle of Maryang San*, HQ Training Command, Sydney, 1991

Brune, Peter, *Those Ragged Bloody Heroes*, Allen & Unwin, Sydney, 1991

—— *We Band of Brothers*, Allen & Unwin, Sydney, 2000

Carlyon, Les, *Gallipoli*, Macmillan, Sydney, 2001

Carthew, Noel, *Voices from the Trenches*, New Holland, Sydney, 2002

Coulthard-Clark, *The Encyclopaedia of Australia's Battles*, Allen & Unwin, Sydney, 1998

Davies, J.B., *Great Campaigns of WWII*, Little Brown, London, 2002

Department of Veteran's Affairs, *Simply Hell Let Loose*, ABC Books, Sydney, 2001

Dornan, Peter, *The Silent Men*, Allen & Unwin, Sydney, 1999

Dunlop, E.E., *The War Diaries of Weary Dunlop*, Penguin, Melbourne, 1986

Dunnigan, James F. & Nofi, Albert, *The Pacific War Encyclopedia*, Checkmark, New York, 1998

Edgar, Bill, *Warrior of Kokoda*, Allen & Unwin, Sydney, 1999

Erickson, Edward J., *Ordered to Die*, Greenwood Press, Westport Connecticut, 2001

Fasih, Mehmet (ed), *Bloody Ridge (Lone Pine) Diary*, Denizler, Istanbul, 1997

Fearnside, G.H. (ed), *Bayonets Abroad*, John Burridge Military Books, Perth, 1993

Feldt, Eric, *The Coastwatchers*, Currey O'Neill, Melbourne, 1975

Flannery, Tim (ed), *The Birth of Sydney*, Text Publishing, Melbourne, 1999

Gallaway, Jack, *The Odd Couple*, University of Queensland Press, Brisbane, 2000

Grey, Jeffrey, *A Military History of Australia*, Cambridge University Press, Cambridge, 1999

Hardie, Robert, *The Burma–Siam Railway*, Imperial War Museum, London, 1983

Holt, Tonie & Valmai, *Gallipoli Battlefield Guide*, Leo Cooper, Barnsley UK, 2000

Horner, David, *Blamey: The Commander-in-Chief*, Allen & Unwin, Sydney, 1998

—— *Crisis of Command*, Australian National University Press, Canberra, 1978

Jackson, Frank, *My War 50 Years On*, self published, 1992

James, Lawrence, *Warrior Race*, Abacus, London, 2002

Johnston, Mark, *That Magnificent 9th*, Allen & Unwin, Sydney, 2002

Keegan, John, *The First World War*, Pimlico, London, 2002

Keogh, E.G., *The South-West Pacific 1941–45*, Grayflower, Melbourne, 1965

Kidd, Neville, *An Impression Which Will Never Fade*, self published, 1999

King, Peter, *Australia's Vietnam*, Allen & Unwin, Sydney, 1983

Lewis, Stephen, *My Vietnam*, My Vietnam Trust, Adelaide, 2002

Lindsay, Patrick, *The Spirit of Kokoda . . . Then & Now*, Hardie Grant, Melbourne, 2002

Lord, Walter, *Lonely Vigil*, Viking, New York, 1977

McAllester, Jim (ed), *Men of the 2/14th Battalion*, self published, Melbourne, 1990

McAulay, Lex, *Blood & Iron*, Hutchinson, Sydney, 1991

—— *The Battle of Long Tan*, Arrow, Sydney, 1986

McGregor, Sandy, *No Need for Heroes*, Calm Books, Sydney, 1993

McKie, Ronald, *The Heroes*, Angus & Robertson, Sydney, 1960

Manchester, William, *American Caesar*, Little Brown, Boston, 1978

Manning, Frederic, *The Middle Parts of Fortune*, Text Publishing, Melbourne, 2000

Miller, William Ian, *The Mystery of Courage*, Harvard, Cambridge Massachusetts, 2000 Nelson, Hank, *Prisoners of War*, ABC Books, Sydney, 1985

Odgers, George, *Army Australia: An Illustrated History*, Child & Associates, Sydney, 1988

—— *100 Years of Australians at War*, Lansdowne, Sydney, 1999 Paull, Raymond, *Retreat From Kokoda*, Heinemann, Melbourne, 1982

Pemberton, Gregory (ed), *Vietnam Remembered*, New Holland, Sydney, 2002

Petersen, Barry, *Tiger Men*, Macmillan, Melbourne, 1988

Reid, Richard, *Gallipoli 1915*, ABC Books, Sydney, 2002

Roberts, Tom, *Will We be Disappointed–After?*, Tom Roberts Books, Adelaide, 1995

Ryan, Peter, *Fear Drive My Feet*, Duffy & Snellgrove, Sydney, 2001

Shephard, Ben, *A War of Nerves*, Pimlico, London, 2000

Slim, Sir William, *Courage and Other Broadcasts*, Cassell, London, 1957

Steel, Nigel & Hart, Peter, *Defeat at Gallipoli*, Pan, London, 2002

Stone, Gerald L., *War Without Honour*, Jacaranda, Brisbane, 1966

Terkel, Studs, *The Good War*, Phoenix, London, 1984

Travers, Tim, *Gallipoli 1915*, Tempus, Gloucestershire UK, 2001

Williams, John F., *Anzacs, the Media and the Great War*, UNSW Press, Sydney, 1999

Wilmot, Chester, *Tobruk 1941*, Penguin, Melbourne, 1993

White, Osmar, *Green Armour*, Angus & Robertson, Sydney, 1945

Acknowledgements

Special thanks to:

Lisa Cotton, for her love, support and help, and her photographs;
Don Murray, for his counsel and enduring friendship;
Deb Callaghan, for her advice and support;
Tom Gilliatt, for his faith and guidance;
Charlie Lynn and Paul Croll for their continued mateship and
    support;
General Peter Cosgrove, for his wisdom and honesty;
Major-General Duncan Lewis, for his candour;
Dennis Ayoub, Sandy McGregor, Noel Pallier, Mike McDer-
    mott, Ted Love, Terry Beaton, Wally Thompson and Ali
    Efe, for their passion and their openness;
Corporal Brett 'Woody' Woodward and the men of the
    Section Two Three Bravo, 5/7 Bn RAR – Billy Boulton,
    Scott Dudley, Joshua Nicholas, Clint Holdsworth, Brent
    Thomson, Matthew McMahon, Wayne Griggs and Nathan
    Charles – for their hospitality;
Lieutenant Colonel Mike Lean, Co AusBatt VII, and Major
    Andrew Hocking, for their hospitality and help in East
    Timor;
Peter and Leigh Hughes, for sharing their remarkable exp-
    eriences; and
Joan Murray, for her friendship and memories.

Index